======

AQUINAS
Summa Theologiae, *Questions on God*

CAMBRIDGE TEXTS IN THE
HISTORY OF PHILOSOPHY

Series editors

KARL AMERIKS
Professor of Philosophy at the University of Notre Dame

DESMOND M. CLARKE
Professor of Philosophy at University College Cork

The main objective of Cambridge Texts in the History of Philosophy is to expand the range, variety and quality of texts in the history of philosophy which are available in English. The series includes texts by familiar names (such as Descartes and Kant) and also by less well-known authors. Wherever possible, texts are published in complete and unabridged form, and translations are specially commissioned for the series. Each volume contains a critical introduction together with a guide to further reading and any necessary glossaries and textual apparatus. The volumes are designed for student use at undergraduate and postgraduate level and will be of interest not only to students of philosophy, but also to a wider audience of readers in the history of science, the history of theology and the history of ideas.

For a list of titles published in the series, please see end of book.

THOMAS AQUINAS

Summa Theologiae
Questions on God

EDITED BY

BRIAN DAVIES
Fordham University

BRIAN LEFTOW
University of Oxford

CAMBRIDGE
UNIVERSITY PRESS

CAMBRIDGE UNIVERSITY PRESS
Cambridge, New York, Melbourne, Madrid, Cape Town, Singapore, São Paulo

CAMBRIDGE UNIVERSITY PRESS
The Edinburgh Building, Cambridge CB2 2RU, UK

Published in the United States of America by Cambridge University Press, New York

www.cambridge.org
Information on this title: www.cambridge.org/9780521528924

© Cambridge University Press 2006

First published 2006

Printed in the United Kingdom at the University Press, Cambridge

A catalogue record for this book is available from the British Library

ISBN-13 978-0-521-82140-7 hardback
ISBN-10 0-521-82140-1 hardback
ISBN-13 978-0-521-52892-4 paperback
ISBN-10 0-521-52892-5 paperback

Contents

v

Contents

Introduction

The thirteenth century brought Western Europe much that was new in Christianity and in the life of the mind. New religious orders for both men and women were founded, including two whose rules stipulated that their members should not be attached permanently to any monastery: the Franciscans and the Dominicans. Thus there came to be friars willing to travel widely in pursuit of their missions. The thirteenth century also fostered a new institution called a 'university'. And it was then that Aristotle was reintroduced to the West, in Latin translation and with commentaries by Islamic and Jewish scholars of the eleventh and twelfth centuries, such as Ibn Sina, Ibn Rushd and Moses Maimonides. The work of Thomas Aquinas (1224?–74) was one fruit of these developments. As a young man he joined the Dominicans, who supported systematic theological studies for their members as a preparation for preaching, especially to non-Christians. He later became a professor in the Theology Faculty of the University of Paris, and Aristotle became the chief philosophical influence on his defence and explanation of Christian theology. If Aquinas is the medieval author who most influenced the development of Christian thought about God, his times helped to make him so.

Though Aquinas lectured in the Theology Faculty, he also wrote a number of purely philosophical books, including (as was usual then) commentaries on Aristotle and other earlier authors. He thus debated philosophy with his contemporaries in the Faculty of Arts, particularly Siger of Brabant, who defended as Aristotle's opinion the view of Averroes (Ibn Rushd) that all humans share a single soul. Still, Aquinas's primary responsibility was to teach theology, and his major work in this context was the *Summa Theologiae* (*ST* for short). He began writing *ST* while teaching in Rome (1265–8), worked on Part II while teaching in Paris (1268–72) and wrote the rest of what he produced (he never completed the project) in Naples during the following year. *ST* covers all the issues that were prominent in medieval theology and were addressed in the standard eight-year course of theology studies. He wrote *ST* for 'beginners'.[1] But it will be obvious that someone embarking on the study of theology in Aquinas's day had to have mastered much else first.

Reading the *Summa*

ST is the size of a multi-volume book. It is divided into three Parts, which are in effect the book's volumes, and its arrangement is inspired by the Neoplatonic theme of all reality flowing from and eventually returning to a divine source. Thus, Part I is about God and about creation as proceeding from him as its source. Part II discusses the return of intelligent creatures to God, and is divided into two major sections: one (usually called the 1a2ae) concerns human actions, morality and grace, while the second (2a2ae) provides a more detailed review of the virtues. Part III is devoted to Christ as the mediator between God and human beings and to the theological implications of the Incarnation, including the Church. The Parts are subdivided into 'questions', which are equivalent to *ST*'s chapters, and are grouped by topic into 'treatises'.

Finally, the questions divide into articles, each a discrete, self-contained discussion of one specific problem under its question's general topic. Each article is a debate in miniature, which reflects the style of formal academic disputation common in medieval universities. The title identifies the issue to be debated and is put in the form of a question that invites a 'yes' or 'no' answer. The debate begins with arguments for both answers. Usually the first set of arguments – the 'objections' – is against the position Aquinas wants to defend, and the following argument(s), introduced by the phrase 'on the contrary', support(s) Aquinas's own view. (Sometimes, though, he rejects the arguments on both sides (e.g. 13.10).[2]) These

---

[1] S. Thomae Aquinatis *Summa Theologiae* (Ottawa: Studii Generalis, 1941), prologue, 1a.

[2] References to material translated in this volume appear in the text, by question and article number. Where I quote Aquinas without giving translation credits, I quote from this volume's translation. To avoid confusion, please note: references to Aquinas always involve at least two numbers, or else a number and an abbreviation like 'q'. Where a single number is given in brackets, this is a reference to a proposition of mine stated in this introduction.

preliminary arguments often rely on brief citations from the Bible, or equally brief references to Christian theologians or philosophers. As a Christian, Aquinas takes biblical texts to express truths revealed by God: thus biblical citations are in effect arguments from the testimony of an unimpeachable witness. Citations of theologians may have the force of authoritative interpretations of that testimony, especially if they are drawn from those early theologians (such as Augustine or Gregory) who came to be known as 'Fathers of the Church'. However, these and the references to philosophers may also be quick ways to refer students (or their teachers) to arguments they could be expected to know. Even where they are simply references to someone's views, they do not represent a blind obeisance to the dead. The mere fact that someone smart finds a certain view plausible has some force as evidence for the view's truth. For at least some of the smart are so in part because they are perceptive, and to be perceptive is to see more, and more clearly, than most.

Following the objections and counter-argument(s) in each article is the body ('*corpus*') of the question. Here Aquinas sets out his own view. Finally, there are responses to the initial objections, in which Aquinas tries to show why they misfire. It is unwise to skip these; some of Aquinas's best points appear in them.

Philosophy and theology

Aquinas wrote *ST* as a Christian theologian. This affects how he frames some issues. When he takes up the existence of God, for instance, he does not raise it as a matter he seeks to settle by argument. He takes it for granted that God exists. Aquinas sees the real issue here as about the kind of justification that belief in God can have. Is the proposition that God exists self-evident (2.1)? Is it one that philosophy can demonstrate (2.2)? Can one show that philosophy can demonstrate it by showing that philosophy has done so (2.3)? Still, Aquinas was a *philosophical* theologian. While the Christian faith provides the claims he seeks to support, the arguments he gives to support them are intended to pass muster with philosophers. So it does not distort Aquinas's intent to see him as providing a philosophical account of God. This account is found in Questions 1–26 of Part I of *ST*, and this account is what I now introduce.

God's nature and existence

Aquinas takes up arguments for God's existence in the second Question of Part I, before he has said anything about what he means by 'God'. This may seem to some readers an odd way to proceed. Philosophers discuss two interrelated questions: (a) how should we conceive of God: what should we mean by the word 'God'? (b) are there good reasons to think that there is a God? One might think that (a) should come first. When we know what something is, we can move immediately to the question about its existence or otherwise. When Jones dies and Jones's lawyer executes the will, the lawyer may ask, did Jones have a sister? The lawyer knows what a sister is, and the real question is whether such a sister exists or not. But it is not clear that we know what sort of thing a God would be, or what the word 'God' means. So it might seem better first to clarify what 'God' means and only then to ask whether there is a God.

Aquinas's own theory of knowledge bolsters this thought. He held that (mystical experience aside)[3] nothing is in the intellect which was not first in the senses: we can by natural means have positive, contentful concepts of the natures only of what we can see, hear, touch, and so forth. We cannot perceive immaterial things: as they cannot reflect light they cannot be seen, as they do not emit sound waves they cannot be heard, and so forth.[4] So on Aquinas's terms we cannot by natural means have positive, contentful concepts of what such things are. We cannot acquire a concept of God – even an inadequate one – by acquaintance, in the way in which we might get a vague concept of what an aeroplane is by seeing one flying by at a great height in the sky. If we cannot perceive God and cannot by natural means have a positive concept of him without perceiving him, and we have not been 'infused' with such a concept by gracious divine action, how then can we say what he is well enough to know what it would take to show that he exists?

Aquinas's answer is that while we do not know what God is, we do know what we mean by the word 'God', a meaning we have built up from our acquaintance with his effects (2.2 *ad* 2). But this just pushes the question back a step: if we do not know what sort of thing God is, how do

---

[3] As Aquinas sees it, in mystical 'rapture', one can 'see' the essence of God (*ST* 2a2ae 175.3).

[4] Of course, God can cause the air to vibrate and so cause us to hear a sound. But he does not *emit* the sound wave, and so there is a distinction between hearing a sound God causes to occur and hearing God.

we know what sorts of effect he would have? One answer here, surely, is that as Aquinas is a Christian theologian, he gets his ideas of God's effects from biblical sources. The Bible tells him that God creates, sustains, provides for and rules over whatever is not God. We may not know much about *how* any of these things work, but if one is a Christian, one accepts that they are so. This tells Aquinas that there are certain roles earlier philosophers had spoken of that God must in fact play. Aristotle, for instance, had argued the existence of an unmoved mover, a first being in his cosmological scheme who was ultimately responsible for all change in the material world. Any being who plays this role has a great deal to do with sustaining and providing for the world. Perhaps the Christian God might delegate this to some eminent creature, but it is at least a reasonable thought too (to a Christian) that if anyone plays this role, God does. So Aquinas takes it that the unmoved mover's effect, the world's motion, is actually a divine effect and so reworks Aristotle's argument for an unmoved mover as an argument to the existence of the Christian God.

This reworking would seem all the more reasonable because earlier Christians shaped the concept of God that his tradition developed under the influence (ultimately) of Aristotle and Plato. Plato had argued for the existence of Forms, entities that he held to be timeless, immutable, simple and divine.[5] Aristotle had modified this picture by depicting God as being like a Platonic Form but everlastingly engaged in thinking about the best possible thing, namely himself.[6] Christian theism took these ideas aboard as it developed during the first Christian centuries. St Augustine (354–430) put the resulting concept of God (often called 'classical theism') so persuasively that it became the unchallenged framework for Christian theology for the subsequent nine hundred years.

Thus when Aquinas begins *ST* with arguments for God's existence, he knows what he aims to prove. So did the students he wrote for, who shared his biblical and philosophical sources.

The Five Ways

Even the decision to begin with proofs of God's existence left other options open. St Anselm (1033–1109) had argued in the *Proslogion* (1078) that by unfolding the content of a particular description of God, one

---

[5] *Phaedo* 78b–c; *Timaeus* 37e–38a.   [6] Aristotle, *Metaphysics* 12.8.

could show that he exists, a style of argument usually called 'ontological'. Aquinas prefers arguments from observable natural effects to their first cause. The Five Ways he offers did not originate with him. The first is based closely on Aristotle. So is the second, for which Maimonides is a more immediate source.[7] Some are not stated fully; the first, for instance, either compresses or excerpts a far longer account of Aristotle's argument given by Aquinas in the earlier *Summa against Gentiles*.[8] Even one of the Ways raises more issues than an introduction can hope to discuss adequately, but it may be helpful to clarify one feature common to the first three by examining how it occurs in the first. Part of the First Way runs as follows:

> Some things . . . undergo change . . . anything in process of change is changed by something else . . . this something else, if in process of change, is itself changed by yet another thing . . . But there has to be an end to this regress of causes, otherwise there will be no first cause of change, and, as a result, no subsequent causes of change. For it is only when acted upon by a first cause that intermediate causes produce change (if a hand does not move the stick, the stick will not move anything else). So, we are bound to arrive at some first cause of change that is not itself changed by anything . . . God. (2.3)

Aquinas does not think that every regress of causes must end in a first cause. For example, while he thinks there was a first human being, he does not think this had to be so. On the contrary, he thinks it possible that every human being could have had human parents, that is, that there was no first human.[9] But he does think that at least one sort of causal series must end in a first cause. He uses the term 'causal series ordered *per se*' (which I shall abbreviate as a '*per se* series') for this kind. The First Way deals with one such causal series.[10]

Let me note three distinctive properties of *per se* series. In a famous series of events, Booth pulls the trigger, this causes the bullet to strike,

[7] For a full historical treatment see William Craig, *The Cosmological Argument from Plato to Leibniz* (New York: Macmillan, 1979).
[8] This may be because Aquinas intended *ST* as an introduction to theology. It may also indicate that sometimes Aquinas briefly refers to an argument whose full version he could expect students already to have met.
[9] *ST* 1a 46.2 *ad* 7. 'It is possible' here does not mean 'for all we know, this might be so'. Aquinas's point is that, although this is not how things are, God could have chosen to have it so.
[10] Ibid.

and the strike causes Lincoln to die. In this series, some causes act before others.[11] In a *per se* series, however, all causes act at once: when the hand moves the stick which moves (say) a stone, hand and stick act at once in moving the stone.[12]

That Abraham begets Isaac and Isaac begets Jacob is another causal series. But though Abraham caused Isaac to exist and so contributed to Isaac's begetting, he did not cause Isaac to beget Jacob. In a *per se* series, however, every cause other than a first is caused to act by another member of the series: the hand causes the stick to cause, that is, to move the stone.

Again, Abraham does not act with Isaac to beget Jacob. In a *per se* series, all causes act together to produce the final effect: the stick moves the stone and the hand also moves the stone. So in a *per se* series, all at once, the stick is acting on the stone because the hand is causing the stick to act on it, because the human is causing the hand to act on the stick, and the human and the hand are acting on the stone because the human is causing the hand to cause the stick to act on the stone.[13]

The argument in the First Way, then, is really the following:

1. Some things are in change at time t.
2. Everything in change at t is at t part of a *per se* causal series and is at t being changed by some cause in this series.[14]
3. If there are any causes in such a series, there is a first cause of change in it.
4. There are causes in these series (from 2). So
5. There is a first cause of change in each such series.

---

[11] In one sense, causes act only when their effects occur: they have not acted until they have had some effect. This is how Aquinas (following Aristotle, *Physics* 3.3) thinks of causes; but speaking as I do in the text smoothes exposition.

[12] Aquinas thinks that in the First Way's case, the first mover in the series will be atemporal. For defence of the claim that one can use 'at once' to speak even of an atemporal being's relation to temporal events, see my *Time and Eternity* (Ithaca, NY: Cornell University Press, 1991).

[13] If only one cause acts to produce its effect, it is trivially the case that all causes act at once, that every cause other than the first is caused to cause by the first (i.e. that there are no causes in the series which are not first and are not caused to cause by the first) and that all causes act together to produce the final effect. If these were the only properties which distinguish a *per se* causal series from the Abraham–Isaac–Jacob sort, we would have to conclude that all causal series consisting of just one cause and one effect are trivially *per se*. I cannot here consider whether these are the only distinguishing marks of *per se* series.

[14] 'Is at t being changed' allows for the claim that the changer does not act at t – a point on which Aquinas insists, as he thinks that the first changer in this series is atemporal. If all one-cause causal series are trivially *per se*, the second conjunct in (2) above entails the first.

6. If a cause of change is in change, it is not first (from 2). So
7. There is an unchanging cause of change.
8. This is God.

This rendering may strike some readers who are familiar with the Five Ways as odd, since it makes no reference to an infinite series of causes: many commentators read the First Way as arguing that because an infinitely extended causal series of a certain sort is impossible, there must be a first cause. But this gets things backwards. The argument, surprisingly, is that 'there has to be an end to this regress of causes [because] otherwise there will be no first cause of change and, as a result, no subsequent causes of change'. It is not that there must be a first cause because there cannot be an infinite series, but that there cannot be an infinite series because there must be a first cause. That the series of causes cannot be infinite is (Aquinas thinks) a corollary of (3).[15] There is something else, not argued here, that stands behind (3). The hand-and-stick illustration alludes to this. Aquinas made the thought behind (3) a bit clearer in his earlier *Compendium of Theology*:

> All changed things are changed by other things, inferiors by superiors, as the elements are by the celestial bodies ... Since whatever is changed by another is as if an instrument of the first changer, were there no first changer, all changers would be instruments ... it is ridiculous ... to suppose instruments to be changed, but not by some first agent. This would be as if someone were to say that a saw or hatchet operates without a carpenter. So there is a first changer.[16]

Like the First Way, this text does not use the term '*per se* series'. But the parallels in the illustrations show that this is what Aquinas has in mind: just as a hand moves the stick that moves the stone, so a hand moves the saw that cuts the wood, and when a hand moves a stick and the stick moves a stone, the hand moves the stone by means of the stick; the stick is the hand's instrument in moving the stone. What supports (3) in

---

[15] Actually, it does not follow from (3). A series can both be infinite and have a first or last member. For example, there is a first natural number and there is an infinite series of them; there is a last negative integer and there is an infinite series of them.

[16] *Compendium of Theology* 1.3, in S. Thomae Aquinatis *Opuscula Omnia*, ed. R. Mandonnet (Paris: LeThielleux, 1927), v. 2, 2–3. Until recently the *Compendium* was taken to postdate *ST* 1a. The consensus now is that the *Compendium* is earlier than *ST*, and perhaps contemporary with the *Summa against Gentiles*.

Aquinas's mind, then, is the idea featured in the *Compendium* argument, that changers in *per se* series that are not first are instruments.

Consider again the distinctive properties of a *per se* series. If the stick is acting on the stone because the hand is causing it to do so, and the hand is acting on the stone because the hand is causing the stick to act on the stone, it is by means of the stick that the hand's power is applied to the stone. The stick is the instrument by which the hand's power moves the stone; in a *per se* series, whatever is being moved or changed by another member of the series is that further thing's instrument. Thus the *Compendium* in effect argues for (3) as follows:

9. Necessarily, in any *per se* series of changers, either it is or it is not the case that all changers in the series are instruments of other changers in the series.
10. Necessarily, if a changer is not an instrument of any other changer in the series, it is a first changer in that series. So
11. Necessarily, in any *per se* series of changers, either there is a first changer or all changers in the series are instruments of other changers in the series.
12. Necessarily, it is not the case that all changers in a *per se* series are instruments of other changers in the series. So
13. Necessarily, in every *per se* series there is a first changer,

(13) is just (3). (9) is obvious. (10) is equally so on reflection. If a changer is not the instrument of another member of the series, but whatever is being moved or changed by another member of the series is that further thing's instrument, the changer is not being moved or changed by another member of the series. But if there *were* further members of the series, they would be moving or changing it. So there are none: the changer that is not an instrument is the series' first member. (9) and (10) together entail (11). We must ask, then, whether (12) is true.

Here is one consideration that favours (12). If our stick is the hand's instrument to move the stone, the hand moves the stone by means of the stick. That is, when we insert 'the hand' into the blank space in the phrase '__ causes the stone to move by means of the stick', we get a true statement that expresses what is going on. This statement describes the entire causal series as causing the final effect. And it should, for the effect is *inter alia* the effect of the entire series: it is true that the stone moves because the stick moves it, and because the hand moves it, and because the entire series (hand and stick) moves it. In fact, it is the statement describing the entire series that seems best to capture what is really going on. It seems that for any *per se* series, there should be a true statement of this sort. For in any such series there is instrumental causality and the entire series is the cause of the final effect.

Now, if nothing is inserted in the blank space in '__ causes the stone to move by means of the stick', these words express no truth or falsehood. They are not the kind of thing that can do so, for they are not a complete sentence. Consider, then, what would be so if there were no first changer in a *per se* series. Now, if this *is* a *per se* series, there is 'instrumental causality' in it. So there should be a true sentence describing the entire series by inserting into the blank space of a sentence-frame of the form: '__ causes effect F by means of C by means of D by means of E . . .' a term referring to a cause. But with no first changer, we could not insert a subject-term in the blank space and have the result be a truth describing the entire series as causing the effect. Suppose we insert 'B' into the sentence-frame just given. The resulting statement will be true, if B is in fact a cause in the series. But if B is not the first cause in the series, this truth will not describe the entire series causing the final effect. For if B is not the first cause, some further part(s) of the series cause(s) B to cause, and the resulting statement will leave out namely whatever part(s) of the series play(s) this role. On the other hand, with nothing plugged into the blank – no term for a first cause – the purported description of what is going on is something that cannot be true. This suggests that there cannot be a true sentence asserting the existence of an entire *per se* causal series with no first changer.[17] Further, if in such a case there is nothing to plug into the blank before the verb 'causes', then there is nothing that does the whole series' causing and therefore the whole series is not a cause of the final effect. But there cannot be a *per se* causal series of which this is true. If every cause in the series save a first is caused to act by prior causes of the series – if every such cause is applying other members' power to the final effect – then the entire series causes the effect, that is, all the members together do.

Thus, at least, one argument for (3). But even if it is sound, there is much more to say about the First Way. Its argument for (2) is

---

[17] This paragraph is heavily indebted to Barry Miller, 'Necessarily Terminating Causal Series', *Mind* 91 (1982), 201–15.

controversial. Again, why see a human as an instrument of a further mover, for example an angel? Perhaps humans can be first causes; in other words, perhaps (2) is not true. It is therefore possible that, even if it is sound, the *Compendium* argument provides less than Aquinas had hoped, for perhaps first movers need not be anything like a divine cause. Still, though many deride them, perhaps there is yet something to be said for Aquinas's First and Second Ways.[18]

Each of the Five Ways concludes that a description is satisfied – that there is an unchanging changer, a first efficient cause, and so on. However, it is not obvious that all five descriptions apply to the same being. Nor is it obvious that 'all call these God' (2.3) (although the Ways assert this), or that if all do call these God they are correct to do so. These assertions are in effect promissory notes. Questions 3–26 try to redeem them by drawing out implications of these five descriptions. In doing so Aquinas tells us what it is to be an unchanging changer, a first cause, and the rest. By the time we reach Question 26, if Aquinas's arguments work, we do have something Godlike on our hands. So these five descriptions provide the foundation of Aquinas's subsequent account of God's nature.

Simplicity

Aquinas begins this account with his doctrine of divine simplicity (of which someone once said: 'if that's His simplicity, I cannot face His complexity'). Something is more complicated or complex the more parts it has. It is simpler the fewer its parts, and wholly simple if it has no parts at all. Aquinas's doctrine of divine simplicity (which I abbreviate 'DDS') asserts that God is wholly simple: he is not put together from parts of any sort. Aquinas places DDS first in his treatment of God's nature because it is basic to the rest of it: DDS leads directly to claims that God is perfect, unchangeable, atemporal, spiritual, and suchlike. These claims (together with DDS) constitute the core of classical theism.

Most theists accept one part of DDS, that God is not made of matter, where 'matter' is used in the familiar sense of the stuff of which physical bodies are composed. (Aquinas also uses the term in a rather different sense, which is discussed below.) If God is not made of matter, he is not composed of extended parts (3.1). But Aquinas also speaks of God as not

---

[18] The Third Way also involves (3). But it has problems which seem to me insuperable.

'composed' of other kinds of part, such as a form, an essence, accidents, a 'subject' of accidents, and existence. Most theists who are not philosophers have no views on this at all. And well they may not, for the terms are strange, as is what Aquinas's use of them in this context presupposes. Parts compose. Wholes are composed. Wholes can consist completely of different sorts of part at once; our bodies consist completely of both molecules and quarks. When Aquinas speaks of things other than God as 'composed' of, for example, essences and accidents, he takes it that concrete things consist completely not only of concrete parts but also of abstract ones – essences and accidents. His discussion of DDS, then, takes the form of denying that God is composed of either concrete or abstract parts.

The sorts of part Aquinas includes are the already-mentioned ordinary material parts and forms,[19] 'prime matter', essences, accidents, and a thing's existence. Forms are either souls or certain sorts of properties, for example shapes, sizes, weights, colours, structures or powers. For Aquinas, forms are particular: as he sees it, it is not the case that all square things share a single form, squareness, but rather that each has its own squareness. Having forms empowers causes to act as they do but, with the possible exception of souls, forms are abstract, that is, they are not the kinds of thing that can act themselves.

As Aquinas understands the term, a 'form' may be either substantial or accidental. The substantial form of any given thing is whatever in it made its matter become – and/or makes it be actually – the kind of thing it is. Aquinas follows Aristotle in thinking of the whole natural world as objectively divided into kinds. When we classify (say) birds as one genus of animal and fish as another, it is not the case that one scheme we might adopt is no better than another: if we saw birds and fish as the same kind of animal, we would be getting it wrong, objectively. So too, for Aquinas, each natural kind is in turn subdivided into more specific kinds (such as sparrows, trout, etc.), and each most specific natural kind has a characteristic form that makes it the kind of thing it is. In this way of thinking, what makes a horse a horse rather than a cow is that it has the substantial form of a horse. Human souls thus are also substantial forms: having a human soul is what makes us belong to the kind 'human'. Kinds

---

[19] Aquinas also uses 'form' to refer to immaterial substances. In this sense of the term, God is a form. In neither sense is it true that he *has* a form.

are intrinsic properties. That means that the kind to which something belongs is determined entirely by itself, not by how other things are in the world outside it.[20] So substantial forms are all intrinsic attributes.

In Aquinas's usage, a form is accidental (an accident) if and only if it is not substantial. He thought of accidental forms as of three sorts.[21] Some are quantities, which make true answers to questions broadly of the 'how much?' sort – such as sizes and weights. While Aquinas thought of all these as intrinsic to their bearers, we no longer think today of all Thomist quantities as intrinsic. For example, an object's weight is a function of the gravity field it is in and so is affected by the world beyond it. Some accidental forms are qualities, which make true answers to questions broadly of the 'how is it?' or 'what is it like?' sort – such as colours and tones. Aquinas thinks of these too as all intrinsic to their bearers. Relational properties – for example being shorter than Socrates – are Aquinas's third sort of accidental form.

I shall now introduce a new term: a truthmaker is an item whose existence makes some truths true. All Thomist forms are truthmakers. So for that matter are ordinary material parts: my left hand's existence makes it true that I have a left hand. The term 'truthmakers' naturally raises such questions as: what is it to make something true? What 'things' are made true? For present purposes one need not answer these questions. The 'things' that are made true might be sentences, sentence-types, propositions – whatever the correct theory of the matter says they are. Likewise, one can say for the moment that 'making true' is whatever the correct theory of truth says it is. If truth is understood as correspondence with reality, for instance, to make something true is to be that with which the truth in question corresponds.[22]

---

[20] At least this is intuitively a plausible claim. There are philosophers who suggest that something is human only if it had the right sort of parents, which is not an intrinsic property. My gloss on being intrinsic represents only the main sort of intuition that developed accounts of the intrinsic try to respect. For one of the most influential contributions to defining 'intrinsic', see David Lewis and Rae Langton, 'Defining "intrinsic"', in David Lewis, *Papers in Metaphysics and Epistemology* (Cambridge: Cambridge University Press, 1999), 116–32.

[21] Aquinas accepts Aristotle's claim that there are nine categories of accidental predicates. But he thinks that the other six apply to things in virtue not of forms in them but of how things are outside them (*Commentary on Aristotle's Metaphysics Book V* 1. 9, #892; *Commentary on Aristotle's Physics Book III* 1. 5, #322; my thanks to Jeff Brower for these references). They do not apply to a thing *A* in virtue of a form in *A* which is of the same category as the predicate.

[22] But for a problem with this claim see David Lewis, 'Forget about the Correspondence Theory of Truth', *Analysis* 61 (2001), 275–80.

For Aquinas, 'matter' is the general term for that which 'bears' or 'receives' forms. If one sculpts a statue from a block of marble, the resulting statue is still made of marble but it acquires its characteristic features as a statue – for example, that it is a statue of Cicero rather than of someone else – from its shape. The change the artist brings about is the imposition of a specific shape or form on the original material. Aristotle and Aquinas took this as a model for all kinds of change; thus Aquinas took a thing's matter to be *inter alia* what gives it the capacity to undergo change, and he used the term 'form' to label whatever attribute matter might acquire. For any material thing, its matter is the stuff of which it is made, the parts of which it is composed or, most generally, whatever was potentially that thing and became actually that thing by coming to have the appropriate form. The matter of any thing is also a truthmaker: it makes true answers to questions such as 'of what does this thing consist?'

Aquinas distinguishes one sort of matter as 'prime' ('first'). To see why and what he means by this, let us consider the 'sculpture' model of change again. If a sculpture gradually changes from pink to grey, it is still the same kind of stuff – marble – that it was. It has just changed in respect of an accident. But there is also change with respect to substantial form: at death, Aquinas held, the human soul (a substantial form) is parted from the human body, and as a result what is left behind, a corpse, no longer belongs to the kind *human being*. If we model this change on a sculpture's changing colour, we shall want to say that there is some stuff (like the marble) that is the same throughout the change, that first was and now is not a human being, as the marble first was and now is not pink. This stuff also belongs to some kind(s): it is (say) organic matter of a particular chemical composition. But we can imagine this stuff too losing its substantial form, as when its constituent molecules break down into atoms.[23] Does every parcel of matter host an infinite number of substantial forms? Since each substantial form places a thing in its kind(s), an infinity of such forms would mean that each thing belongs to an infinity of natural kinds; there seems no good reason to believe this. But if there are a finite number of substantial forms in any bit of matter, there is a 'first' form,

[23] Aquinas did not believe in molecules or atoms; this is a not an illustration he would have used.

one all the others presuppose.[24] Suppose one believes this, and believes too that any bit of matter has the capacity to change with respect to every substantial form it bears. If this is a *change*, then there must be something that continues throughout, existing both at the start and at the end of the change. Were there no such thing, this would be merely a case of substituting a new bit of matter for an old, not the old bit of matter changing its form. If this is change in a material thing, what continues must be some sort of matter. But we are talking now about the matter that bears (and changes with respect to) the very first, most basic substantial form in a thing. So this must be matter that has of itself no substantial form at all, that is, matter that is not of itself any *kind* of matter at all, but a mere receiver of forms. This is Aquinas's 'prime matter'. It is supposed to be the ultimate receiver of all attributes and a necessary condition for change in respect to the most basic substantial form.

To continue this quick survey of Aquinas's terms, the essence of any being is what makes it the kind of thing it is, so it is that which makes true the answer to the question 'what is this?' Things with essences come to exist when matter receives a particular substantial form. Aquinas thinks of essences, like forms, as abstract particulars. Finally, a subject is that which receives or bears a form.[25]

Aquinas's arguments for DDS try to show that none of the ways in which things divide into multiple truthmakers apply to God. For present purposes, then, Aquinas's DDS may be summarized as follows: in the case of God, every intrinsic non-Trinitarian truth is true in virtue of exactly the same truthmaker, which is identical with God. Leaving the Trinity aside, God has no internal structure of truthmakers at all: God is just one undivided truthmaker for all these truths. One may wonder just how a Christian of Aquinas's orthodox stripe could leave the Trinity aside here. On standard Trinitarian doctrine, God is Father, Son and Holy Spirit. It is not obvious that this is compatible with the Thomist account of divine simplicity. To make an incredibly long story short, for

---

[24] Actually, Aquinas believed that there was *just* one substantial form in any bit of matter (*ST* 1a 76.4). But one need not accept this particular view of his to feel the more general conceptual pressure to which talk of prime matter responds, and it is to show this that I am abstracting from his particular view.

[25] What of existence? The existence of something *x* is also supposed to be a truthmaker for the proposition '*x* exists'. But one can be pardoned the thought that *x* itself makes '*x* exists' true, and so a further truthmaker (existence) is otiose.

Aquinas, following a particular reading of an important Christian creed, the divine Persons are not supposed to be parts into which God divides. Each Person is all of God. All of God is Father, all of God is Son, and yet Father and Son are not identical. On Aquinas's approach, it is more nearly correct to say that God makes up the Persons of the Trinity rather than that the Persons make up God: very roughly, God eternally, necessarily and intrinsically plays the roles of Father, Son and Spirit. But I cannot say more than this; one cannot summarize Aquinas's account of the Trinity in a few paragraphs, and the Trinity does not come up in the Questions I am introducing.

Immutability

Aquinas's DDS shapes the rest of his account of God. It entails, for instance, God's being intrinsically immutable (9.1). Aquinas relies in this context on a distinction between intrinsic and extrinsic changes. To change intrinsically is to gain or lose some but not all intrinsic properties. To see why 'some but not all' is required, suppose that some item, George, loses all its intrinsic properties. George has the property of being identical with George. This property is intrinsic: whether George has it does not depend on how things are in the world outside George's boundaries. If George loses all its intrinsic properties, it loses the property of being identical with George. But if George loses this property, there no longer is anything identical with George. George has ceased to exist and been replaced by something else, rather than merely changing, that is, continuing to exist in a changed form. Thus to change intrinsically, a thing must lose some intrinsic property and also retain at least one other intrinsic property. Since no one property can both remain and not remain, intrinsic change requires a real distinction between the intrinsic properties of the thing that changes. In a simple being such as God, however, there can be no such distinction.

DDS does not rule out 'extrinsic' change, a change in the way that other things are related to God. Since this would not involve God's having had or developing any internal complexity, such changes can be attributed to God (13.7). However, it is worth asking whether Aquinas should admit even extrinsic change in God. Suppose that at a certain point in time we are the same height, and you later grow taller so that I am then shorter than you. This is a mere extrinsic change in me. But it still follows that at one time something is true of me that is not true of me at another time, and this may entail my being in time. Yet Aquinas wants God's immutability to entail God's being atemporal (10.2). Aquinas also thinks that DDS rules out ceasing to exist. In Question 9.2 he suggests that this follows because ceasing to exist is a change in the thing that ceases. This is in tension with his claim (at *ST* 1a 45.2 *ad* 2) that coming into existence is not a change in the thing that comes into existence, because his argument for this claim would apply equally to ceasing to exist.

Timelessness

As Aquinas sees it, 'time is the numbering of before and after in change (*motus*)' (10.1). For Aquinas, a '*motus*' is an intrinsic change or a spatial movement. Thus time is a sequence of locations for this sort of event, which are ordered like the real numbers. Just as (in his eyes) spaces are locations for material objects, times are locations for events. Other items such as properties are in space due to their relations to material things. For example, the colours red, white and blue are in a certain place only because there is an American flag there. If there were no flag or anything else red there, there could not be any redness there. In a similar way, according to Aquinas, if things other than *motus* exist at times, this is only because they do or can have *motus* at those times (10.4 *ad* 3). Accordingly, if a thing does not at least possibly change intrinsically or move, it is not located in time.

Aquinas's account of time is one premise in his argument that God is atemporal. The other premises come from his treatment of God. As we have seen, the Thomist God is intrinsically immutable. In arguing for God's immutability, Aquinas does not discuss spatial motion because he thinks that other things he has already argued eliminate this. Because God is immaterial (3.1), he does not occupy any place as material things do and so does not move from place so filled to place so filled. This is necessarily so, as he is immaterial by nature. Because he is omniscient and the Creator and sustainer of all things, he is also omnipresent in the sense of being 'in' all things and places in virtue of his power over and knowledge of them (8.2–3). In this peculiar way of being in place, he is already in every place to which we might think he could move. There is no place for him to go and, for that reason too, he does not move from place to place. This too is necessarily so if any place exists: he is omniscient by nature, and he is by nature such that he creates and sustains whatever coexists with him. So necessarily, Aquinas's God does not move from place to place.

Aquinas's account of time, together with his claims about God, imply that God is atemporal (10.2). However, one might query the account of time on which he relies here. Perhaps (we may think) if time passes, everything gets older, not just things that do or might undergo *motus*. Again, Aquinas explicitly allows that God can undergo extrinsic change, as when God becomes Lord of a new creature simply because a new creature comes to exist (13.7). At one point in time, for instance, he is not the Lord of Moses and subsequently he comes to be such after Moses is born. It is a good question why being able to change extrinsically is not enough to place God in time.

God's knowledge

The First Way leads Aquinas to say that nothing in God either is or realizes a passive potentiality (3.1), where 'passive potentiality' is understood as that by virtue of which something may be acted on by something else.[26] The denial of passive potentiality in God has implications for Aquinas's account of divine knowledge. If nothing can act on God then God does not know things outside himself by perceiving them, because perceptual knowledge is knowledge that one is caused to have. When we see a tree, for instance, light reflected from the tree enters our eyes and stimulates various nerves. On Aquinas's account, therefore, God cannot literally observe the world. If God cannot 'look' outside himself to know things, the only way he could have knowledge is by looking within. Accordingly, Aquinas holds that in some sense God knows all he knows by knowing himself (14.5–6). We know some of our mental states by introspection: we are just immediately aware that we are thinking certain things or are in pain, for instance. For Aquinas, via DDS, everything in God is identical with his mental states: otherwise there would be a real distinction within him, between his mental states and something else. So if God can know his mental states immediately, just by having them, God can have the same immediate grasp of everything about him. Aquinas holds in consequence that God can 'look within' for knowledge

---

[26] *Commentary on Aristotle's Metaphysics Book IX* 1. 1, #1782.

of both possible and necessary truths. Aquinas holds that God is omnipotent, meaning by this that he can bring about all states of affairs whose
obtaining does not entail a contradiction (25.3).[27] So, on his account, God
can know all that is possible simply by understanding fully the range of
his own power.[28] He might also know all that is necessarily true by
introspection, since necessary truths are simply those that would be
true given any possible state of affairs whatever. So when he looks within
himself and sees what he can bring about, he sees the content of every
possible world. He knows by looking within himself that what he can
make actual is a world containing contingent truths that he helps make
true and necessary truths that he does not make true, but which would be
true if he made the contingent truths true.

Thus Aquinas may be able to provide an account of God's knowledge
of what is possible and necessary, and perhaps DDS allows us to call all
this knowledge introspective. But it is not clear how God can look within
himself and come to know contingent states of affairs in creation.
Aquinas argues that God must be able to do this, but does not say
much about how he can do so. Question 14.5 and 14.8 might suggest
an answer along these lines: God knows what he wills to be the case by
looking within himself. God knows by knowing his own nature that
whatever he wills to be the case is the case. So God knows by looking
within himself premises from which he could infer what is the case
outside himself. God does not perform any inferences (14.7). But God
'sees' without inference, 'in' these premises, what anyone else would have
to infer from them (19.5).

This account implies that God wills the occurrence even of our free
choices, with a power that cannot be obstructed. It also seems to entail
God's not (so to speak) waiting to see what we choose and then cooperat-
ing in causing it to happen, but rather determining from all eternity what
we choose. This seems to put the freedom of our choices in jeopardy. But
if Aquinas's account of how God knows what is contingently the case
outside himself is not broadly of this sort, it is not clear what else it might
be. True, when Aquinas comes to discuss the relation between divine

---

[27] For some apparent qualifications see *Summa against Gentiles* II 25.
[28] Aquinas holds that it is not in God's power to do evil (25.3 *ad* 2). It would seem to follow that he
could not know of possible evil states of affairs by understanding the range of his power. To
pursue this by way of a look at Aquinas on God's knowledge of evils, see 14.10; *Summa against
Gentiles* I 71; *On Truth* 2.15.

foreknowledge and human freedom (14.13), he does not speak of God's will. He speaks instead as if God knew about our free actions by observing them. But on Aquinas's terms, as we have seen, God cannot literally observe anything.

Divine ideas

There are eternal, necessary truths, for example that $2 + 2 = 4$ or that courage is a virtue. Plato gave an influential theory of what makes these things true: they are true, he held, because there are timeless entities, the Forms or Ideas, whose relations make them true: courage is a virtue because the Idea of Courage has a particular relation to the Idea of Virtue. Augustine, whose theology was in many ways the framework within which Aquinas worked, had been a Platonist before he became a Christian. So he was concerned to fit the Ideas he had believed in within a Christian metaphysic: Augustine asked how the Ideas relate to God. His answer was that Plato's Ideas were ideas in the mind of God. But Augustine, like Aquinas, held DDS. This posed a question: how can an internally simple being have many ideas in his mind? Augustine never answered the question. Aquinas does. To understand his answer, let us distinguish two sorts of 'meaning' a term can have. A term's *sense* is the sort of meaning a definition of the term might express: the sense of 'the Morning Star' is 'the last star to disappear in the morning'. 'The Morning Star' refers to Venus: a term's *reference* is what those who use that term as the subject of an assertive sentence are talking about, and if I say 'the Morning Star is a planet', I am talking about Venus. Aquinas's answer to our question is that ' "idea" is not the name for God's essence as such, but only in so far as it is the likeness or intelligible nature of this or that thing' (15.2 *ad* 1). That ' "idea" is not the name for God's essence as such' asserts that when we speak of (say) a divine idea of Jones, we are referring to God's nature (as 'the Morning Star' names Venus). As DDS implies that God *is* his nature, Aquinas's point here is really that in these cases we are talking about God. That 'idea' names God 'as . . . the likeness or intelligible nature of this or that thing' asserts that the sense of 'divine idea of Jones' is 'God *qua* likeness . . . of Jones'. For Aquinas, then, there really are not many distinct divine ideas. There is only God. Aquinas purges divine ideas from his ontology. When DDS collides with the claim that God has many ideas, the latter yields.

The will of God

Due to DDS, Aquinas holds that God's occurrent knowing (14.4) and willing (19.2 *ad* 1) are identical with God's essence and so with each other. This seems implausible, as one would think there are things that God knows but does not will. God knew that Hitler was killing the Jews, but (we might think) this surely was not something that he willed. So too, he knows that $2 + 2 = 4$, but what God wills, we might think, he brings about – and if it is necessarily true that $2 + 2 = 4$, that $2 + 2 = 4$ would seem not to need bringing about by anyone. As to the first problem, the claim that God did not will that Hitler kill the Jews is misleading short-hand. God certainly did permit it, and permitting is an act of will. Further, God also kept Hitler in existence, kept the gas in the chambers lethal (by upholding the laws of nature), and so on. When we say that God did not will the Jews' deaths, then, we can mean only that he did not think that this was good or that he commanded that we not do such things. But all this raises another question. If all God's acts of will are identical with his essence, God has only one act of will, since he has only one essence. So one may wonder how the one act can cause the gas to be lethal, permit the SS men to operate the chamber and prevent the doing of even worse evil, which seem three different kinds of activity.

Here is one approach. For Aquinas, what makes necessary truths true is identical with the divine essence (14.5–6; 25.3): the same simple reality makes it true that God is divine and that $2 + 2 = 4$. It follows that God's willing does not bring it about that necessary truths are true, because they are identical with God's willing (19.2 *ad* 1) and because God's willing does not bring it about that his essence exists. He knows that such things are true introspectively, and his willing them can be called a rejoicing that they are so, in so far as he rejoices in being God.[29] In the case of contingent things that God knows/wills, he either causes or merely permits them. He causes them if they do not involve either free creaturely action or natural or moral evil. If they involve any of the latter, he merely permits them. All distinctions here depend on the content of what God knows/wills. There is the one simple divine act, which is directed to all actual and possible states of affairs. Whether it is a rejoicing, a causing or a permitting of some particular state of affairs depends entirely on what

---

[29] *Summa against Gentiles* 1 90.

the state of affairs is. But this strategy is troubling. Sometimes, when we cause good things and merely permit evils, this is because our attitude towards the two differs in tone or quality: we approve of the goods and disapprove of the others, and these attitudes' really differing explains why we only permit the evils. On the strategy just outlined, God's inner attitudes (knowing/willing) towards a good he positively wills and an evil he merely permits are just identical. So to speak, one could not tell that he was for one and against the other by a qualitative tone. There is nothing in the attitude he takes to explain his only permitting the evils, for there is no difference in the attitudes involved at all, intrinsically. So it seems that something important has been lost.

Aquinas's picture of God as perfect (q. 4) and simple sets him other problems about God's will. Someone who is perfect in all respects lacks nothing. But to will something seems to imply that one wants it, and (one might think) one wants only what one does not have. So being perfect seems to exclude having a will (19.1 obj. 1). Aquinas replies that God wills to possess only himself (19.1 *ad* 1, and 2) and so always has what he so wants as to will it. But then can he will things outside himself (19.2)? Yes, Aquinas argues, because it is natural to things to seek to 'spread their own good to others so far as they can' and so 'much more is it the characteristic of God's will to share his goodness with others (so far as this is possible)' (19.2). The idea, it seems, is that God wills only what he does not lack – his goodness – but wills there to be more of it by making other things which reflect it (19.3). But before he made them, did not God lack those other things and that reflection? What Aquinas really needs here is the thought that God's own possession of his goodness cannot be added to, and so his decision to share with others is sheer generosity.[30] In any case, this answer imperils the claim that God has free choice. It seems to make God's willing other things something that he does by nature and to require an explanation and defence of the claim that God is free (19.10).

Aquinas asks whether God necessarily wills whatever he wills (19.3) and whether he acts by will at all (19.4). These are for Aquinas really two aspects of a single question, since on his account, anything that does not act by will acts by nature (19.4) and a thing necessarily does whatever it

---

[30] *Summa against Gentiles* I 93.

does by nature. This question arises in part from DDS (19.3 obj. 3 *et* 6). According to DDS, God's willing is identical with God's essence (19.1 *ad* 3), and things have their essences necessarily. So it might seem to follow that God has his act of will necessarily. But if he necessarily has the very act of will he has, it seems to follow that he necessarily wills exactly what he does. If he does, he acts by nature, not will.

Aquinas replies that God wills with absolute necessity only his own goodness. Since in order to possess his own goodness he does not need other things to exist, he need not will the latter (19.3). Yet Aquinas also recognizes a way in which it is necessary that God will anything he wills, and this muddies the waters. In addition to absolute necessity, Aquinas speaks of hypothetical necessity:

> We judge something to be absolutely necessary on the basis of some relation holding between terms . . . 'Socrates is sitting' is not necessary in this way, and is, therefore, not absolutely necessary. But we can say that 'Socrates is sitting' is hypothetically necessary in the sense that it is true that if Socrates is sitting, he is sitting. (19.3)

Absolute necessity is the sort had by truths of logic and mathematics: if it were absolutely necessary that Socrates sit, that Socrates not be sitting would be as impossible as that $2 + 2 = 5$. Hypothetical necessity is necessity 'given the truth of a particular hypothesis'. It is not absolutely necessary that Socrates sit, but suppose we take as true the hypothesis that he is sitting. While Socrates sits, it is not possible that he is also not sitting. Thus, on the supposition that Socrates sits, for Socrates not to sit would entail a contradiction, namely that Socrates sits and does not sit at the same time. Hypothetical necessity is the same sort as is involved when Aquinas asks whether God can change the past. He cannot do so, Aquinas thinks, because given that Socrates sat, for God to bring it about that he did not sit would imply God's bringing it about that he sat and did not sit at the same time (25.4). Aquinas thinks that hypothetical and absolute necessities are necessary for the same reason: something is necessary whose contradictory implies a contradiction (25.3). There is a difference, however, in that hypothetical necessity is time-relative. From the fact that with hypothetical necessity Socrates sits, nothing follows about whether Socrates will sit or was sitting at some other time. By contrast, if humans are animals with absolute necessity, they are always animals.

Aquinas thinks that it is absolutely necessary that God will his own goodness, but that he need not will anything to exist outside himself. Nonetheless, if God has willed that Socrates sit, this has hypothetical necessity – in his eternal present (10.1), it is necessarily so while it is so – and in this case this does entail his willing it at all future times, since his will is immutable (19.3). (This raises a further question, of how God can will changes without changing his will, which Aquinas takes up in 19.7.) Now, the reason this muddies the waters emerges precisely from the fact that Aquinas sees hypothetical necessities as necessary due to their connection to contradictions, just as absolute necessities are. For then it seems that the proper way to distinguish the two cases is this: absolute necessities are necessarily necessary. Their contradictories are contradictions and could not have failed to be so. Hypothetical necessities are necessary, but only contingently necessary. Their contradictories are contradictions, but could have failed to be such. If this is so, then God necessarily wills everything that he wills. But this is not because he needed to, and he need not have necessarily willed it. If I have interpreted the modality correctly here – a big if, because Aquinas's thinking about modality is hard to puzzle out – Aquinas does not actually save the claim that God wills contingently anything he wills. But oddly enough, this does not matter much. There is no problem in the claim that God did not need to act as he did and that it is up to him what is necessarily true of him 'hypothetically'. These things leave God's action healthily free.

Still, Aquinas does want to say that God wills some things with absolute necessity and some with only hypothetical necessity. Does this entail God's having two acts of will, then? We can see what Aquinas would say here from what he says in a parallel case. God wills some things to be so at all times, for example, that there be the outermost heaven (10.6). He wills others to be so now and not later, for example, that a certain human being is alive. So it seems that his will changes. Aquinas replies that, on the contrary, he has one changeless act of will, which changelessly wills changes to occur, so that some things are so only now (and then otherwise later), while others are always so (19.7). A difference in the temporal status of the object of will does not entail a different act of will. In the same way, Aquinas would say that a difference in the modal status of the object of will does not entail a modally different act of will. God has one act of will, which wills states of affairs of both kinds.

Classical theism after Aquinas

With Aquinas, classical theism reached its apogee. Shortly after his death in 1274, the position began to lose its appeal. Duns Scotus (*c.* 1265–1308) launched influential arguments against Aquinas's DDS and his atemporalism at the end of the thirteenth century. William of Ockham (*c.* 1285–1347/9) subsequently defended a version of DDS but dropped Aquinas's atemporalism. Meanwhile, the *Summa Theologiae* became the standard textbook for the teaching of theology. This ensured that the later Middle Ages knew Aquinas's views, but not that it accepted them. Thomists (i.e. those who aligned themselves with Aquinas) continued to defend classical theism. Scotists and nominalists (i.e. those whose philosophy and theology aligned broadly with Ockham) continued to assault parts of it to the close of the period. The first generation of Protestant theologians, including Luther and Calvin, tended to support late-medieval nominalism, but later generations gradually reabsorbed more elements of Aquinas's views. Today Aquinas is the most important figure in orthodox Catholic theology, and many Catholic philosophers still consider themselves Thomists. There has been a revival of sympathy for Aquinas and classical theism among analytic philosophers, among whom Aquinas has always been a central presence in debates in the philosophy of religion. There cannot be many medieval authors who are as lively a presence in their fields of study as Aquinas remains today in philosophical theology.[31]

BRIAN LEFTOW

---

[31] My thanks to Jeff Brower and Brian Davies for comments on this introduction.

Chronology

1268–72   again Master in theology, Paris
      Disputed Questions on Evil, Commentary on Aristotle's On Interpretation, Commentary on Aristotle's Nicomachean Ethics, Commentary on Aristotle's Physics, Commentary on Aristotle's Posterior Analytics, Summa Theologiae 2a, *On the Unicity of the Intellect, On the Eternity of the World*

1272–3   in Naples
      Commentary on Aristotle's Metaphysics, On Separated Substances, Summa Theologiae 3a.
      6 December 1273 – mystical experience; stops writing

1274   leaves for Council of Lyons in February; injures head *en route*, near Borgonuovo in mid-month; dies 7 March at Fossanuova

Further reading

On Aquinas's life, the standard work is now J-P. Torrell, *St Thomas Aquinas: the Person and His Work* (Washington, DC: Catholic University of America Press, 1996); there is also James Weisheipl, *Friar Thomas D'aquino* (Washington, DC: Catholic University of America Press, 1983). If you happen to read Latin, the primary sources for Aquinas's life are in A. Ferrua (ed.), *Thomae Aquinatis vitae fontes praecipuae* (Alba: Edn Dominicane, 1968). For some of these in English see Kenelm Foster (ed.), *The Life of Thomas Aquinas* (London: Longmans, Green and Co., 1959).

Several essays in *The Cambridge Companion to Aquinas*, ed. Norman Kretzmann and Eleonore Stump (Cambridge: Cambridge University Press, 1993) provide overviews of Aquinas's relations to his historical sources and to his contemporaries. Almost any treatment of Aquinas will include discussion of his Aristotelianism. His Platonist aspects are less well appreciated; on these there is W. J. Hankey, *God in Himself* (Oxford: Oxford University Press, 1987).

On the form of the *Summa*, its context and how to read it, see, for example, Otto Bird, 'How to Read an Article in the *Summa*', *The New Scholasticism* 27 (1953); Leonard Boyle, *The Setting of the* Summa Theologiae *of Saint Thomas* (Toronto: Pontifical Institute of Medieval Studies, 1982); and M. D. Chenu, *Toward Understanding Saint Thomas*, trans. A. M. Landry and D. Hughes (Chicago: Regnery, 1964).

General introductions to Aquinas's thinking vary in level and degree of comprehensiveness. For a brief, pithy, readable account, see Geach's essay in Elizabeth Anscombe and Peter Geach, *Three Philosophers* (Oxford: Basil Blackwell, 1961). F. C. Copleston's *Aquinas* (Harmondsworth:

Penguin, 1955) is clear but offers less analysis. At greater length are Brian Davies, *The Thought of Thomas Aquinas* (Oxford: Oxford University Press, 1994), and Robert Pasnau and Christopher Shields, *Thomas Aquinas* (Boulder, CO: Westview, 2004). The latter is a bit dismissive of what Thomas has to say about God. Eleonore Stump, *Aquinas* (London and New York: Routledge, 2003) provides a more in-depth and analytical treatment of many aspects of Aquinas's thought. It is clear, precise and penetrating, and although it is at a more advanced level than the others I have mentioned it still manages to be very readable. Most essays in Anthony Kenny's *Aquinas: Critical Essays* (London: Macmillan, 1969) have been superseded by more recent work, but Geach's 'Form and Existence' and the papers of Brown and Deck are still worth a look. Brian Davies (ed.), *Thomas Aquinas* (Oxford: Oxford University Press, 2002), collects a variety of more recent papers.

General metaphysics

No one book encompasses all that Aquinas had to say in metaphysics. Traditional Thomists (basically those not influenced by analytic philosophy) tend to focus on issues that current analytic philosophy either does not discuss or does not know that it is discussing, for example the relation between essence and existence. Representative of this approach are Reginald Garrigou-Lagrange, *Reality* (Chicago: Herder, 1953); John Wippel, *The Metaphysical Thought of St Thomas Aquinas* (Washington, DC: Catholic University of America, 2000); Etienne Gilson, *Being and Some Philosophers* (Toronto: Pontifical Institute of Medieval Studies, 1952); Joseph Owens, *An Elementary Christian Metaphysics* (Houston: Center for Thomistic Studies, 1985). Brian Leftow focuses on issues of more concern to analytic philosophy in *Aquinas on Metaphysics* (Oxford: Oxford University Press, 2006); so do the relevant chapters of Stump (*Aquinas*). Traditional Thomists tend to think well of Aquinas's understanding of existence. Anthony Kenny's *Aquinas on Being* (Oxford: Oxford University Press, 2003) decidedly does not.

The existence of God

The few paragraphs of Aquinas's 'Five Ways' are one of the most heavily discussed passages in all of philosophy: most textbooks and anthologies in philosophy of religion have something to say about them. It is worth looking at the comparable arguments in the *Summa against Gentiles*; many would say that they flesh out at least some of the Ways. James Weisheipl's *Nature and Motion in the Middle Ages* (Washington, DC: Catholic University of America Press, 1985) has a number of essays that provide useful background. Anthony Kenny's *The Five Ways* (Notre Dame: University of Notre Dame Press, 1969) is sharply critical. More sympathetic is Robert Fogelin, 'A Reading of Aquinas's Five Ways', *American Philosophical Quarterly* 27 (1990). Two particularly good articles are Scott MacDonald, 'Aquinas' Parasitic Cosmological Argument', *Medieval Philosophy and Theology* 1 (1991), 134–73, and Barry Miller, 'Necessarily Terminating Causal Series', *Mind* 91 (1982), 201–15. Some say that Aquinas gives another argument for God's existence in *On Essence and Existence*; this is discussed in Wippel (*Metaphysical Thought*), and Scott MacDonald, 'The Esse/Essentia Argument in Aquinas's *De ente et essentia*', *Journal of the History of Philosophy* 22 (1984), 157–72.

The nature of God

Aquinas is the best representative of 'classical theism', a broad approach to God's nature that was almost unchallenged from Augustine until about 1300. Because of this, almost anything written on the divine attributes in the last decades is *de facto* relevant to his views even if it does not mention him by name. The best overall treatment of Aquinas on this is Norman Kretzmann, *The Metaphysics of Creation* (Oxford: Clarendon, 1997). Kretzmann gives a sympathetic account of most main theses Aquinas defends, but the argument for God's existence that he develops may not really be Aquinas's; it employs a principle of sufficient reason that I believe Aquinas rejects. Traditional Thomist treatments include Reginald Garrigou-Lagrange's *The One God* (St Louis, MO: Herder, 1943), which provides commentary on all the questions in this volume, and *God: His Existence and Nature* (St Louis, MO: Herder, 1934), and also Leo Elders, *The Philosophical Theology of St Thomas Aquinas* (Leiden: E. J. Brill, 1990). The most thoroughgoing, careful critique of Aquinas on God's nature is Christopher Hughes, *On a Complex Theory of a Simple God* (Ithaca, NY: Cornell University Press, 1989), though perhaps Hughes gives up on Aquinas rather quickly at points. The most widely discussed recent criticisms of divine simplicity have been Alvin Plantinga's *Does God Have a Nature?* (Milwaukee: Marquette University Press, 1980) and Thomas Morris, 'On God and Mann', reprinted in his *Anselmian Explorations* (Notre Dame: University of Notre Dame Press, 1987). On divine simplicity the best defence available is the relevant chapter of Stump (*Aquinas*); she also advances an interesting but controversial account of God's knowledge. David Burrell's *Aquinas: God and Action* (Notre Dame: University of Notre Dame Press, 1979) is idiosyncratic, but interesting on simplicity. The most influential works critical of the timelessness that Aquinas defends have been Nelson Pike's *God and Timelessness* (New York: Schocken, 1970) and Nicholas Wolterstorff's 'God Everlasting', in Steven Cahn and David Shatz (eds.), *Contemporary Philosophy of Religion* (Oxford: Oxford University Press, 1982), 77–98. Aquinas's account of God's eternality is given its most careful defence in the relevant chapter of Stump (*Aquinas*). Extended defences not specifically keyed to Aquinas include Paul Helm, *Eternal God* (Oxford: Oxford University Press, 1988) and Brian Leftow, *Time and Eternity* (Ithaca, NY: Cornell University Press, 1991).

The most-discussed recent argument against divine immutability was resurrected in Norman Kretzmann, 'Omniscience and Immutability', *Journal of Philosophy*. (The argument's earliest appearance was in the Muslim philosopher al-Ghazzali.) Richard Gale rings the changes on this sort of argument at length in his *On the Existence and Nature of God* (Cambridge: Cambridge University Press, 1991). A traditional Thomist account of immutability is Michael Dodds, *The Unchanging God of Love* (Fribourg: Editions Universitaires Fribourg Suisse, 1986). Aquinas's account of freedom and foreknowledge is largely an endorsement of the 'Boethian' approach to it. For sympathetic discussions see Linda Zagzebski, *The Dilemma of Freedom and Foreknowledge* (Oxford: Oxford University Press, 1991) and Brian Leftow, 'Timelessness and Foreknowledge', *Philosophical Studies* (US) 63 (1991), 309–25. Recent discussions of omnipotence tend to bring Aquinas's account forward as a 'first approximation' and then introduce successive qualifications. The most widely discussed account is in Fred Freddoso and Thomas Flint, 'Maximal Power', in Alfred Freddoso (ed.), *The Existence of God* (Notre Dame: University of Notre Dame Press, 1983), 81–113; see also Edward Wierenga, *The Nature of God: an Inquiry into Divine Attributes* (Ithaca, NY: Cornell University Press, 1989).

Talk about God: the theory of analogy

The best work by a traditional Thomist is Ralph McInerny, *The Logic of Analogy* (The Hague: Martinus Nijhoff, 1961), and *Aquinas and Analogy* (Washington, DC: Catholic University of America Press, 1996). A good recent account and critique is William Alston, 'Aquinas on Theological Predication', in Eleonore Stump (ed.), *Reasoned Faith* (Ithaca, NY: Cornell University Press, 1993), 145–78.

Editors' and translator's note

The translation of this text was prepared by Brian Davies, and the introduction and essay on further reading are by Brian Leftow. The editorial footnotes are the result of collaboration between Brian Davies and Brian Leftow.

The translation

Between 1964 and 1981 a fifty-nine-volume edition of Aquinas's *Summa Theologiae* was published under the auspices of the English Dominican friars. Its general editor was the late Thomas Gilby OP. Apart from the final volume, it was published by Eyre and Spottiswoode (London) and the McGraw-Hill Book Company (New York). (Volume 59, an Index, was only published by Eyre and Spottiswoode.) The edition contained a Latin text of the *Summa Theologiae* and a facing English translation produced by a number of different people (some Dominicans, some not). It also included many explanatory and reference notes together with a large number of appendices expounding or commentating on Aquinas's thinking. This multi-volume translation became known as the Blackfriars edition.

Having recently acquired the rights to the Blackfriars edition (now out of print), Cambridge University Press invited me to correct part of its translation for publication in Cambridge Texts in the History of Philosophy. What follows is my revision of most of the translation of Aquinas to be found in volumes 1–5 of the Blackfriars edition. These cover 1a (*prima pars*) 1–26 and (following a question in which Aquinas ruminates on what he calls 'sacred doctrine') basically give us Aquinas's treatise on God considered without special reference to uniquely Christian teaching.

The Blackfriars edition of Aquinas is very known, has been favourably reviewed and has been much used by professional medievalists and by students seeking to learn about what is probably Aquinas's greatest intellectual achievement. It was a great project. Before it appeared, the only complete English version of the *Summa* was *St Thomas Aquinas, 'Summa Theologica'*, translated by the Fathers of the English Dominican Province (in reality, translated by a single and largely unacknowledged Dominican called Laurence Shapcote, who lived from 1864 to 1947) and originally published by Burns, Oates and Washbourne (London) in 1911.

Yet the Blackfriars translation is not without its faults. In some ways it was a distinct improvement on its predecessor. It reads much more easily to general readers; it seems more modern and less technical; for many people it has made Aquinas come alive as never before. But it often (and sometimes very misleadingly) paraphrases where a more literal rendition is called for. And it does not always help readers to note where Aquinas is changing (or not changing) his terminology, or where a translation using an unfamiliar word might help readers to see what Aquinas is actually talking about. Also, even though it appeared relatively recently, the Blackfriars translation (of 1a 1–26 at any rate) is now somewhat less than colloquial when it comes to contemporary English. So, while retaining a good part of what I have been asked to go over, I have also modified it quite substantially, and in many places dramatically. The result, I hope, is both a more accurate and a more readable rendition of Aquinas's text, one which should prove especially useful to students approaching Aquinas for the first time and with no knowledge of Latin.

Four questions of 1a 1–26 are missing from the present volume: 16 (on truth), 17 (on falsity), 23 (on predestination) and 24 (on the 'Book of Life'). These passages have been omitted partly for reasons of space and partly because they are not essential to Aquinas's major topic in this section of the *Summa Theologiae*. From 1a 2 onwards (1a 1 being a 'scene-setting' introduction to the *Summa Theologiae* as a whole, and, therefore, worth including below), this can be put in the form of the question 'What can reason alone tell us about God?', and, in the translation that follows, readers will find all that is most central to Aquinas's answer to this question in the *prima pars*.

The Latin text used in the Blackfriars edition did not claim to be a critical one, though it noted a small number of variations between different printed editions of the *Summa Theologiae*. In what follows

I have simply worked from the Latin text preferred by the Blackfriars translators (which is a perfectly respectable one given that we still lack a definitive critical edition of the *Summa Theologiae*). I have also: (a) often revised their translations of biblical texts quoted by Aquinas in accordance with the Latin he gives for them; and (b) modified the layout of the Blackfriars translation to make for what, I hope, is an easier read. Commentary and explanatory notes to be found in volumes 1–5 of the Blackfriars edition are omitted below, though the translation comes with new explanatory notes designed to help readers to make sense of what Aquinas is arguing and to give them the dates of authors referred to by him. I should add that notes to the translation employ only three abbreviations: *PL* (Migne, *Patrologia Latina*); *PG* (Migne, *Patrologia Graeca*); and 1a (*Summa Theologiae*, Part I (*prima pars*)). I should also add that when Aquinas cites Scripture he is referring to the Vulgate edition of the Bible and that references accompanying Aquinas's citations in this volume follow him accordingly.

I have rendered all titles of Latin texts into English. Since English translations of some of the texts in question vary and others are not available in English editions, the translations of the titles are intended simply to assist readers who cannot consult the original texts.

For helpful comments on my reworking of the Blackfriars translation of 1a 1–26 I am grateful to Desmond Clarke, Joseph Koterski SJ, Brian Leftow, Robert Pasnau, Richard Regan SJ and Thomas Williams. The remaining mistakes, of course, are all mine.

BRIAN DAVIES

Summa Theologiae, Questions on God

Question 1

The nature and scope of sacred doctrine

In order to confine the scope of my inquiry, I must first investigate the nature and range of sacred doctrine,[1] on which I have ten questions to raise:

1. Is there any need for this teaching?
2. Is it a science?[2]
3. Is it one science or many?
4. Is it theoretical or practical?
5. How does it compare with other sciences?
6. Is it wisdom?
7. What is its subject?
8. Does it employ arguments?
9. Does it rightly employ metaphorical or figurative language?
10. Can we interpret its sacred writings in different senses?

Article 1: Is any teaching needed apart from what philosophy provides?

1. It seems that we need no teaching beyond that of philosophy. For we should not seek to know what lies beyond our reason. As Ecclesiasticus

---

[1] I.e. Christian theology, the setting forth of what the Christian faith teaches about various matters.

[2] Aquinas uses 'science' to describe bodies of truths, not a method of discovering truths. Aquinas thinks of sciences as deductive systems; the conclusions of a science deduce conclusions from its primary assertions or 'first principles' and so unfold their contents. To know a proposition by grasping its deduction from a science's 'first principles' is to know it 'scientifically' within that science; the 'first principles' are either self-evident or accepted from another science. To know a proposition which is not self-evident 'scientifically' is to know it in the best possible way.

3

says, 'Do not seek after things above you.'[3] But philosophy deals well enough with what lies within the range of reason. So, additional teaching seems unnecessary.

2. Moreover, we can only be taught about some being or other. For we only know the true, and the true and being are convertible.[4] But the philosophical sciences[5] deal with all beings, even God. So we call a part of philosophy 'theology', or 'the science of God', as the Philosopher makes clear in his *Metaphysics*.[6] So, there is no need for teaching other than what philosophy can provide.

On the contrary, 2 Timothy says, 'All divinely inspired scripture is useful for teaching, reproving, correcting, and instructing in righteousness.'[7] But divinely inspired Scripture does not belong to the branches of philosophy which come from human reasoning. So it is useful to have a divinely inspired science over and above philosophical ones.

Reply: It was necessary for human salvation that there should be instruction by divine revelation in addition to the philosophical sciences pursued by human reasoning – chiefly because we are ordered to God as an end beyond the grasp of reason. As Isaiah says, 'Without you, God, no eye has seen what you have prepared for those who love you.'[8] But we have to know about an end before we can direct our intentions and actions towards it. So, it was necessary for the salvation of human beings that truths surpassing reason should be made known to us through divine revelation.

We also stood in need of being instructed by divine revelation even in matters to do with God which human reason is able to investigate. For the truth about God that reason investigates would have occurred only to few, and only after a long time, and only with many mistakes mixed in. But our salvation, which lies in God, depends on us knowing the truth about him. So, in order that our salvation might be effected more suitably and surely, we needed to be instructed by divine revelation concerning God. We had, therefore, to have sacred doctrine by revelation – teaching over and above that given to us by philosophical sciences.

---

[3] Ecclesiasticus 3:22.
[4] I.e. whatever is true is something that exists, and whatever exists is something that is true.
[5] The disciplines of philosophy, particularly metaphysics. 'Sciences' indicates the grade of knowledge Aquinas thinks they provide.
[6] Aristotle (384–322 BC), *Metaphysics* 6.1, 1026a19; 1.2, 983a10. Also, possibly not authentic, 11.7, 1062b2 and 12.6–7, 1071b3–1073a12.
[7] 2 Timothy 3:16.   [8] Isaiah 64:4.

Hence:

1. Human reason should indeed not pry into things above human knowledge. But we should welcome them in faith when God reveals them to us. As the passage in Ecclesiasticus continues, 'You are shown many things that are above the understanding of human beings.'[9] And sacred doctrine contains such things.

2. When there is more than one aspect under which a given item can be known, there will be more than one science concerning it. After all, both an astronomer and a natural scientist might demonstrate the same conclusion – that the earth is round, for instance. The former, however, employs a middle term that is mathematical (i.e. one that prescinds from matter), whereas the latter employs a middle term that takes matter into account. So, there is nothing to stop what is treated by philosophical sciences (in so far as it can be known by natural reason) from also being dealt with by another science (in so far as it is known by the light of divine revelation). The theology that belongs to sacred doctrine therefore differs in kind from the theology ranked as a part of philosophy.

Article 2: Is sacred doctrine a science?

1. It seems that sacred doctrine is not a science. For every science advances from self-evident first principles.[10] But sacred doctrine advances from articles of faith,[11] which are not self-evident since not everybody grants them. As 2 Thessalonians says, 'not all have faith'.[12] So, sacred doctrine is not a science.

2. Again, a science is not concerned with individual things. But sacred doctrine deals with individual events and people (the lives of Abraham, Isaac, Jacob, and so on). So, sacred doctrine is not a science.

On the other hand, Augustine says that 'this science alone is credited with begetting, nourishing, protecting, and strengthening the most saving faith'.[13] These functions belong only to the science of sacred doctrine. So, sacred doctrine is a science.

---

[9] Ecclesiasticus 3:23.   [10] The primary premises from which conclusions in a science are deduced.
[11] The assertions of the Apostles' and Nicene Creeds.   [12] 2 Thessalonians 3:2.
[13] St Augustine (354–430), *On the Trinity* 14.7. *PL* 42.1037.

Reply: Sacred doctrine is a science. Yet bear in mind sciences differ from each other. Some work from first principles known by the natural light of the intellect – such as arithmetic, geometry, and the like. Others, however, work from principles known by the light of a higher science. Optics, for instance, begins from geometrical principles, and music proceeds from arithmetical ones.

Sacred doctrine is a science in the second sense here, for it proceeds from principles made known by a higher science – that of God and the blessed. So, just as music relies on principles taken from arithmetic, sacred doctrine relies on principles revealed by God.

Hence:

1. The first principles of any science are either self-evident in themselves or can be traced back to what a higher science recognizes. Such are the principles of sacred doctrine, as I have noted.
2. Sacred doctrine deals with individual things not because it is primarily concerned with them but to introduce examples for our lives (as in moral sciences), and to make clear the authority of the people through whom divine revelation (on which sacred Scripture or teaching is based) has come down to us.

Article 3: Is sacred doctrine a single science?

1. It seems that sacred doctrine is not a single science. For, according to Aristotle, 'one science has one kind of subject'.[14] But the creator and creature, both treated of in sacred doctrine, are not contained in one kind of subject. So, sacred doctrine is not a single science.
2. Moreover, sacred doctrine treats of angels, bodily creatures, and human conduct – all of which belong to different philosophical sciences. So, sacred doctrine is not a single science.

On the contrary, sacred Scripture refers to it as a single science: 'He gave him the science of sacred things.'[15]

Reply: Sacred doctrine is a single science. For we gauge the unity of a faculty[16] or habit[17] by its object, considered not with regard to matter,[18]

---

[14] *Posterior Analytics* 1.28, 87a38.   [15] Wisdom 10:10.
[16] A power, e.g. the powers to think or sense.
[17] A disposition to use a power in a particular way, e.g. the habit of doing arithmetic correctly.
[18] The particular things a power or disposition deals with.

but with respect to some formal characteristic.[19] Thus, for example, people, donkeys and stones all share one formal characteristic, that of being coloured, and colour is the object of sight. Now since, as I have already noted,[20] sacred Scripture looks at things with respect to them being divinely revealed, all divinely revealed things share in the one formal aspect which is the object of this science. They are, therefore, included under sacred doctrine as under a single science.

Hence:

1. Sacred doctrine does not draw conclusions about God and creatures equally. It is chiefly concerned with God, and it turns to creatures considered as being in relation to him, their origin and end. So, its unity as a science is not compromised.

2. Nothing prevents lower faculties or habits from being diversified by different subject matters that all fall under one higher power or habit, for the higher is related to its object under a more universal formality. Take, for instance, the common sense.[21] Both visual and audible phenomena (perceptible to the senses) are included in its object. Yet, while gathering in all the objects of the five external senses, it remains a single faculty. Likewise, different classes of object separately treated by different philosophical sciences can be treated by sacred doctrine that retains its unity in so far as all of them are brought into the same focus, namely, in so far as they are divinely revealed. In effect, therefore, sacred doctrine is like an imprint of God's own knowledge, which is a single and simple knowledge of everything.

Article 4: Is sacred doctrine a practical science?

1. It seems that sacred doctrine is a practical science. For Aristotle says that 'a practical science has action as its end'.[22] But according to the letter of James, sacred doctrine is directed to action: 'Be doers of the word and not only hearers.'[23] So, sacred doctrine is a practical science.

---

[19] The trait in virtue of which particular things become the 'objects' of a power or disposition. It is because they are coloured that people, etc. are objects of sight, i.e. things that can be seen.
[20] 1a 1.2.
[21] That which integrates the inputs of the five particular senses into a single sensory picture of the world.
[22] *Metaphysics* 2.1, 993b21. [23] James 1:22.

2. Moreover, sacred doctrine is divided into the Old Law and the New Law. But law relates to moral science, which is practical. So, sacred doctrine is a practical science.

On the contrary, every practical science is concerned with what people can do. Thus ethics is concerned with human acts, and architecture is concerned with buildings. Sacred doctrine, however, is chiefly about God, whose first and foremost work is people. So, it is a theoretical science rather than a practical one.

Reply: As I have already said,[24] sacred doctrine, while remaining single, nevertheless extends to things belonging to different philosophical sciences because of the common formal factor that it considers in all things, namely, their knowability by illumination from God. While some philosophical sciences are theoretical and others are practical, sacred doctrine is both – in this being like the single science by which God knows himself and the things that he makes.

All the same, it is more theoretical than practical. For it is more concerned with divine things than with what people do. It deals with human acts only in so far as they prepare us for the perfect knowledge of God in which our eternal bliss consists.

This makes it clear how the objections noted above should be answered.

Article 5: Is sacred doctrine more noble than any other science?

1. It seems that sacred doctrine is not more noble than any other science. For certainty is part of a science's value. But the other sciences (whose first principles are indubitable) look more assured and certain than sacred doctrine, whose first principles (the articles of faith) are open to doubt. So, these other sciences seem more noble.

2. Again, a lower science draws on a higher, as, for example, music draws on arithmetic. But sacred doctrine draws on philosophical learning. Jerome says that 'the ancient writers so filled their books with the theories and verdicts of philosophers that at first you are at a loss which to admire more: their secular erudition or their knowledge[25] of

---

[24] 1a 1.3.   [25] The Latin here is 'scientia', translated 'science' elsewhere.

the Scriptures'.[26] So, sacred doctrine has a lower standing than other sciences.

On the contrary, Proverbs describes the other sciences as its maidservants: 'Wisdom has sent her maidservants to extend an invitation to the tower.'[27]

Reply: Since the science of sacred doctrine is partly theoretical and partly practical, it ranks above any other science, whether theoretical or practical.

We reckon one theoretical science to be more noble than another first because of the certitude it brings, and then because of the dignity of its subject matter. The science of sacred doctrine surpasses the others on both counts. As to certainty, because theirs comes from the natural light of human reason, which can make mistakes, whereas sacred doctrine is held in the light of God's knowledge which cannot be mistaken. As to nobility of subject matter, because their business is only with things that reason can grasp, whereas sacred science leads to heights to which reason cannot climb.

And the practical science that is ordered to a further purpose is more noble than other practical sciences. Hence, for example, the science of governing is nobler than military science since the good of the military is directed to the good of the state. Now, in so far as sacred doctrine is a practical science, its aim is eternal happiness, and this is the final end to which all the ends of other practical sciences are ordered.

Hence it is clear that from every standpoint sacred doctrine is nobler than all other sciences.

Hence:

1. There is nothing to stop something more certain as to its nature from being less certain in relation to us because of the weakness of our intellect (which, as Aristotle notes, 'blinks at the most evident natural things like owls in the sunshine').[28] So, doubt about the articles of faith, which falls to the lot of some, is not because the reality they talk about is at all uncertain, but because human understanding is feeble. Nevertheless, as Aristotle also points out, the smallest grasp we can form of the highest things is more desirable than even a thorough grasp of the lowest ones.[29]

---

[26] St Jerome (*c.* 345–420), Letter 70. *PL* 22.668.   [27] Proverbs 9:3.
[28] *Metaphysics* 2.1, 993b10.   [29] *On the Parts of Animals* 1.5, 644b31.

2. Sacred doctrine can borrow from philosophical disciplines, not from any need to beg from them, but in order to make itself clearer. For it takes its first principles directly from God through revelation, not from other sciences, and it therefore does not rely on them as though they were its superior. Their role is subsidiary and ancillary, as is that of a tradesman to an architect or a soldier to a statesman. And that it turns to them accordingly is not from any lack or insufficiency within itself, but because of a lack in our intellect, which is more easily led to what lies beyond reason (and is set forth in sacred doctrine) by things known through natural reason (from which the other sciences begin).

Article 6: Is this teaching wisdom?

1. It seems that this teaching is not wisdom. For no teaching which takes its principles from elsewhere deserves the name of wisdom. As Aristotle remarks, 'the office of the wise is to govern others, not to be governed by them'.[30] But sacred doctrine takes its first principles from elsewhere, as I said earlier.[31] So, it is not wisdom.
2. Moreover, it is wisdom's job to prove the principles of the other sciences, which is why we call it 'the chief of the sciences',[32] as Aristotle makes clear. But sacred doctrine does not prove the first principles of the other sciences. So, it is not wisdom.
3. Again, this teaching is acquired from study. Wisdom, however, is acquired by infusion,[33] and is therefore numbered among the seven Gifts[34] of the Holy Spirit (as is clear from Isaiah).[35] So, this teaching is not wisdom.

On the contrary, at the beginning of the Torah Deuteronomy says, 'This is our wisdom and understanding in the sight of the peoples.'[36]

Reply: Among all human wisdom, this body of doctrine especially is wisdom, not only in some particular respect but unconditionally.

---

[30] *Metaphysics* 1.2, 982a18.   [31] 1a 1.2.   [32] *Nicomachean Ethics* 6.7, 1141a16.
[33] Direct divine bestowal.
[34] Unearned benefits that God confers to aid the Christian life, including courage, piety, fear, counsel, understanding, knowledge, wisdom.
[35] Isaiah 11:2.   [36] Deuteronomy 4:6.

It belongs to the wise person to regulate and judge, and one judges lesser matters in the light of a higher cause. So people are wise in some area of inquiry if they consider the highest cause in that area. Take, for example, architecture. We apply the terms 'wise' and 'expert builders' to the artists who plan the form of a house, not to their employees who cut the stones and mix the mortar. Hence the reference in 1 Corinthians: 'Like a wise architect, I have laid the foundation.'[37] Then again, when it comes to human living in general we call prudent people wise because they direct human acts to their due end. Thus Proverbs says 'Prudence in a person is a form of wisdom.'[38] So, we say that one who considers without qualification the highest cause of the entire universe (God), is supremely wise, which is why we say that wisdom consists in knowledge of divine things, as is clear from what Augustine writes.[39]

Now, sacred doctrine most properly treats of God in so far as he is the highest cause – not only because of what is knowable about him from creatures, which philosophers have recognized (cf. Romans: 'What was known of God is manifest in them'),[40] but also because of what he alone knows about himself and communicates to others by revelation. So, sacred doctrine is called wisdom in the highest degree.

Hence:

1. Sacred doctrine takes its first principles from no human science, but from God's own knowledge,[41] by which, as by supreme wisdom, all our knowledge is governed.

2. The first principles of other sciences are either self-evident[42] (in which case they cannot be proved) or are proved in some other science through natural reason. What is distinctive to the knowledge of the science of sacred doctrine is that it comes through revelation, not through natural reasoning. For this reason, its function is not to establish the first principles of the other sciences but to judge them. For whatever we encounter in the other sciences which is incompatible with its truth we condemn as false. Hence 2 Corinthians alludes to 'destroying counsels and every height that rears itself against the knowledge of God'.[43]

3. Since wisdom's role is to judge, there are two kinds of wisdom according to the two ways of passing judgement. It happens that

---

[37] 1 Corinthians 3:10.   [38] Proverbs 10:23.   [39] *On the Trinity* 12.14. *PL* 42.1009.
[40] Romans 1:19.   [41] 'Scientia' or science.   [42] See q. 2, a. 1c.   [43] 2 Corinthians 10:4–5.

one may judge on the basis of an inclination, as when people who possess the habit of virtue rightly judge what should be done in accordance with it because they are already drawn to those things. Hence Aristotle remarks that the virtuous person sets the measure and standard for human acts.[44] Alternatively, a judgement may be arrived at through a cognitive process, as when people soundly instructed in moral science make judgements about some acts reflecting a particular virtue even though they do not themselves have the virtue in question.

The first way of judging divine things belongs to that wisdom which is classed among the Gifts of the Holy Spirit. So 1 Corinthians says, 'The spiritual person judges all things.'[45] And Dionysius says that 'Hierotheus was taught by the experience of divine things, not only by learning about them.'[46] The second way of judging pertains to sacred doctrine to the extent that it can be gained by study. Even so, its first principles come from revelation.

Article 7: Is God the subject of this science?

1. It seems that God is not the subject of this science. For, according to Aristotle, every science should begin by defining its subject matter.[47] But this science does not start with a definition of God. As Damascene remarks, 'In God's case, we cannot say what he is.' So, God is not the subject of this science.[48]
2. Again, all matters about which a science reaches settled conclusions enter into its subject. But sacred Scripture has conclusions to offer about many other things than God – creatures and human conduct, for instance. So, God is not the subject of this science.

On the contrary, the subject of a science is what it discusses. But sacred doctrine discusses God, and is therefore called theology – 'talk about God in some sense'. So, God is the subject of this science.

Reply: God is the subject of this science. For a subject is to a science as an object is to a faculty or habit. Now, to designate the object of a faculty or habit properly is to note why anything is related to the faculty or habit

---

[44] *Nicomachean Ethics* 10.5, 1176a17. [45] 1 Corinthians 2:15.
[46] Dionysius the Areopagite (*c.* 500), *The Divine Names* 2.9. PG 3.648.
[47] *Posterior Analytics* 1.4, 71a13.
[48] St John Damascene (*c.* 655–*c.* 750), *On the Orthodox Faith* 1.4. PG 94.797.

in question. Thus a man or a stone is related to sight in that both are coloured, so being coloured is the proper object of the sense of sight. Now, sacred doctrine deals with all things in terms of God, either because they are God himself or because they are related to him as their origin and end. So, God is truly the object of this science.

This is also clear from the fact that the first principles of this science are the articles of faith, and faith is about God. The subject of the first principles of a science is the same as that of the science as a whole, since the whole of a science is contained virtually in its first principles.

Some writers, however, preoccupied with the things treated of by sacred doctrine rather than with its formal interest, have indicated its subject matter otherwise, assigning it to things and signs, or to the works of redemption, or to the whole Christ (head and members). And sacred doctrine certainly deals with all these, but only as they are ordered to God.

Hence:

1. Though we cannot know what God is, sacred doctrine, in place of a definition, uses divine effects (whether of nature or of grace) with respect to what it deals with concerning God – just as some of the philosophical sciences demonstrate something about a cause by means of its effects, using the effects instead of a definition of the cause.

2. All other things that are settled in sacred Scripture are included under God – not that they are parts, or species, or accidents of him, but because they are somehow related to him.

Article 8: Does this teaching employ arguments?

1. It seems that this teaching does not employ arguments. Ambrose says, 'Away with arguments when seeking faith.'[49] Faith is the principal concern of this teaching, so we find St John saying, 'These things are written that you may believe.'[50] So, sacred doctrine does not employ arguments.

2. Again, were it to advance arguments, they would be either from authority or from reason. If from authority, then the process would be unbefitting its dignity, for, according to Boethius, authority is the weakest ground of proof.[51] If from reason, then the process would not

---

[49] St Ambrose (*c.* 339–97), *On the Catholic Faith* 1.13. *PL* 16.370.   [50] John 20:31.
[51] Boethius (*c.* 480–*c.* 524), *On Cicero's 'Topics'* 1. *PL* 64.1166.

correspond with its purpose, for according to Gregory, 'Faith has no merit where the reason presents actual proof from experience.'[52] So, sacred doctrine does not employ arguments.

On the contrary, Titus requires of a bishop that he should 'embrace the faithful word which is according to teaching, that he may be able to exhort in sound teaching and convince those who argue against it'.[53]

Reply: Just as the other sciences do not argue to prove their first principles, but work from them to bring out other things in their field of inquiry, sacred doctrine does not argue to establish its first principles (the articles of faith) but advances from them to prove something else – as when St Paul adduces the resurrection of Christ to prove the general resurrection.[54]

Bear in mind, however, that among the philosophical sciences lower ones neither prove their chief premises nor controvert those who deny them. They leave these functions to a higher science. Yet the supreme science among them (i.e. metaphysics) can dispute the denial of its first principles with opponents who will concede something – though if they concede nothing, debate is at an end, albeit that the opponents' objections can be answered.

So, sacred Scripture, which has no higher science over it, disputes the denial of its first principles. It argues on the basis of those truths held by revelation that an opponent admits, as when (debating with heretics) it appeals to received authoritative texts of sacred doctrine and uses one article of faith against those who reject another. But if an opponent believes nothing of what has been divinely revealed, no way lies open for proving the articles of faith. All that can be done is to solve the difficulties against faith that the opponent may bring up. For since faith rests on infallible truth, and since the contrary of truth cannot be demonstrated, it is clear that alleged proofs against faith are not successful demonstrations but charges that can be refuted.

Hence:

1. Though arguments of human reason play no role in proving matters of faith, nevertheless, as I have said, sacred doctrine does work from articles of faith to infer other things.

---

[52] St Gregory the Great (*c.* 540–604), *On the Gospel* 2.26. *PL* 76.1197.
[53] Titus 1:9.   [54] 1 Corinthians 15:12.

2. Argument from authority is the method most appropriate to this teaching in that its first principles are held through revelation. So, we ought to acknowledge the authority of those to whom this revelation was given. This does not detract from sacred doctrine's dignity, for though weakest when based on what human beings have to say, the argument from authority excels when based on what God declares.

All the same, sacred doctrine also uses human reasoning, not indeed to prove the faith (for that would take away from faith's merit) but to clarify some of its message. As grace does not abolish nature but brings it to perfection, natural reason should assist faith as the natural inclination of the will yields to charity. St Paul speaks of 'bringing into captivity every understanding into the service of Christ'.[55] So, sacred doctrine uses the authority of philosophers who have been able to perceive the truth by natural reasoning – as when St Paul quotes the saying of Aratus, 'As some of your poets have said, we are God's offspring.'[56] Yet sacred doctrine employs such authorities only in order to provide, as it were, extraneous and probable arguments. When it argues conclusively, its own proper authority is canonical Scripture. It has other proper authorities (the doctors of the Church), and it looks to these as its own – but for arguments that carry no more than probability. For our faith rests on the revelation made to the prophets and apostles who wrote the canonical books, not on a revelation, if such there be, made to any other teacher. In this sense Augustine wrote to Jerome, 'Only to those books or writings which we call canonical have I learnt to pay such honour that I firmly believe that none of their authors have erred in composing them. Other authors, however, I read to such effect that, no matter what holiness and learning they display, I do not hold what they say to be true because those were their sentiments.'[57]

Article 9: Should sacred doctrine employ metaphorical or figurative language?

1. It seems that sacred doctrine should not use metaphors. For what is proper to the lowest teaching appears ill-suited to this one, which, as

---

[55] 2 Corinthians 10:5. [56] Acts 17:28. [57] Letter 82.1. *PL* 33.277.

I have already said, holds the highest place.[58] But to employ various similitudes and images is proper to poetry, the least of all disciplines. So, to make use of such similitudes is ill-suited to the science of sacred doctrine.

2. Moreover, sacred doctrine seems intended to make truth clear; and there is a reward held out to those who do so: 'Those who explain me shall have everlasting life.'[59] But such similitudes obscure the truth. So, it is not in keeping with this teaching to convey divine things under the likeness of bodily ones.

3. Again, the nobler a creature is, the closer it approaches God's likeness. So, if properties of creatures are to be read into God, then they should be chiefly the more excellent ones, not the baser ones so commonly found in Scripture.

On the contrary, Hosea writes, 'I have multiplied visions, and I have used similitudes by the ministry of the prophets.'[60] But to teach something by means of imagery is to use metaphor. So, sacred doctrine uses metaphors.

Reply: Sacred Scripture fittingly teaches about divine and spiritual things by means of likenesses drawn from physical things. For God provides for all things according to their nature. Now it naturally belongs to us to reach intelligible things through sensible ones, for all our cognition originates from the senses. It is, then, appropriate for sacred Scripture to teach spiritual things to us by means of metaphors drawn from bodily things. This is what Dionysius says: 'The divine rays cannot enlighten us except wrapped up in many sacred veils.'[61]

Then again, sacred Scripture is intended for all of us in common, as we read in Romans ('I am a debtor both to the learned and the ignorant').[62] And it fittingly puts forward spiritual things under bodily likenesses so that they may be grasped by the uneducated (i.e. people who are not capable of understanding intellectual realities in their own terms).

Hence:

1. Poetry employs metaphors for the sake of representation, in which we all naturally delight. Sacred doctrine, on the other hand, adopts them for their indispensable usefulness, as I have just explained.

---

[58] 1a 1.5.   [59] Ecclesiasticus 24:31.   [60] Hosea 12:10.
[61] *The Celestial Hierarchy* 1.2. PG 3.121.   [62] Romans 1:14.

2. As Dionysius says, the beam of divine revelation is not extinguished by the sense imagery that veils it, and its truth does not flicker out. For the minds of those given the revelation are not allowed to remain arrested with the images. They are lifted up to their meaning and enabled to instruct others. So, truths expressed metaphorically in one passage of Scripture are explained more expressly elsewhere. Yet even the figurative disguising serves a purpose – as a challenge to those eager to find out the truth, and as a defence against unbelievers ready to ridicule. As we read in Matthew, 'Do not give what is holy to dogs.'[63]

3. As Dionysius teaches, in the Scriptures the figures of base bodies (rather than those of higher bodies) more happily serve the purpose of conveying divine things to us.[64] And this for three reasons. First because human thinking is thereby better protected from error. For the expressions obviously cannot be taken literally and be crudely ascribed to divine things (which might be doubtful if divine realities were described by comparison with noble bodies, especially for people who cannot think of anything more noble than bodies). Second, because this way of talking is more appropriate when it comes to our present knowledge of God. For in this life what he is not is clearer to us than what he is. So, from the likenesses of things farthest removed from him we can more fairly estimate how far above our speech and thought he is. Third, because divine matters are thereby more effectively screened against those unworthy of them.

Article 10: Can one passage of sacred Scripture bear several senses?

1. It would seem that a single text of sacred Scripture does not bear several senses – namely, the historical or literal, the allegorical, the tropological or moral, and the anagogical. Multiple senses for single passages of Scripture lead to confusion and deception, and they undermine the firmness of the arguments. An argument proceeding from propositions with many senses is not valid but contains some fallacy or other. Sacred Scripture, however, should effectively display

---

[63] Matthew 7:6.   [64] *The Celestial Hierarchy* 2.2. PG 3.136.

truth without any kind of fallacy. So, one text of Scripture should not bear various senses.

2. Moreover, Augustine holds that 'we can divide the Scripture which we call the Old Testament into history, etiology, analogy and allegory'.[65] But these four divisions seem quite different from the four senses just mentioned. So, it does not seem fitting to elucidate a passage of sacred Scripture in accordance with those four senses.

3. Again, there is also a parabolic sense not included among the senses just listed.

On the contrary, Gregory declares that 'sacred Scripture transcends all other sciences by its very style of expression, in that one and the same discourse, while narrating an event, also transmits a mystery'.[66]

Reply: The author of sacred Scripture is God, who has the power, not only of adapting words to convey meanings (which we can also do), but also of adapting things themselves to convey meanings. Words have meaning in every science, but what is distinctive of sacred doctrine is that the things meant by the words themselves also mean something. That first meaning, whereby the words signify things, belongs to the first sense, namely the historical or literal. But we call that meaning by which the things signified by the words in their turn signify other things 'the spiritual sense'. And it is based on and presupposes the literal sense.

Now, this spiritual sense is divided into three. For, as St Paul says, the Old Law is a figure of the New.[67] And, as Dionysius says, the New Law is itself 'a figure of the glory to come'.[68] Then again, under the New Law the deeds wrought by our Head (Christ) are also signs of what we ourselves should do.

Well then, the allegorical sense is brought into play when the things of the Old Law signify the things of the New Law; the moral sense when the things done in Christ and in those who prefigured him are signs of what we should carry out; and the anagogical sense when the things that lie ahead in eternal glory are signified.

Now, because the literal sense is that which the author intends, and because the author of sacred Scripture is God (who comprehends everything all at once in his understanding), it is not surprising, as Augustine

[65] *On the Usefulness of Believing* 3. PL 42.68.   [66] *Morals* 20.1. PL 76.135.
[67] Cf. Hebrews 10:1.   [68] *The Ecclesiastical Hierarchy* 5.2. PG 3.501.

observes, that many meanings are present even in the literal sense of one passage of Scripture.[69]

Hence:

1. These various readings do not produce equivocation or any other kind of mixture of meanings. For, as I have explained, they are many, not because one term signifies many things, but because the things signified by the terms can themselves be the signs of other things. So, no confusion results in sacred Scripture since all the senses are based on one – the literal sense. An argument can be drawn only from this, and not, as Augustine remarks in his letter to Vincent the Donatist, from things said by allegory.[70] Nor does this result in anything being lost from sacred Scripture. For nothing necessary for faith is contained under the spiritual sense that is not elsewhere conveyed through the literal sense.

2. These three (history, etiology and analogy) are grouped under the one general heading of the literal sense. For as Augustine explains in the same place, we have history when any matter is straightforwardly recorded; etiology when its cause is indicated (as when our Lord pointed to men's hardness of heart as the reason why Moses allowed them to set aside their wives);[71] analogy when the truth of one Scriptural passage is shown not to clash with the truth of another. Of the four senses listed in the objection, allegory stands alone for the three spiritual senses. Thus Hugh of St Victor included the anagogical sense under the allegorical and he enumerated just three senses – the historical, the allegorical and the tropological.[72]

3. The parabolical sense is included in the literal sense, for words (taken in the literal sense) can signify either strictly or figuratively. In the second case the literal sense is not the figure of speech itself, but what the figure means. When Scripture speaks of the arm of God, the literal sense is not that he has a physical limb of this kind, but that he has what 'arm' signifies, namely, the power of doing and making. This example brings out how nothing false can underlie the literal sense of sacred Scripture.

---

[69] *Confessions* 12.31. *PL* 32.844.   [70] Letter 93.8. *PL* 33.334.   [71] Matthew 19:8.
[72] Hugh of St Victor (d. 1142 AD), *On the Sacraments* I, prol. 4. *PL* 176.184.

Question 2

Does God exist?

With respect to this question there are three points of inquiry:

1. Is it self-evident that God exists?
2. Can we demonstrate that God exists?
3. Does God exist?

Article 1: Is it self-evident that God exists?

1. It seems that 'God exists' is self-evidently true. For we say that things are self-evident to us when we know them by nature, as by nature we know first principles. But as Damascene observes when beginning his book, 'the knowledge that God exists is implanted by nature in everybody'.[1] So, 'God exists' is self-evidently true.

2. Moreover, a proposition is self-evident if we perceive its truth immediately upon perceiving the meaning of its terms – a characteristic of first principles of demonstration (according to Aristotle).[2] For example, when we know what wholes and parts are, we know at once that wholes are always bigger than their parts. But once we understand the meaning of the word 'God', we immediately see that God exists. For the word means 'that than which nothing greater can be signified'. So, since what exists in thought and fact is greater than what exists in thought alone, and since, once we understand the word 'God', he exists in thought, he must also exist in fact. It is, therefore, self-evident that God exists.

---

[1] *On the Orthodox Faith* 1.1. PG 94.789.   [2] *Posterior Analytics* 1.2, 72a7–8.

20

3. Again, it is self-evident that truth exists, for even denying so would amount to admitting it. If there were no such thing as truth, it would be true that there is no truth. So, something is true and, therefore, there is truth. But God is truth itself: 'I am the way, the truth, and the life.'[3] So, it is self-evident that God exists.

On the contrary, as Aristotle's discussion of first principles makes clear, nobody can think the opposite of what is self-evident.[4] But we can think the opposite of the proposition 'God exists.' For 'the fool' in the Psalms 'said in his heart: "There is no God." '[5] So, it is not self-evident that God exists.

Reply: A proposition can be self-evident in two ways: (a) in itself, though not to us, and (b) both in itself and to us. For a proposition is self-evident when its predicate forms part of its subject's definition (thus, for example, it is self-evident that human beings are animals since being an animal is part of the meaning of 'human being'). And if everyone knows the essence of the subject and predicate, the proposition will be self-evident to everybody. This is clearly the case with first principles of demonstration, which employ common terms known to all of us (such as 'being' and 'non-being', 'whole' and 'part', and the like). But if some people do not know the essence of its subject and predicate, then a proposition, though self-evident in itself, will not be so to them. This is why Boethius can say that 'certain notions are self-evident and common-places only to the learned, as, for example, that only bodies can occupy space'.[6]

So, I maintain that the proposition 'God exists' is self-evident in itself, for, as I shall later show,[7] its subject and predicate are identical since God is his own existence. But, because we do not know what God is, the proposition is not self-evident to us and needs to be demonstrated by things more known to us, though less known as far as their nature goes – that is, by God's effects.

Hence:

1. Knowledge that God exists is not implanted in us by nature in any clear or specific way. Admittedly, we naturally know what we

---

[3] John 14:6.   [4] *Metaphysics* 4.3, 1005b11; *Posterior Analytics* 1.10, 76b23–7.
[5] Psalms 13:1. The numbering of the Psalms follows that of the Latin Vulgate.
[6] *How Substances Are Good in Virtue of Their Existence without Being Substantial Goods* (*De Hebdomadibus*). PL 64.1311.
[7] 1a 3.4.

naturally desire, and we naturally desire happiness, which is to be found only in God. But this is not to know unequivocally that there is a God any more than to be aware of someone approaching is to be aware of Peter (even if it is really Peter who is approaching). Many, in fact, believe that the ultimate good that will make us happy is riches, or pleasure, or some such thing.

2. Someone hearing the word 'God' may very well not understand it to mean 'that than which nothing greater can be thought'. Indeed, some people have believed God to be something material. And even if someone thinks that what is signified by 'God' is 'that than which nothing greater can be thought', it does not follow that the person in question thinks that what is signified by 'God' exists in reality rather than merely as thought about. If we do not grant that something in fact exists than which nothing greater can be thought (and nobody denying the existence of God would grant this), the conclusion that God in fact exists does not follow.

3. It is self-evident that there is truth in general. But it is not self-evident to us that there is a First Truth.

Article 2: Can we demonstrate that God exists?

1. It seems that we cannot demonstrate[8] that God exists. For it is an article of faith that God exists, and we cannot demonstrate matters of faith since demonstration causes knowledge while faith, as St Paul says, is concerned with 'the unseen'.[9] So, it is impossible to demonstrate that God exists.

2. Moreover, the middle term[10] in a demonstration is what something is. But, as Damascene tells us, we do not know what God is, only what he is not.[11] So, we cannot demonstrate that God exists.

3. Again, if we could demonstrate God's existence, the demonstration would have to proceed by reference to his effects. But God and his effects are incommensurable, for God is infinite and his effects finite, and the finite cannot measure the infinite. So, since a cause cannot be

---

[8] I.e. prove by deducing from known premises.   [9] Hebrews 11:1.
[10] The term in an Aristotelian syllogism that lets one link the subject of one premise with the predicate of another. Thus in the argument 'S is P, all Ps are Qs, so S is Q', the middle term is 'P'.
[11] *On the Orthodox Faith* 1.4. *PG* 94.800.

demonstrated by effects that are incommensurate with it, it does not seem possible to demonstrate that God exists.

On the contrary, St Paul tells us that 'the invisible things of God can be clearly seen, being understood from what he has made'.[12] And if that is right, then we must be able to demonstrate that God exists from what he has made, for that something exists is the first thing we need to know about it.

Reply: There are two kinds of demonstration. One kind, 'demonstration why' something is so, argues from cause to effect and proceeds by means of what is unqualifiedly first. The other, 'demonstration that' something is so, argues from effect to cause and proceeds by means of what is first so far as we are concerned (for when an effect is more apparent to us than its cause, we come to know the cause through its effect). But, in cases where the effect is better known to us, any effect of a cause demonstrates that the cause exists, for effects depend on causes and can occur only if their causes exist. So, from effects that we know we can demonstrate what in itself is not self-evident to us, namely, that God exists.

Hence:

1. The truths about God that St Paul says we can know by our natural powers of reasoning (that God exists, for example) are not articles of faith.[13] They are presupposed by them. For faith presupposes natural knowledge, just as grace does nature, and just as all perfections presuppose that which they perfect. But there is nothing to stop people from accepting on faith some demonstrable truth that they cannot personally demonstrate.

2. When we demonstrate a cause from its effect, the effect takes the place of what the case is in the proof that the cause exists, especially if the cause is God. For, when proving that something exists, the middle term is not what the thing is (we cannot even ask what it is until we know that it exists) but what we are using the name of the thing to mean. But when demonstrating from effects that God exists, we are able to start from what the word 'God' means, for, as I shall later explain,[14] what we predicate of God is derived from these effects.

---

[12] Romans 1:20.   [13] Romans 1:19–20.   [14] 1a 13.1ff.

3. Effects can give comprehensive knowledge of their cause only when they are commensurate with it. But, as I have said, any effect can make it clear that a cause exists. So, God's effects can serve to demonstrate that God exists, even though they cannot help us to know him comprehensively for what he is.

Article 3: Does God exist?

1. It seems that there is no God. For if one of two contraries were infinite, the other would be completely destroyed. But by the word 'God' we understand a certain infinite good. So, if God existed, nobody would ever encounter evil. But we do encounter evil in the world. So, God does not exist.
2. Moreover, anything that can be caused by few principles is not caused by many. But it seems that we can fully account for everything we observe in the world while assuming that God does not exist. Thus we explain natural effects by natural causes, and intentional effects by human reasoning and will. So, there is no need to accept that God exists.

On the contrary, Exodus represents God as saying, 'I am who am.'[15]

Reply: There are five ways in which we can prove that there is a God.

The first and most obvious way is based on change. It is certain, and clear to our senses, that some things in the world undergo change. But anything in process of change is changed by something else. For nothing can be undergoing change unless it is potentially[16] whatever it ends up being after its process of change – while something causes change in so far as it is actual[17] in some way. After all, to change something is simply to bring it from potentiality to actuality, and this can only be done by something that is somehow actual: thus fire (actually hot) causes wood (able to be hot) to become actually hot, and thus it changes and modifies it. But something cannot be simultaneously actually x and potentially x, though it can be actually x and potentially y (something actually hot, for

---

[15] Exodus 3:14. [16] See introduction.
[17] Aquinas's claim is that causes cause due to a property they have, not one they lack. When we say that the pilot's absence caused the shipwreck, then, Aquinas would parse this more precisely by saying that what caused the shipwreck was the storm and the hidden reef, but the pilot's absence permitted these causes to operate.

instance, cannot also be potentially hot, though it can be potentially cold). So, something in process of change cannot itself cause that same change. It cannot change itself. Necessarily, therefore, anything in process of change is changed by something else. And this something else, if in process of change, is itself changed by yet another thing; and this last by another. But there has to be an end to this regress of causes, otherwise there will be no first cause of change, and, as a result, no subsequent causes of change. For it is only when acted upon by a first cause that intermediate causes produce change (if a hand does not move the stick, the stick will not move anything else). So, we are bound to arrive at some first cause of change that is not itself changed by anything, which is what everybody takes God to be.

The second way is based on the notion of efficient causation.[18] We find that there is an order of efficient causes in the observable world. Yet we never observe, nor ever could, something efficiently causing itself. For this would mean that it preceded itself, which it cannot do. But an order of efficient causes cannot go back infinitely. For an earlier member in it causes an intermediate, and the intermediate causes a last (whether the intermediate be one or many). If you eliminate a cause, however, you also eliminate its effect. So, there cannot be a last cause, nor an intermediate one, unless there is a first. If there is no end to the series of efficient causes, therefore, and if, as a consequence, there is no first cause, there would be no intermediate efficient causes either, and no last effect, which is clearly not the case. So, we have to posit a first cause, which everyone calls 'God'.

The third way is based on the possible and the necessary, and it runs as follows. Some of the things we encounter are able to be or not to be, for we find them generated and perished (and, therefore, able to be or not to be). But not everything can be like this. For something that is capable of not being at some time is not. So, if everything is able not to be, at some time there was nothing in the world. But if that were true, there would be nothing even now, for something that does not exist is only brought into being by something that does exist. Therefore, if nothing existed, nothing could have begun to exist, and nothing would exist now, which is patently not the case. So, not everything is the sort of thing that is able to be or not to be. There has got to be something that must be. Yet a thing

---

[18] Causation in the usual sense.

that must be either does or does not have a cause of its necessity outside itself. And, just as we must stop somewhere in a series of efficient causes, so we must also stop in the series of things which must be and owe this to something else. This means that we are forced to posit something which is intrinsically necessary, owing its necessity to nothing else, something which is the cause that other things must be.

The fourth way is based on the gradations that we find in things. We find some things to be more and less good, more and less true, more and less noble, and so on. But we speak of various things as being more or less F in so far as they approximate in various ways to what is most F. For example, things are hotter and hotter the closer they approach to what is hottest. So, something is the truest and best and most noble of things, and hence the most fully in being.[19] For, as Aristotle says, the truest things are the things most fully in being.[20] But when many things possess some property in common, the one most fully possessing it causes it in the others. To use Aristotle's example, fire, the hottest of all things, causes all other things to be hot. So, there is something that causes in all other things their being, their goodness, and whatever other perfection they have, and we call this 'God'.

The fifth way is based on the governance of things. For we see that some things that lack intelligence (i.e. material objects in nature) act for the sake of an end. This is clear from the fact that they always, or usually, act in the same way so as to achieve what is best (and therefore reach their goal by purpose, not by chance). But things lacking intelligence tend to a goal only as directed by one with knowledge and understanding. Arrows, for instance, need archers. So, there is a being with intelligence who directs all natural things to ends, and we call this being 'God'.

Hence:

1. As Augustine says, 'Since God is supremely good, he would not permit any evil at all in his works, unless he were sufficiently powerful and good to bring good even from evil.'[21] So, it belongs to the limitless goodness of God that he permits evils to exist and draws good from them.

---

[19] *Metaphysics* 2.1, 993b30.   [20] *Metaphysics* 2.1, 993b25.
[21] *A Handbook on Faith, Hope and Love (Enchiridion)* 11. PL 40.236.

2. Since nature acts for definite ends under the direction of a higher cause, its effects must be traced to God as the first of all causes. Similarly, even things done intentionally must be traced back to a higher cause than human reasoning and will, for these are changeable and lacking. And, as I have said, we must trace all such things back to a first cause that cannot change and is intrinsically necessary.

Question 3
God's simplicity

Having recognized that something exists, we still have to investigate the way in which it exists, so that we may come to understand what it is that exists. But we cannot know what God is,[1] only what he is not. We must therefore consider the ways in which God does not exist rather than the ways in which he does. So, now I consider:

> First, the ways in which God is not;
> second, the ways in which we know him;
> third, the ways in which we describe him.

The ways in which God is not will become apparent if we rule out everything unfitting to him, such as being composite, changing, and the like. So, I shall ask:

First, about God's simplicity, thus ruling out composition.[2] And because simplicity implies imperfection and incompleteness in the material world, I shall then ask;

> second, about God's perfection;
> third, about his limitlessness;

---

[1] According to Aquinas, we know that God necessarily satisfies many descriptions – that he is omnipotent, omniscient, etc. But God satisfies these because he is divine. For Aquinas these descriptions do not tell us what it is to be divine; it is not the case that to be divine is to be omniscient, omnipotent, etc. Deity is some property other than any of these. Aquinas's claim here is that we cannot intellectually grasp this property. We can know what it is to be omniscient or to be human, but we cannot know what it is to be divine.

[2] Literally consisting of or having been put together from parts. We usually think of parts as concrete things from which other concrete things are assembled. But the same thing can consist completely of different sorts of part: books, say, of both quarks and molecules. Aquinas thinks that concrete things consist completely of concrete parts, but also abstract ones – essences, accidents, and the like.

fourth, about his unchangeableness;
fifth, about his oneness.

About the first of these questions there are eight points of inquiry:

1. Is God a body? Is he, that is to say, composed of extended parts?
2. Is he composed of form and matter?
3. Is he composed of 'whatness' (essence or nature) and subject?
4. Is he composed of essence and existence?
5. Is he composed of genus and difference?
6. Is he composed of substance and accidents?
7. Is there any way in which he is composite, or is he altogether simple?
8. Does he enter into composition with other things?

Article 1: Is God a body composed of extended parts?

1. It would seem that God is a body. For a body is something with three dimensions, and sacred Scripture ascribes three dimensions to God: 'He is higher than heaven and what will you do? He is deeper than hell and how will you know? His measure is longer than the earth and broader than the sea.'[3] So, God is a body.

2. Moreover, everything with shape is a body, for shape is characteristic of extended things as such. But God seems to have a shape, for in Genesis we read, 'Let us make human beings in our image and likeness',[4] where 'image' means 'figure' or 'shape' as in Hebrews: 'who is the brightness of his glory, and the figure [that is to say, image] of his substance'.[5] So, God is a body.

3. Moreover, anything with bodily parts is a body. But Scripture ascribes bodily parts to God, saying in Job, 'Have you an arm like God?',[6] and in the Psalms, 'The eyes of the Lord are towards the righteous'[7] and 'the right hand of the Lord does valiantly'.[8] So, God is a body.

4. Moreover, only bodies can assume postures. But Scripture ascribes certain postures to God: thus Isaiah 'saw the Lord sitting',[9] and says that 'the Lord stands to judge'.[10] So, God is a body.

---

[3] Job 11:8–9.   [4] Genesis 1:26.   [5] Hebrews 1:3.   [6] Job 40:4.
[7] Psalms 33:16.   [8] Psalms 117:16.   [9] Isaiah 6:1.   [10] Isaiah 3:13.

5. Again, nothing can be the starting-point or finishing-point of a spatial movement unless it is a body or bodily. But Scripture refers to God as the finishing-point of a spatial movement ('Come to him and be enlightened')[11] and as a starting-point ('Those that depart from you shall be written in the earth').[12] So, God is a body.

On the contrary, John writes: 'God is spirit.'[13]

Reply: God is in no way a body, and we can show this in three ways.

First, no body causes change without itself being changed, as can be shown inductively. But I have shown above that God is the unchanging first cause of change.[14] So, God is clearly not a body.

Second, the first being must of necessity be actual and in no way potential. For, although in any one thing that passes from potentiality to actuality, the potentiality temporally precedes the actuality, actuality, absolutely speaking, precedes potentiality, for nothing can be changed from a state of potentiality to one of actuality except by something actual. Now we have seen that the first being is God.[15] So, there can be no potentiality in God. In bodies, however, there is always potentiality, because the extended is as such divisible. So, God cannot be a body.

Third, God is the most noble of beings, as is clear from what I have already said.[16] But a body cannot be the most noble of beings. For bodies are either living or non-living, and living bodies are clearly the more excellent. Yet a living body is not alive simply in virtue of being a body (otherwise all bodies would be living); it is alive because of some other principle (in our case, the soul). Such a principle will be more excellent than body as such. So, God cannot be a body.

Hence:

1. As I remarked earlier, sacred Scripture uses bodily metaphors to convey truth about God and spiritual things.[17] So, in ascribing three dimensions to God they are using bodily extension to signify the extent of God's power: depth, for example, signifies his power to know what is hidden; height, the loftiness of his power above all other things; length, the lasting quality of his existence; breadth, the universality of his love. Or there is Dionysius's explanation of depth as the incomprehensibility of God's essence, length as the penetration of

---

[11] Psalms 33:6.   [12] Jeremiah 17:13.   [13] John 4:24.   [14] 1a 2.3.
[15] 1a 2.3.   [16] 1a 2.3.   [17] 1a 1.9.

all things by God's power, and breadth as the boundless reach of God's guardianship enveloping all things.[18]

2. We say that human beings are in God's image, not because they have bodies, but because of their superiority to other animals. And this is why Genesis, after saying, 'Let us make human beings in our image and likeness', adds, 'that they may have dominion over the fishes of the sea',[19] and so on. Human beings owe this superiority to reason and intellect. So, they are in God's image because of their intellect and reason, which are incorporeal.

3. The Scriptures ascribe bodily parts to God by a metaphor drawn from their functions. Eyes, for example, see; so, when we attribute an 'eye' to God it refers to his power of seeing things in an intelligible rather than a sensory manner. And similarly with other parts of the body.

4. The ascribing of posture to God is again simply metaphor. He is said to be sitting, for instance, because of his unchangeableness and authority. He is said to be standing because his might triumphs in the face of all opposition.

5. One approaches God, and one draws away from him, not by bodily movement, since he is everywhere, but by movement of the heart. In this context, 'approaching' and 'drawing away' are metaphors that picture being moved in spirit as if it were like being moved in space.

Article 2: Is God composed of form[20] and matter[21]?

1. God seems to be composed of form and matter. For since soul is the form of the body,[22] anything with a soul is composed of matter and form. But the Scriptures ascribe soul to God; thus in Hebrews we find

---

[18] *The Divine Names* 9.5. *PG* 3.913. [19] Genesis 1:28.

[20] A real attribute 'in' the thing. Aquinas thinks of forms as abstract constituents, as particular as their bearers: Socrates' humanity is something abstract that is 'in' and particular to Socrates. Forms are either substantial or accidental. For any x, x′ substantial form is that in x which made x′ matter (q.v.) become and/or makes it be actually x′ kind of thing. The substantial form of water, for instance, is a structure which makes of a group of atoms an instance of the kind *water molecule*. A form is accidental just if it is not substantial. A form may be, for example, a shape, a structure, a power, a quality or a soul.

[21] That which 'bears' or 'receives' forms. For any x, x′ matter is the stuff of which x is made, the parts of which x is composed, or most generally that which was potentially x and became actually x.

[22] For Aquinas, for any x, x′ form is that in x which made (or makes) x′ matter (q.v.) become (or be) actually x′ kind of thing. Every soul is a form: a dog's soul is that in the dog which made and makes its matter a living canine body, and so a dog. But not every form is a soul. Water has a form but no soul.

31

quoted, as if from the mouth of God, 'my righteous one shall live by faith, and if he shrinks back my soul will have no pleasure in him'.[23] So, God is composed of matter and form.

2. Moreover, according to Aristotle, anger, joy, and the like, are passions of something made up of parts.[24] But the Scriptures ascribe such passions to God: 'the anger of the Lord,' says the psalm, 'was kindled against his people'.[25] So, God is composed of matter and form.

3. Again, matter is what makes a thing an individual. But God seems to be an individual, not something predicable of many individuals. So, God is composed of matter and form.

On the contrary, since having dimensions is one of the primary properties of matter, anything composed of matter and form must be a body. As I have shown, however, God is not a body.[26] So, he is not composed of matter and form.

Reply: God cannot contain matter.

First, because matter is potential, while God, as I have shown, is sheer actuality with no potentiality.[27] So, God cannot be composed of matter and form.

Second, in things composed of form and matter, their form gives them perfection and goodness. Such composite things therefore only participate in goodness, for matter participates in form. But the first and best good (i.e. God) does not participate in goodness, for being good by essence is prior to being good by a kind of participation.[28] So, God cannot be composed of matter and form.

Third, all agents act in virtue of their form, so the way in which they are agents will depend on the type of form they have. What is primarily and essentially an agent must therefore be primarily and intrinsically form. Yet God is the primary agent, since, as I have explained, he is the first efficient cause.[29] So, God is essentially form and is not composed of matter and form.

Hence:

1. Scripture ascribes soul to God by a metaphor drawn from its activity. For since soul is the seat of volition in us, we call what is pleasing to God's will 'pleasing to his soul'.

---

[23] Hebrews 10:38.   [24] *On the Soul* 1.1, 403a3ff.   [25] Psalms 105:40.   [26] 1a 3.1.   [27] 1a 3.1.
[28] Something 'participates in' a form just if it bears the form and is not identical with it.   [29] 1a 2.3.

2. Scripture ascribes anger and the like to God by a metaphor drawn from their effects. For it is characteristic of anger that it stimulates us to requite wrong. Divine retribution is therefore metaphorically called 'anger'.
3. The forms of material things are individualized by matter, which cannot be predicable of a subject since it is itself the first underlying subject – though a form as such (unless something interferes) can be received by many things. But a form which cannot be received in matter, and is self-subsisting, is individualized just because it cannot be received in a subject, and God is such a form. So, it does not follow that there is matter in God.

Article 3: Is God composed of 'whatness' (that is, essence[30] or nature) and subject[31]?

1. It seems that God is not the same as his essence or nature. For nothing is in itself. But we say that God's essence or nature (his divinity) is in God. So, it seems that God must differ from his essence or nature.
2. Moreover, effects resemble their causes, for what a thing does reflects what it is. But individual created things are other than their natures (a particular human being, for instance, is not humanity). So, it seems that God is not divinity.

On the contrary, we speak of God not only as living but as life: 'I am the way, the truth and the life.'[32] But divinity bears the same relationship to God as life does to the living. So, God is divinity itself.

Reply: God is the same as his essence or nature.

We shall understand this when we note that things composed of matter and form cannot be the same as their natures or essences. For essence or nature in these things includes only what falls within the definition of a species – as humanity includes what falls within the definition of human being, for this makes us to be human and is what humanity signifies

---

[30] For any x, x' having its essence makes x the kind of thing it is, and so is that which makes true the answer to the question 'what is x?' Things acquire their essences by acquiring their substantial forms: a water molecule acquires its essence, *being water*, by coming to host the distinctive structure of a water molecule. Aquinas thinks of essences as abstract constituents, as particular as their bearers: Socrates' humanity is something abstract that is 'in' and particular to Socrates.
[31] That which receives or bears an essence. When hydrogen and oxygen atoms come to make up a water molecule, the atoms are the subject that receives the essence (that is, come to be structured as water molecules are) and the resulting water is the subject that bears the essence.
[32] John 14:6.

(i.e. what makes human beings to be human beings). But we do not define the species of anything by the matter and properties peculiar to it as an individual. We do not, for example, define human beings as things that have *this* flesh and *these* bones, or are white, or black, or the like. *This* flesh and *these* bones, and the properties peculiar to them, belong indeed to *this* human being, but not to its nature. Individual human beings therefore possess something that human nature does not, and particular human beings and their nature are not, therefore, altogether the same thing. 'Human nature' names the formative element in human beings; for what gives a thing definition is formative with respect to the matter that gives it individuality.

However, the individuality of things not composed of matter and form cannot derive from this or that individual matter. So, the forms of such things must be intrinsically individual and themselves subsist as things. Such things are therefore identical with their natures.

In the same way, then, God, who, as I have said, is not composed of matter and form,[33] is identical with his own divinity, his own life, and with whatever else is similarly predicated of him.

Hence:

1. When we talk about simple things we have to use the composite things from which our knowledge derives as models. So, when talking about God we use concrete nouns to signify his subsistence (since the subsistent things with which we are familiar are composite), and we use abstract nouns to express his simplicity. Therefore, when we talk of divinity, or life, or something of that sort, residing in God, we should not attribute the diversity that this implies to God himself, but to the way in which we conceive of him.
2. God's effects resemble God as far as they can, but not perfectly. This failure in resemblance is due to the fact that they can represent only by many what, in itself, is simple and one. As a result they are composite and cannot, therefore, be identified with their natures.

Article 4: Is God composed of essence and existence?

1. It seems that essence and existence are not the same when it comes to God. If they were, there would be nothing added to God's existence.

---

[33] 1a 3.2.

But existence to which nothing is added is existence in general (the existence that is predicated of everything), and, if essence and existence are the same in God, the word 'God' would mean 'existence in general' (the existence we can predicate of everything). But this is not so. As the book of Wisdom says, 'they gave the incommunicable name to wood and stones'.[34] So, God's existence is not his essence.

2. Moreover, as I said earlier, we can know that God exists, but we cannot know what he is.[35] So, God's existence is not the same as what God is – his essence or nature.

On the contrary, Hilary writes, 'Existence is not an accident in God; it is subsisting truth.'[36] So, what subsists in God is his existence.

Reply: I have shown that God is his own essence.[37] That he is also his own existence can be shown in a number of ways.

First, what belongs to a thing over and above its essence must be caused: either from the principles of the essence itself, as accidents peculiar to a particular species (as the sense of humour characteristic of human beings derives from human nature), or from an external cause (as heat in water derives from some fire). So, if the existence of something is other than its essence, it must derive from the thing's essence, or it must have an external cause. But it cannot be caused by the principles of the thing's essence, for nothing of which the existence is derived can bring itself into being. If a thing's existence differs from its essence, therefore, its existence must be caused by something other than the thing in question. But this cannot be so in God's case, for, as we have seen, he is the first efficient cause.[38] So, we cannot say that God's existence is something other than his essence.

Second, existence is what makes every form or nature actual (which is why we only express the actuality of goodness or human nature by speaking of them as existing). So, when a nature is not what amounts to existence as such, then, it must exist potentially. Now, as I have shown, God does not contain potentialities.[39] In him, therefore, essence cannot differ from existence, and existence is his essence.

Third, anything on fire, without being fire itself, participates in fire. Similarly, anything existing, without being 'existence as such', participates

---

[34] Wisdom 14:21.   [35] 1a 2.2.
[36] St Hilary of Poitiers (*c.* 315–*c.* 368), *On the Trinity* 8. *PL* 10.208.
[37] 1a 3.3.   [38] 1a 2.3.   [39] 1a 3.1.

in existence. Now, God and his essence are the same, as I have shown.[40] And if God is not 'existence as such' (if existence is not what his essence amounts to), then he only participates in existence and will not therefore be the primary existent, which he clearly is. So, God is not only his own essence, but also his own existence.

Hence:

1. We can understand 'something to which nothing is added' in two ways. We can take it as implying that further addition is excluded by definition (as reason is excluded by definition from irrational animals). We can also take it as implying that further addition is just not included in the definition (as reason is not included in the definition of animals in general, though neither is it excluded). Understood in the first way, divine existence is existence without addition. Understood in the second way, existence without addition is existence in general.

2. We use the verb 'to be' in two ways: to signify the act of existence, and to signify the mental uniting of predicate to subject which constitutes a proposition. Now, we cannot know what God's act of existence amounts to any more than we can know his essence. But we can know God's being in the second sense in so far as we know ourselves to be speaking truly when we say that God exists. As I have said, we know that we are speaking truly here because of God's effects.[41]

Article 5: Is God composed of genus and difference?

1. It seems that God does belong to a genus. For the definition of a substance ('something self-subsistent') is most fully applicable to God. So, God belongs to the genus of substance.

2. Moreover, any measure must belong to the same genus as the things it measures (lengths are measured by length, and numbers by number). But it seems from what Averroes says that God is the measure of all substances.[42] So, God must belong to the genus of substance.

On the contrary, a genus is logically prior to the things that exemplify it. But nothing is prior to God in either reality or understanding. So, God does not belong to a genus.

---

[40] 1a 2.3.   [41] 1a 2.2, especially *ad* 2.
[42] Ibn Rushd, also known as Averroes (1126–98), *Commentary on Aristotle's Metaphysics* 10.7.

Reply: There are two ways of belonging to a genus: strictly and without qualification, as do the species that fall under a genus; and by way of reduction, as principles and privations do. For example, unity and the point are reduced to the genus of quantity as principles of quantity; and blindness, like all other defects, is reduced to the genus of its corresponding. But God belongs to a genus in neither of these ways.

We can show that he cannot be a species within a genus in three ways.

First, because we define species by differentiating some generic notion. Such differentiation is always based on some actualization of the potentiality that gave rise to the generic notion. Thus sense-life, envisaged in the concrete, gives rise to the notion of animal (an animal being something that lives by sense-perception), while mental life gives rise to the notion of a reasoning creature (a creature which lives by its mind). But the mind-life of human beings realizes potentialities of their sense-life. And we see the like in other cases. So, since realization of potentialities does not occur in God, he cannot be a species within a genus.

Second, since the genus of something states what the thing is, a genus must express a thing's essence. But God's essence is to exist, as I have shown.[43] So, the only genus to which God could belong would be the genus of being. Aristotle, however, has shown that there is no such genus: for genera are differentiated by factors not already contained within those genera, and no differentiating factor could be found that did not already exist (it could not differentiate if it did not exist).[44] So, we are left with no genus to which God could belong.

Third, all members of a genus share one essence or nature: that of the genus stating what they are. As existing things, however, they differ, for some particular horse is not some particular man, and this man is not that man. So, when something belongs to a genus, its nature, or what it is, must differ from its existence. As I have shown, though, this difference does not exist in God.[45] God, therefore, clearly cannot be a species within a genus.

And this shows why we cannot assign either genus or difference to God, nor define him, nor demonstrate anything of him except by means of his effects; for definitions are composed of genus and difference, and demonstration depends upon definition.

[43] 1a 3.4.   [44] *Metaphysics* 3.3, 998b22.   [45] 1a 3.4.

It is also clear that God does not belong mediately to a genus by initiating or generating it. For anything that initiates a genus in such a way that it mediately belongs to it is ineffective outside that genus: only the point generates extension, and only unity generates number. But God initiates everything that is, as I shall later show.[46] So, he does not initiate any particular genus so as to belong to it.

Hence:

1. The word 'substance' does not mean baldly that which exists of itself, for existence is not a genus, as I have shown. Rather, 'substance' means 'that which is possessed of an essence such that it will exist of itself, even though to exist is not its essence'. So, it is clear that God does not belong to the genus of substance.

2. This argument supposes that like is measured by like. Strictly speaking, however, God is not like anything, though he is called the measure of all things in as much as the closer things come to God the more fully they exist.

Article 6: Is God composed of substance[47] and accidents[48]?

1. It seems that there are accidents in God. For Aristotle says that 'substance is never accidental to anything'.[49] So, something that is accidental in one thing cannot be the substance of another. The fact that heat, for example, is an accidental form of some things proves that it cannot be the substantial form of fire. But wisdom, power, and the like, which we ascribe to God, are accidents in us. So, there are accidents in God.

2. Moreover, in every genus there is a principal member. But there are many genera of accidents. So, if the principal members of these genera are not in God, there will be many other principal members besides God; and this does not seem right.

---

[46] 1a 44.1.   [47] A concrete particular thing that bears attributes.

[48] Attributes (forms) that are not essences or substantial forms. Aquinas thinks of accidents as abstract constituents, as particular as their bearers: Socrates' weight is something abstract that is 'in' and particular to Socrates. As Aquinas sees it, all real accidents are either quantities (which make true answers to questions in the 'how much?' family), qualities (which make true answers to questions in the 'how is it?' or 'what is it like?' families) or relations (which make true answers to questions about how things are related).

[49] *Physics* 1.3, 186b1–4.

38

On the contrary, every accident is an accident of some subject. But God cannot be a subject, since, as Boethius says, 'no simple form can be a subject'.[50] So, there cannot be accidents in God.

Reply: What I have already said makes it clear that accidents cannot exist in God.

First, because accidents realize some potentialities of their subject, since an accident is a mode in which the subject achieves actuality. But, as I have said, we must entirely rule out potentiality from God.[51]

Second, because God is his own act of existence, and as Boethius says, 'you may add to an existent, but you cannot add to existence itself'[52] (just as a hot thing may have other properties besides being hot – such as whiteness – but heat itself cannot be otherwise than hot).

Third, because what exists by nature is prior to what is accidental, so that if God is the absolutely prime existent, nothing can exist in him by accident. Nor can there be accidents existing in him by nature (as, for example, people have a sense of humour by nature). For such accidents derive from a subject's essential nature. But there is nothing derived in God. All derivation starts from him. It therefore follows that God contains no accidents.

Hence:

1. As I shall explain later, we do not ascribe power and wisdom to God and to us in the same sense.[53] So, it does not follow that accidents exist in God as they do in us.

2. Since substance is prior to accidents, the principles of accidents are reducible to the principles of substance as to something prior. And although God is not first in the genus of substance, he is still first with respect to all being, transcending all genera.

Article 7: Is there any way in which God is composite, or is he entirely simple?

1. It seems that God is not entirely simple. For the things that derive from God resemble him: thus everything deriving from the first being

---

[50] *On the Trinity* 2. PL 64.1250.   [51] 1a 3.1.
[52] *How Substances Are Good in Virtue of Their Existence without Being Substantial Goods* (*De Hebdomadibus*). PL 64.1311.
[53] 1a 13.5.

exists, and everything deriving from the first good is good. But nothing deriving from God is entirely simple. So, God is not entirely simple either.

2. Moreover, we should ascribe whatever is better to God. But, in the world with which we are familiar, composite things are better than simple ones: compounds are better than elements, for example, and elements are better than their constituent parts. So, we should not assert that God is altogether simple.

On the contrary, Augustine says that God is truly and absolutely simple.[54]

Reply: There are many ways of showing that God is entirely simple.

First, relying on what I have already said, God is not composed of extended parts (since he is not a body), nor of form and matter, nor does he differ from his own nature, nor his nature from his existence. Nor can we distinguish in him genus and difference, nor substance and accidents. It is therefore clear that God is in no way composite. Rather, he is entirely simple.

Second, everything composite is subsequent to its components and dependent on them. But God, as I have shown, is the first of all beings.[55]

Third, everything composite is caused; for elements diverse of themselves do not combine unless made to do so by a cause. As I have said, though, God is not caused since he is the first efficient cause.[56]

Fourth, in any composite there is a realizing of potentialities such as cannot occur in God: for either the potentialities of one component are realized by another, or, at any rate, all the components together are potentially the whole.

Fifth, we cannot predicate anything composite of its own component parts. This is obvious in composites made up of different parts, for no part of a man is a man, and no part of a foot is a foot. And although in composites made up of similar parts certain ways of describing the whole apply also to the parts (every bit of air, for example, is air, and every drop of water is water), other ways do not (thus if a unit of water occupies two cubic feet, no part of it will do so). So, in all composites there is some element that is not the composite itself. Now, even if we grant that a thing possessed of a form may contain something that is not itself (e.g. that a

---

[54] *On the Trinity* 4.4–8. *PL* 42.927–9.   [55] 1a 2.3.   [56] 1a 2.3.

white thing contains elements not included in the concept of whiteness), in the form itself there is nothing other than itself. But God is form itself, indeed existence itself. So, he can in no way be composite. And this was what Hilary was pointing out when he said, 'God, being power, is not made up of things that are weak; and, being light, is not pieced together from things that are darkness.'[57]

Hence:

1. Things deriving from God resemble him as effects resemble a primary cause. But it is in the nature of an effect to be composite in some way, because even at its simplest its existence differs from its essence, as I shall later explain.[58]
2. In the world with which we are familiar composite things are better than simple ones, because created perfection is found in many things, not just one. But divine perfection is found in one simple thing, as I shall shortly show.[59]

Article 8: Does God enter into composition with other things?

1. It seems that God does enter into composition with other things. For Dionysius declares that 'the existence of everything is the divine nature, which is beyond being'.[60] But the existence of everything enters into the composition of each. So, God enters into composition with other things.
2. Moreover, God is a form, for Augustine says that 'the Word of God' (which is God) 'is unformed form'.[61] But form is a component of things. So, God must be a component of something.
3. Again, things which exist without differing are identical. But God and prime matter[62] exist without differing and are, therefore, completely

---

[57] *On the Trinity* 7. *PL* 10.223.   [58] 1a 50.2, *ad* 3.   [59] 1a 4.2, *ad* 1.
[60] *The Celestial Hierarchy* 4.1. *PG* 3.177.   [61] Sermons 38. *PL* 38.662.
[62] The ultimate receiver of all attributes. Suppose with Aquinas that there are four elements – earth, air, fire and water – and that some earth can change into some water. If this is one body of stuff changing, rather than being replaced by another body of stuff, something must be there throughout that first bears the attribute of being earth and then bears the attribute of being water. But if earth and water are *elements*, they are ultimate kinds of chemical matter: they are not made up of some more fundamental chemical stuff. Aquinas infers that there is a more basic kind of matter than chemical elements, and he calls it prime matter. Since for Aquinas every physical thing is composed of elements, for Aquinas, every physical thing contains prime matter.

identical. Yet prime matter enters into the composition of things. So, God must do so too. – To prove the middle step in this argument: things that differ do so by certain differentiating factors, and must therefore be composite. But God and prime matter are altogether simple and, therefore, they are identical.

On the contrary, Dionysius says that 'nothing can touch God, nor is there any union with him by mingling part with part'.[63]

Reply: On this point three mistakes have been made. As we learn from Augustine, some people have held that God is the soul of the world.[64] We can include with these people those who said that God is the soul of the outermost heaven.[65] Others have said that God is the form of all things – the reputed view of Amaury of Bène and his followers. The third mistake was the really stupid thesis of David of Dinant – that God is prime matter. All these opinions are clearly wrong. God cannot enter into composition with anything in any way, whether as a formal principle or as a material one.

First, because God is the first efficient cause of things, as I have already said.[66] But the form of an effect, though specifically similar to its efficient cause (e.g. people beget people), is not numerically identical with the efficient cause. Matter and efficient causes are neither numerically nor specifically identical, for matter is in potentiality while efficient causes are actual.

Second, since God is the first efficient cause, efficient activity belongs to him primarily and essentially. But a component is not an efficient cause primarily and essentially. Thus a hand does not act. Rather, human beings act by means of their hands, and it is fire which warms by virtue of its heat. So, God cannot be a component of anything.

Third, no part of something composite can be the first being. Nor can the matter or form of composite things (their first parts) be the first among beings. For matter is in potentiality, and potentiality is unqualifiedly secondary to actuality, as I have shown.[67] Again, form, when a part of something composite, is a form which participates in something. Now something that participates in *x* is posterior to that which is essentially *x*.

---

[63] *The Divine Names* 2.5. PG 3.643.   [64] *The City of God* 7.6. PL 41.199.
[65] Aquinas accepted Aristotle's cosmology, in which the earth was surrounded by a series of crystalline spheres, the heavens.
[66] 1a 2.3.   [67] 1a 3.1.

For example, the fire that is in things that are on fire is posterior to that which is by nature fire. But I have already shown that God is the primary being, without qualification.[68]

Hence:

1. Dionysius means that God's nature is the existence of all things by efficient causality and as an exemplar, not by its essence.
2. The Word is not a component form but an exemplary one.[69]
3. Simple things do not differ from one another because of differences. That is the case only with composites. Hence, although the factors 'rational' and 'irrational' differentiate people and horses, these factors themselves do not require further factors to differentiate them one from another. Strictly speaking, therefore, simple things are not *different*, but *diverse*. According to Aristotle, things that are diverse are absolutely distinct, but things that are different are different in some respect.[70] Strictly speaking, then, God and prime matter are not *different* but *diverse*. So, it does not follow that they are identical.

[68] 1a 2.3.   [69] The prototype or model in accordance with which things are made.
[70] *Metaphysics* 10.3, 1054b24.

43

Question 4
God's perfection

Having considered God's simplicity, I now turn to his perfection. And since perfect things are called 'good', I shall discuss

first, God's perfection,
second, his goodness.

About the first of these questions there are three points of inquiry:

1. Is God perfect?
2. Is his perfection all-embracing, containing, so to say, the perfection of everything else?
3. Can we say that creatures resemble God?

Article 1: Is God perfect?

1. 'Perfect' does not seem a suitable term to apply to God. Its literal meaning is 'thoroughly made', but we would not say that God is made. So, we should not say that he is perfect.
2. Moreover, God is the first origin of things. But things have imperfect origins. Plants and animals, for example, begin from seed. So, God is imperfect.
3. Moreover, as I have shown, God's essence is existing itself.[1] But simply to exist is seemingly most imperfect (the most common of all things). So, God is not perfect.

---

[1] 1a 3.4.

44

On the contrary, we read in Matthew, 'Be perfect, as your heavenly Father is perfect.'[2]

Reply: Aristotle tells us that certain ancient philosophers (the Pythagoreans and Speusippus) did not predicate 'best' and 'most perfect' of the first source because they paid attention only to the matter out of which things originated, and the first matter out of which things originated is the most imperfect.[3] For matter as such is only potential, and the first material source is therefore the most potential and, therefore, the most imperfect.

But we take God to be the first source in so far as he is an efficient cause, not in so far as he is something material. And a first efficient cause has to be the most perfect of things. For as matter as such is potential, an efficient cause as such is actual. So, the first origin of all activity must be the most actual, and therefore the most perfect, of all things. For we call things perfect when they have achieved actuality (a perfect thing being that in which nothing required by its particular mode of perfection fails to exist).

Hence:

1. What is not made cannot properly be called perfect. But as Gregory says, 'stammering, we echo the heights of God as best we can'.[4] So, because we call things that are made 'perfect' when they are drawn from mere potentiality into actuality, we extend the word to refer to anything not lacking in actuality, whether made or not.

2. The imperfect matter from which the things around us originate is not their ultimate origin. It is preceded by something perfect. For even when an animal is generated from seed, the original seed derives from some previous animal or plant. Anything potential must be preceded by something actual, since only that which is actual can actualize something that exists potentially.

3. Existence is the most perfect thing of all, for everything else is potential compared to it. For nothing achieves actuality unless it exists, and the act of existing is therefore the actuality of everything, even of every form. Thus it is that things acquire existence and that existence does not acquire things. For in the phrases 'the existence of man' or 'of a horse' or 'of some other thing', it is existence that is

---

[2] Matthew 5:48.   [3] *Metaphysics* 7.7, 1072b30.   [4] *Morals* 5.36. *PL* 75.715.

regarded as an acquisition like a form, not the thing to which existence belongs.

Article 2: Is God's perfection all-embracing, containing, so to speak, the perfection of everything else?

1. It seems that God does not contain the perfections of everything. For God, as I have shown, is simple,[5] while the perfections of things are many and diverse. So, God does not contain every perfection of things.

2. Moreover, opposites cannot coexist in one and the same thing. But things have contrary perfections, for each species is perfected by that which differentiates it from other species in the same genus (and such constitutive differences are contrary to each other). So, it seems that, because opposites cannot exist together in the same thing, God does not contain all the perfections of things.

3. Again, a living thing is more perfect than a merely existent thing. And something wise is more perfect than something that is merely alive. To live, therefore, is more perfect than to be, and to be wise is more perfect than to live. But God's essence is existing as such. So, he does not have the perfections of life and wisdom and other similar perfections.

On the contrary, we have Dionysius saying that 'God pre-contains in one all existing things.'[6]

Reply: The perfections of everything exist in God. That is why he is said to be universally perfect, for, as Averroes says, he lacks no excellence found in any kind of thing.[7] And there are two ways of showing that this is so.

First, because any perfection found in an effect must also be found in the effective cause of that effect – either as it exists in the cause, when cause and effect are of the same sort (as when people beget people), or in a more perfect manner, when cause and effect are not of the same sort (as when the sun's power produces things having a certain likeness to the sun). Now, effects obviously pre-exist potentially in their efficient causes. And though to pre-exist potentially in a

---

[5] 1a 3.7.   [6] *The Divine Names* 5.9. PG 3.825.   [7] *Commentary on Aristotle's Metaphysics* 5.21.

material cause[8] is to pre-exist in a more imperfect way (matter, as such, being imperfect, and an agent, as such, being perfect), to pre-exist potentially in an efficient cause is to pre-exist in a perfect way, not an imperfect one. So, since God is the primary effective cause of all things, the perfections of everything must pre-exist in him in a higher manner. Dionysius touches on this line of thinking when he says that God is not 'this and not that' but 'is everything, inasmuch as he is everything's cause'.[9]

Second, because, as I have shown, God is existence itself subsisting through itself,[10] he therefore necessarily contains within himself the full perfection of existing. For if something hot falls short of the full perfection of heat, this is clearly only because it does not fully partake of the nature of heat. But if heat were to subsist through itself, nothing of the power of heat could be lacking in it. So, since God is subsistent existence itself, he can lack nothing of the perfection of existing. Yet every perfection is a perfection of existing, for things are perfect in so far as they have existence in some way. God, therefore, cannot lack the perfection of anything. And Dionysius is touching upon this argument when he says that 'God does not exist in any particular way, but possesses all being in himself – absolutely, limitlessly, and in a uniform way.' He goes on to say that 'God is the being of all that subsists.'[11]

Hence:

1. As Dionysius says, if the sun 'possesses in itself, primordially and without diversity, the different qualities and substances of the things that we can sense, while yet maintaining the unity of its own being and the homogeneity of its light, how much more must everything pre-exist in unity of nature in the cause of all?'[12] So, things that are diverse and opposite in themselves pre-exist as one in God without detriment to his simplicity.
2. The above answer suffices for this argument also.
3. In the same chapter Dionysius also tells us that existence as such, when distinguished conceptually, is more perfect than life as such, and that life as such is more perfect than wisdom as such, but that it is still the case that something alive is more perfect than something

---

[8] The matter of or from which a thing is made.   [9] *The Divine Names* 5.8. *PG* 3.824.   [10] 1a 3.4.
[11] *The Divine Names* 5.4. *PG* 3.817.   [12] *The Divine Names* 5.8. *PG* 3.824.

which simply exists, for living things both live and exist, and the same goes for things with intelligence.[13] So, although existence in general does not include in itself being alive or wise (something that has existence need not have it in every mode of existing), existence itself does involve life and wisdom (for subsistent existence itself cannot lack any existing perfection).

Article 3: Can we say that creatures resemble God?

1. It seems that no creature can resemble God. For the psalm says 'Lord, there is none like you among the gods.'[14] But the creatures to which we extend the word 'god' are among the more excellent ones. So, it is even less the case that other creatures can be said to resemble God.

2. Moreover, resemblance is a sort of comparison. But things belonging to different genera cannot be compared with each other and so cannot be alike. Hence, for example, nobody talks of a resemblance between sweetness and whiteness. But no creature can belong to the same genus as God since he, as I have shown, is not a member of any genus.[15] So, no creature resembles God.

3. Moreover, things are said to be alike when they agree in form. But nothing is similar to God in respect of its form because nothing apart from God has as its essence simply to exist. So, no creature can resemble God.

4. Again, resemblance is mutual, for like is similar to like. So, if some creature were like God, God would be like a creature, which Isaiah denies: 'to whom will you liken God?'[16]

On the contrary, we read in Genesis: 'Let us make human beings in our image and likeness.'[17] And in 1 John we find, 'When he appears we shall be like him.'[18]

Reply: Since resemblance results from similarity of form, there are as many sorts of resemblance as there are ways of sharing a form.

We say that some things are alike since they share a form of the same type to the same degree (and we call such things 'exactly alike', not

---

[13] *The Divine Names* 5.3. PG 3.817.   [14] Psalms 85:8.   [15] 1a 3.5.   [16] Isaiah 40:18.
[17] Genesis 1:26.   [18] 1 John 3:2.

'merely alike'). So, we say that two equally white things resemble one another in whiteness. And this is the most perfect kind of likeness.

We speak of other things as alike because they share a form of the same type, though to different degrees. So, we say that something less white resembles something more white – an imperfect likeness.

Third, we say that things are alike when they share a form, but in different ways. An example would be an agent and its effect when they are not in the same genus. For what a thing produces reflects what it is. And since a thing is active in virtue of its form, its effect must bear a likeness to that form. So, if agent and effect belong to the same species, their similar forms will be of the same specific type – as when human beings beget human beings. But if the agent is outside the species to which its effect belongs, the forms will be alike, though not of the same specific type – as a likeness of sorts obtains between the sun and the things that it produces, even though these do not receive a form similar in appearance to that of the sun. So, if there is an agent that is not in any genus, its effects will bear an even more remote resemblance to the agent. The likeness will not now be of the same specific or generic type as the form of the agent. It will display the sort of analogy that holds between all things because they have existence in common. And this is how things receiving existence from God resemble him. As possessing existence, they resemble the primary and universal source of all existing.

Hence:

1. As Dionysius says, when sacred Scripture states that nothing is like God, 'it is not denying all likeness to him. For the same things are like and unlike God: like in so far as they imitate as best they can the one whom it is not possible to imitate perfectly; unlike in so far as they fall short of their cause'[19] – not only in degree (as less white falls short of more white), but also because they do not share a common species or genus.

2. Creatures are not related to God as to a thing of a different genus, but as to something outside of and prior to all genera.

3. We do not say that creatures resemble God because they share a form of the same specific or generic type. Rather, we speak analogically –

[19] *The Divine Names* 9.7. *PG* 3.916.

inasmuch as God is a being by his essence, while other things are beings by participation.

4. Although we may admit in a way that creatures resemble God, we can in no way admit that God resembles creatures. For, as Dionysius points out, 'mutual likeness obtains between things of the same order, but not between cause and effect'.[20] That is why we call a portrait of someone a likeness of a human being, but not vice versa. Similarly, we can say that creatures resemble God in a way, but not that God resembles creatures.

---

[20] *The Divine Names* 9.6. *PG* 3.913.

Question 5
The general notion of good

Now I consider goodness:

> first, goodness in general;
> second, God's goodness.

There are six points of inquiry when it comes to the first question:

1. Is good really the same as being?
2. Assuming that they differ merely as ideas, which idea is the more fundamental?
3. Assuming that being is more fundamental, is every being good?
4. What kind of causality is implicit in the notion of goodness?
5. Is goodness a matter of mode, species and order?
6. The division of goodness into the worthy, the useful and the delightful.

Article 1: Is good really the same as being?

1. It seems that there is a real difference between good and being. For Boethius says, 'I observe that it is one thing for things to be good, another for them to exist.'[1] So, there is a real difference between good and being.

---

[1] *How Substances Are Good in Virtue of Their Existence without Being Substantial Goods (De Hebdomadibus). PL* 64.1312.

2. Moreover, nothing gives form to itself. Yet a comment on the *Book of Causes* says that to be good is to have the form of being.[2] So, being and good really differ.

3. Again, there are degrees of goodness but not of being. So, good and being must really differ.

On the contrary, Augustine says that 'inasmuch as we exist, we are good'.[3]

Reply: As I shall now make clear, goodness and being are really the same. They differ only conceptually.

The goodness of something consists in its being desirable. Hence Aristotle's dictum that 'good is what everything desires'.[4] But desirability evidently follows upon perfection, for things always desire their perfection. And the perfection of a thing depends on the extent to which it has achieved actuality. So, something is obviously good inasmuch as it is a being, for, as I have shown, it is by existing that everything achieves actuality.[5] So, good clearly does not really differ from being, though the word 'good' expresses a notion of desirability not expressed by the word 'being'.

Hence:

1. Although 'good' and 'being' signify a single reality, we do not in the same way say that something is a being without qualification and good without qualification. For 'good' and 'being' have different meanings. 'Being' signifies actuality in the strict sense, which is related to potentiality. We therefore call something a being without qualification as, to start with, we distinguish it from what is only potential. Now, something's existence as a substance distinguishes it from what is potential. So, we call things 'beings without qualification' because they exist as substances. On the other hand, though, we speak of things existing 'in a certain respect' because of added actualities. For example, being white means existing in a certain respect, for being white does not take away an unconditionally potential existence, since it is something that already exists that comes to be white. But 'good' signifies perfection or desirability and, therefore, finality. Thus we say that something completely

---

[2] *Book of Causes* 19. Largely excerpts from the *Elements of Theology* (*Elementatio theologica*) of Proclus, translated into Latin by an unknown author either from the Greek or Arabic in the twelfth century.
[3] *On Christian Doctrine* 1.32. PL 34.32.   [4] *Nicomachean Ethics* 1.1, 1094a3.   [5] 1a 3.4; 4.1, *ad* 3.

perfect is good without qualification. Furthermore, we do not say that something that lacks the final perfection that it ought to have (even though it has some perfection in so far as it is actual) is perfect without qualification. Nor do we call it 'good without qualification'. We say that it is perfect and good in a certain respect.

So we speak of things as beings without qualification and as good in a certain respect in so far as they exist substantially (by existing to start with); and we speak of things as beings in a certain respect and as good without qualification when thinking of their final actuality. Hence, Boethius's remark that 'it is one thing for things to be good and another for them to exist' refers to being without qualification and to good without qualification. For something is a being without qualification because of its first actuality, and it is good without qualification because of its final actuality. Yet something is in some way good by its first actuality, and it is in some way a being by its final actuality.

It therefore follows that when we consider the initial existence of something as a substance we speak of it as existing without qualification and as being good in a certain respect (namely, inasmuch as it exists). But when we consider the actualization which completes a thing we speak of that thing existing in a certain respect and as being good without qualification. Hence Boethius's remark that 'it is one thing for things to be good and another for them to exist' refers to existing and being good understood without qualification. For to exist without qualification is to achieve an initial actuality, and to be good without qualification is to achieve complete actuality. But a thing is in some way good by its initial actuality, and it is in some way a being by the actuality completing it.

2. We call something good when it receives a form. Similarly, we understand it to be good without qualification when it achieves complete actuality.

3. Similarly again, degrees of goodness result from actuality over and above existence, such as knowledge or virtue.

Article 2: Which idea is the more fundamental: good or being?

1. Good seems to be a more fundamental idea than being because the order of names corresponds to the order of the things that they

signify. But Dionysius, among God's other names, lists 'good' before 'being'.[6] So, good is a more fundamental idea than being.

2. Moreover, the more fundamental idea is the one with wider application. But good is of wider application than being, for, as Dionysius says, 'good extends to things that exist and things that do not exist, while being only extends to things that exist'.[7] So, good is a more fundamental idea than being.

3. Moreover, the more universal an idea is the more fundamental it is. But good seems more universal than being, for it conveys the notion of desirability, and even non-existence is desirable to some (thus we read of Judas that 'it would have been good for him never to have been born').[8] So, good is a more fundamental idea than being.

4. Again, it is not only existence that is desirable. The same is true of life, wisdom and many similar things. So, existing seems to be only one of many desirable goods, and good is, without qualification, a more fundamental idea than being.

On the contrary, the *Book of Causes* says that 'existing is the first created thing'.[9]

Reply: Being is a more fundamental idea than good. For the idea expressed in a word is something that the intellect conceives about things and expresses in speech. So, a more fundamental idea is one that is more basic in the intellect's conceptualization. But the most basic idea we meet with in intellectual conceptualization is that of being, for, as Aristotle says, in order to be known, a thing must actually be.[10] This is why being is the proper object of intellect and, therefore, the most intelligible thing, just as sound is the most fundamental object of hearing. Being, therefore, is a more fundamental idea than good.

Hence:

1. Dionysius is concerned with divine names with an eye on God considered as a cause. For, as he says, God's names are drawn from creatures, as those of other causes are drawn from their effects.[11] But 'good', conveying as it does the notion of desirability, implies being an end or goal, and this is where causality starts – for no agent acts except for some end, and no matter acquires form unless some agent acts

[6] *The Divine Names* 3.1. PG 3.680.   [7] *The Divine Names* 5.5. PG 3.816.   [8] Matthew 26:24.
[9] *Book of Causes* 4.   [10] *Metaphysics* 9.9, 1051a31.   [11] *The Divine Names* 1.7. PG 3.596.

(hence we call the end 'the cause of causes'). In causation, then, the good precedes being as end precedes form. Any list of names signifying divine causality will, therefore, put 'good' before 'being'.

Dionysius also places goodness before being because the Platonists, not differentiating between matter and privation, said that matter was non-existent and consequently held that goodness is partaken of more widely than being. Their idea was that since prime matter desires good, it shares in it (what a thing desires reflects what it is), but it does not share in being since it is non-existent. Hence Dionysius says that 'we apply "good" to things that do not exist'.[12]

2. What I have just said clearly answers the second argument also. Or we might instead say that it is not to good as predicate but to good as cause that both existent and non-existent things are subject – understanding by 'non-existent' not total and absolute non-existence but potential existence not yet actualized. For the good is a goal – not only one in which things that have achieved actuality come to rest, but one towards which that which is non-actual but only in potentiality moves. Being, on the other hand, is related only to a formal cause, whether intrinsic or exemplary. And this causality extends only to actual things.

3. Non-existence is desirable not in itself but only incidentally – in so far as the removal of an evil is desirable, and in so far as its removal calls for non-being. But removing evil is desirable only because evil is a lack of some sort of existence. So, the desirable thing itself is existence, and non-existence is desirable only incidentally, inasmuch as people can no longer abide the lack of an existence they desire. We speak of non-existence as good for such incidental reasons.

4. We desire life, knowledge, and so on in so far as they are actual. What we desire from them, therefore, is some kind of existence. So nothing is desirable except being, and, therefore, only being is good.

Article 3: Is every being good?

1. It seems that not every being is good. For my previous discussion has shown that good adds something to being.[13] But whatever is added to

---

[12] *The Divine Names* 5.1. *PG* 3.816.   [13] 1a 5.1.

being (such as substance, quantity, quality, and the like) limits it. So, goodness limits being and not every being is good.

2. Moreover, nothing bad is good: think of Isaiah, crying 'woe to those who call evil good'.[14] But we call some beings bad. So, not every being is good.

3. Moreover, goodness, by definition, is desirable. But prime matter does not have the nature of being desirable, only that of desiring. So, prime matter is not good, and, therefore, not every being is good.

4. Again, Aristotle says that there is no such thing as goodness when it comes to mathematics.[15] But the objects of mathematics are beings of some sort (given that there is a science of them). So, not every being is good.

On the contrary, every being other than God is created by God. Yet, according to 1 Timothy, 'All of God's creatures are good.'[16] And God himself is supremely good. So, every being is good.

Reply: Every being, considered as such, is good. For every being, considered as such, is actual and therefore in some way perfect (all actuality being a sort of perfection). Now, I have already shown that anything perfect is desirable and good.[17] So, every being, considered as such, is good.

Hence:

1. Substance, quantity, quality, and everything included in them, limit being by applying it to some essence or nature. Good, however, does not add to being in this way. It merely adds the notion of desirability and perfection associated with the very existence of things, regardless of the kinds to which they belong. Being good, then, does not limit being.

2. We do not call anything bad because it is a being but because it fails to exist in some way – as when we call people bad when they fail to be virtuous, or as when we call an eye bad when its vision fails.

3. Just as prime matter is a being only potentially, so it is only potentially good. Although, according to followers of Plato, we can speak of prime matter as non-being because of the privation connected with it, prime matter still shares in something of being – namely, the

---

[14] Isaiah 5:20.   [15] *Metaphysics* 3.2, 996a29.   [16] 1 Timothy 4:4.   [17] 1a 5.1.

ordering towards or capacity for good. This is why prime matter, though not desirable, nevertheless desires.

4. Mathematical objects do not really subsist as separate things. If they did, their existence itself would be good. But they are only distinct things conceptually. When we reflect on them, we ignore matter and change, and, as a consequence, we ignore any idea of an end or a goal motivating change. But it is acceptable to think of something in this way without reference to its good or to the idea of good. For, as I have said, the idea of being is more fundamental than the idea of good.[18]

Article 4: What kind of causality is implicit in the notion of goodness?

1. 'Good' seems to imply not so much being an end or goal (being a final cause) as being one of the other kinds of cause. For Dionysius says that 'we praise the good as beautiful'.[19] But beauty involves the notion of formal causality. So, goodness does the same.

2. Moreover, goodness tends to pour itself forth, as Dionysius indicates when he says that 'goodness is the source by which everything subsists and exists'.[20] But the notion of pouring out implies the idea of an efficient cause. To be good, therefore, is to be an efficient cause.

3. Again, Augustine says, 'we exist because God is good'.[21] But we exist from God acting as an efficient cause. So, being good implies being an efficient cause.

On the contrary, we have the words of Aristotle: 'that for the sake of which things exist is their good and their goal'.[22] So, goodness involves being an end or goal (being a final cause).

Reply: Since goodness is what all things desire, and since this involves the idea of a goal, being good clearly involves being a goal. Yet, the idea of goodness presupposes the notions of efficient and formal causality. For we observe that what is first in the idea of what is to be caused is last as actually caused. Thus fire begins by heating other things, and then produces the form of fire in them. Yet, in the case of fire, heat follows upon a thing's substantial form. Now, in an act of causation we begin

---

[18] 1a 5.2. [19] *The Divine Names* 5.7. PG 3.701. [20] *The Divine Names* 4.4. PG 3.700.
[21] *On Christian Doctrine* 1.32. PL 34.32. [22] *Physics* 2.3, 195a23–4.

with a good end which moves an efficient cause. Then follows the action of an agent producing a form, and finally there arises a form. Necessarily, then, the opposite order is found within something caused. First, there occurs a form itself, which gives something existence; then there occurs the thing's operative power through which it comes to perfection of existence (for Aristotle says that something is perfect in being when it can reproduce itself);[23] and finally the characteristic of goodness comes about, on which what has been perfected in the being is based.

Hence:

1. A good thing is also a beautiful thing, for goodness and beauty have the same basis in reality, namely, form; and this is why 'we praise the good as beautiful'. Yet the words 'good' and 'beautiful' are not synonymous. For good ('what all things desire') has properly to do with desire, and therefore involves the idea of end (since desire is a kind of movement towards something). Beauty, on the other hand, has to do with cognition, for we call something beautiful when it pleases the eye of a beholder. So, beauty is a matter of right proportion, for the senses delight in rightly proportioned things as similar to themselves (the sense-faculty being itself a sort of proportion, like all other knowing faculties). Now, since cognition is achieved by assimilation, and since similarity has to do with form, beauty properly involves the notion of formal causality.

2. We say that goodness tends to pour itself forth in the same way that we say that ends cause movement.

3. We say that beings with will are good when their wills are good, for will determines the use to which everything else in us is put. So, good people are not those with good intellects but those with a good will. But the will's special function is the pursuit of ends. So, to say that 'we exist because God is good' is to refer to final causality.

Article 5: Is goodness a matter of mode, species and order?

1. It seems that goodness is not a matter of mode, species and order. For, as I have said, good and being are conceptually different.[24] But mode, species and order seem part of a being's nature. For the book of

---

[23] *Meteorology* 4.3, 380a12ff.   [24] 1a 5.1.

Wisdom declares, 'you have created everything by number, weight and measure'[25] – a threefoldness that Augustine shows to be the basis of species, mode and order when he says, 'measure determines the mode of everything, number supplies species, and weight gives it rest and stability'.[26] So, goodness does not consist of mode, species and order.

2. Moreover, mode, species and order are themselves goods of a certain sort. So, if being good consists in mode, species and order, each of these must have mode, species and order of its own. And so on for ever.

3. Moreover, evil is the privation of mode, species and order. But something evil never lacks goodness altogether. So, goodness does not consist in mode, species and order.

4. Moreover, we cannot say that something containing goodness is bad. But we talk of a bad mode, a bad species and a bad order. So, goodness does not consist in mode, species and order.

5. Again, mode, species and order are caused by weight, number and measure, as the above quotation from Augustine shows. But some good things do not possess weight, number and measure, for Ambrose says that 'it is the nature of light not to be created in number, weight and measure'.[27] So, goodness does not consist in mode, species and order.

On the contrary, Augustine says that 'these three – mode, species and order – are goods always found in everything that God makes; where these three are great, there are great goods; where they are of small account, things are of little good; where they are totally absent there is no good'.[28] Now, none of this would be so unless goodness consisted in these three things. So, goodness consists in mode, species and order.

Reply: For us to call them 'good', things must be perfect, for only then are they desirable, as I have said.[29] Now, being perfect means lacking nothing requisite to one's own mode of perfection. But its form determines what a thing is, and the form presupposes certain things and has certain necessary consequences. So, to be perfect and good, a thing must possess form, together with the prerequisites and consequences of form.

[25] Wisdom 11:21.   [26] *On the Literal Interpretation of 'Genesis'* 4.3. *PL* 34.299.
[27] *On the Days of Creation (In Hexaemeron)* 1.9. *PL* 14.143.
[28] *On the Nature of the Good* 3. *PL* 42.553.   [29] 1a 5.1.

Now, form presupposes that the principles of something, whether material or efficient, are adapted to or commensurate with the form, and this is expressed in the word 'mode', which is why we say that measure determines mode.[30] To express form itself Augustine used the word 'species', since form determines the species of things. And this is why we say that number suggests species; for according to Aristotle definitions of species are like numbers, and just as the addition or subtraction of a single unit changes the species of a number, so adding or subtracting a differentiating factor changes definitions.[31] Finally, form issues in an inclination to some end or action or the like, for activity follows upon actuality, and things gravitate towards what is natural to them. And this is expressed by 'weight' and 'order'. So, because good consists in being perfect, it also consists in being in mode, species, form and order.

Hence:

1. These three do not follow upon being unless it is perfect and is, on that account, good.
2. We call mode, species and order good, and we speak of them as beings, not because they are subsisting things in their own right, but because other things are both beings and good through them. Nevertheless, they are good without being so constituted in goodness. For we do not call them good as being formally constituted good by something else, but because other things are formally constituted good by them. In the same way we say that whiteness is a being not because it exists in some way but because something exists as a white thing by virtue of it.
3. Every way of existing is determined by some form. So mode, species and order accompany every way in which a thing exists. Thus people have one mode, species and order as people, and another mode, species and order again as white, or as virtuous, or as knowledgeable, or as anything else that they are. Now, something gone bad, like a blind eye, lacks some particular way of being (in the case of an eye, being able to see). So it loses, not every mode, species and order, but only the mode, species and order associated with being able to see.
4. Augustine says that 'mode as such is always good' (and the same could be said of species and order), 'but we call mode, species and order bad

---

[30] *On the Literal Interpretation of 'Genesis'* 4.5. *PL* 34.299. [31] *Metaphysics* 8.3, 1043b34.

60

either because they fall short of what they should be, or because they are unfitted for the things for which they are meant, and are thus bad in the sense of foreign and incongruous'.[32]

5. No one says that it is in the nature of light altogether to lack number, weight and measure, but only as compared to bodies; for light is all-pervasive in its influence on bodies, being the form of energy proper to the ultimate physical source of change, namely, the heavens.

Article 6: The division of goodness into the worthy, the useful and the delightful

1. It seems wrong to divide good into the worthy, the useful and the delightful. For, as Aristotle says, goods are divided into ten categories,[33] in each of which we can find worthy, useful and delightful things.[34] Such a division is therefore inappropriate.

2. Moreover, all division results from contraries. But these three classes of goods do not seem contrary, for worthy things are delightful, and, as Cicero says, nothing unworthy is useful[35] (although the worthy and the useful would have to be contrary if the division were by contraries). So, the suggested division is inappropriate.

3. Again, things related as means to end are really one. But the useful is good only as a means to either the delightful or the worthy. So, we should not divide the useful from the delightful and the worthy.

On the contrary, Ambrose divided goodness in this way.[36]

Reply: This division seems properly to apply to human good. Nevertheless, a deeper and more general consideration of goodness reveals that the division properly applies to goodness as such. For a thing is good because it is desirable and because movements of desire terminate in it. Now, we can consider the termination of such movements by analogy with the movements of physical bodies. Physical movement terminates, simply speaking, at its final point; but it terminates also at intermediate places through which it moves to its final point; these may

---

[32] *On the Nature of the Good* 22–3. PL 42.558.
[33] This is an allusion to Aristotle's doctrine that all predicates (or attributes) fall into just one of ten ultimate sorts. Aquinas thinks that Aristotle's ten in fact reduce to four: substance, quantity, quality and relation.
[34] *Nicomachean Ethics* 1.6, 1096a23.   [35] Marcus Tullius Cicero (106–43 BC), *On Duties* 2.3.
[36] *On Duties* 1.9. PL 16.35.

be called final points in some sense because part of the movement terminates there. Moreover, we can consider that which finally stops the movement to be either the actual thing aimed at (a place, say, or a form), or rest in that thing. By analogy then, things desirable in movements of desire (since they put a partial stop to the movements, being part way towards some other thing) we call 'useful'. That which is desirable as putting a full stop to the movement of desire because it is the actually desired thing itself we call 'worthy', for 'worthy' means 'desirable in itself'. That which puts a stop to the movement of desire because it is at rest in the desired thing is 'delight'.

Hence:

1. We divide goods into ten categories in so far as good and being are the same. But the division into worthy, useful and delightful applies to what is characteristic of goodness itself.

2. The division is based not on contrary things but contrary concepts. Yet we are right to say that things that give delight are, as such, desirable – even though they can, at times, be harmful and unworthy. And we say that what is useful is desirable not in itself but only as a means to something else (e.g. the drinking of bitter medicine). We call things worthy, however, when they are desirable in themselves.

3. We do not use the word 'good' in exactly the same sense within these three divisions, but in a graded sequence of analogical senses. The primary sense of 'good' is 'worthy', the second 'delightful', and the third 'useful'.

Question 6

God's goodness

I now turn to God's goodness.

Here there are four points of inquiry:

1. Can we associate goodness with God?
2. Is God supremely good?
3. Is only God essentially good?
4. Does God's goodness make everything good?

Article 1: Can we associate goodness with God?

1. It seems that we should not associate goodness with God. For goodness consists in mode, species and order, which seem out of place in God, who is immeasurable and not ordered to anything. So, we should not associate goodness with God.
2. Moreover, 'the good is what everything desires'.[1] But not everything desires God, because not everything knows him, and one can only desire what one knows. So, we should not associate goodness with God.

On the contrary, we read in Lamentations, 'The Lord is good to those who hope in him, to the soul that seeks him.'[2]

Reply: We should especially associate goodness with God. For something is good in so far as it is desirable. But everything desires its perfection, and an effect's perfection and form consists in resembling its efficient cause (since every efficient cause produces an effect like itself). So an efficient cause is desirable and may be called good because

---

[1] Aristotle, *Nicomachean Ethics* 1.1, 1094a3.   [2] Lamentations 3:25.

what is desired from it is that the effect share its goodness by resembling it. Clearly then, since God is the first efficient cause of everything, goodness and desirability belong to him. That is why Dionysius ascribes goodness to God as to the first efficient cause, saying that we call God good 'as the source of all subsistence'.[3]

Hence:

1. Mode, species and order belong to the essence of caused good. But goodness belongs to God as a cause, so he imposes mode, species and order on others. These three are in God as their cause.

2. In desiring its own perfection everything desires God himself, for the perfections of all things somehow resemble divine existence, as I have said.[4] And so, of the things that desire God, some know him in himself (this is the privilege of reasoning creatures), others know his goodness as participated somewhere or other (which is possible even to sense-knowledge), while yet other things, having no knowledge, desire God by nature, directed to their goal by a higher being with knowledge.

Article 2: Is God supremely good?

1. It seems that God is not supremely good. For supreme goodness is something over and above goodness, otherwise every good would be supremely good. Now, adding one thing to another produces something composite. The supreme good is therefore composite. As I have already shown, however, God is simple.[5] So, he is not supremely good.

2. Moreover, 'good is what everything desires', as Aristotle says.[6] Now the only thing that everything desires is the goal of all things, namely, God. So, nothing except God is good. This is also apparent from something Matthew says: 'No one is good but God alone.'[7] But calling something 'supreme' involves comparing it with other things: the supremely hot, for example, with all hot things. So, we cannot call God supremely good.

3. Again, 'supreme' implies comparison. But one can only compare things belonging to the same genus. It seems odd, for example, to

---

[3] *The Divine Names* 4.4. PG 3.700.   [4] 1a 4.3.   [5] 1a 3.   [6] *Nicomachean Ethics* 1.1, 1094a3.
[7] This quotation is closer to the text of Luke 18:19. The text St Thomas references is Matthew 19:17.

say that sweetness is bigger or smaller than a line. So, since God and other good things are not in the same genus (as is clear from what I have already said),[8] it seems that he cannot be called supremely good by comparison with them.

On the contrary, Augustine tells us that the three divine persons 'are the supreme good seen by the supremely clean of heart'.[9]

Reply: God is not supremely good only within a particular genus or order of reality. He is the absolutely supreme good. For, as I have said, we attribute goodness to God as being the first source of every perfection that things desire.[10] And these perfections, as I have shown, flow from God, not as from an efficient cause in the same genus as its effects, but as from an efficient cause that does not agree with its effects either in species or in genus.[11] Now, an agent in the same genus as its effects mirrors them with unchanged form, but an agent not in the same genus as its effects mirrors them more perfectly: the heat of the sun, for example, excels that of fire. So, since God (not himself in a genus) is good as the first source of everything, he must be good in the most perfect manner possible; and we call him supremely good for this reason.

Hence:

1. What supreme goodness adds to goodness is something not absolute but merely relative. Now, the relations that God is said to bear to creatures, although we represent them mentally as existing in God, really exist not in God but in creatures, just as we call things objects of knowledge not because they are related to our knowledge, but because our knowledge is related to them. So the supreme good does not have to be composite, but other good things must fall short of that good.

2. The assertion that 'good is what everything desires' does not mean that everything desires every good, but that whatever is desired is good. And, as I shall presently explain, the assertion that 'no one is good but God alone' refers to essential goodness.[12]

3. There is no way of comparing things that are not in the same genus, if they are actually in different genera. But we say that God is not in the same genus as other goods, not because he belongs to another genus, but because he exists outside all genera and is their source. We

---

[8] 1a 3.5; 4.3, *ad* 3.   [9] *On the Trinity* 1.2. *PL* 42.822.   [10] 1a 6.1.   [11] 1a 4.3.   [12] 1a 6.3.

therefore compare him to other things as something surpassing them; and this is the comparison implied by supreme goodness.

Article 3: Is only God essentially good?

1. It seems that not only God is essentially good. For, as I noted previously, 'one' and 'being' are convertible, as are 'good' and 'being'.[13] But Aristotle shows that every being is essentially one.[14] So every being is essentially good.
2. Moreover, if 'good is what everything desires', the being of a thing is its good, for everything desires being. But everything is essentially a being. So everything is essentially good.
3. Again, everything is good by its own goodness. So if something is not essentially good, its goodness cannot be its essence. Yet, because it exists in some way, that goodness must itself be good, and if it is good by some goodness different from itself, we must go on to ask about this other goodness. The only way of stopping this process is to arrive at some goodness that is not good by another goodness. But then we might as well have begun with this – that everything is good by its own goodness. So everything is essentially good.

On the contrary, Boethius says that everything other than God participates in goodness. So only God is essentially good.[15]

Reply: God alone is essentially good.

For we call things good in so far as they are perfect. Now, there is a threefold perfection in things: first, they are established in existence; second, they possess in addition certain accidents necessary to perfect their activity; and a third perfection comes when they attain some extrinsic goal. Thus the primary perfection of the fire lies in existing according to its own substantial form, a secondary perfection consists in heat, lightness, dryness, and so on; and a third perfection is being at rest in its appropriate place.

Now, this threefold perfection belongs essentially to no caused thing, but only to God; for only in him is essence the same as existence, and in him there are no added accidents (as I have noted, power, wisdom, and

---

[13] 1a 5.1–3. [14] *Metaphysics* 4.2, 1003b32.
[15] *How Substances Are Good in Virtue of Their Existence without Being Substantial Goods* (*De Hebdomadibus*). *PL* 64.1313.

the like, which are accidental to other things, belong to him essentially).[16] And he is not disposed towards some extrinsic goal but is himself the ultimate goal of all other things. So it is clear that only God essentially possesses every kind of perfection and alone is essentially good.

Hence:

1. Being one does not involve being perfect, but only being undivided; and everything is essentially this. But the essences of simple things are both undivided and indivisible, and the essences of composite things are at least undivided. So while everything is essentially one, not everything is essentially good, as I have shown.
2. Although things are good inasmuch as they exist, existence is not the essence of any created thing. So it does not follow that created things are essentially good.
3. The goodness of something created is not its essence, but something additional: either its existing, or an added perfection, or a relatedness to a goal. Yet we call this added goodness 'good' just as we call it 'being'. But we call it 'being' because it is something, not because it exists because of something else. So we say that it is good because it is something good, not because it possesses some other goodness that makes it good.

Article 4: Does God's goodness make everything good?

1. It seems that God's goodness makes everything good. For Augustine writes: 'Consider this good and that good; abstract from the this and the that and gaze simply at good, if you can; you will then see God, the good of all things, himself not good by any other good.'[17] So everything is good by the good that we call God.
2. Moreover, and as Boethius says, we call things good because they have God as their goal, and this is because of God's goodness.[18] So it is God's goodness that makes everything good.

On the contrary, things are good inasmuch as they exist. But we say that things exist not by divine existence but by their own. So things are good, not by God's goodness, but by their own.

---

[16] 1a 3.6.   [17] *On the Trinity* 8.3. *PL* 42.949.
[18] *How Substances Are Good in Virtue of Their Existence without Being Substantial Goods* (*De Hebdomadibus*). *PL* 64, 1313.

Reply: There is nothing to stop us from naming things by reference to others, if the name is a relative term – as when we say that things are 'in place' by reference to place, or 'measured' by reference to measure. But there have been different opinions concerning non-relative terms. Plato believed that the Forms of things exist separately, and that we name individual things after these separate Forms, in which they participate in some way – that, for example, we call Socrates a 'man' by reference to some separate Form of man. And just as he believed in separate Forms of man and horse, calling them 'Man Himself' and 'Horse Itself', Plato also believed in separate Forms of being and unity ('Being Itself' and 'Unity Itself') by participating in which everything is said to be or to be one. The existent Good Itself and Unity Itself he believed to be the supreme God, by reference to whom we say that all things are good by participation. And although, as Aristotle repeatedly proves, the part of this opinion that postulates separate, self-subsistent forms of natural things appears to be unreasonable, it is absolutely true that there exists some first thing (God), good by essence, as I have shown[19] (a judgement with which Aristotle also agrees).

So we may call things good and existent by reference to this first thing, existent and good by essence, inasmuch as they somehow participate in and resemble it, even if distantly and deficiently (as I pointed out earlier).[20] In this sense we say that all things are good by God's goodness, which is the pattern, source, and goal of all goodness. Nevertheless, the resemblance to God's goodness that leads us to call something good is inherent in the thing itself, belonging to it as a form and, therefore, naming it. So there is one goodness in all things, and yet many.

And this clears up the difficulties.

---

[19] 1a 6.3 (also 1a 3.4 if the reading 'existent and good by nature' is adopted).   [20] 1a 4.3.

Question 7

God's limitlessness

Next for consideration we have God's limitlessness, and then his existence in things. For we say that God exists everywhere in everything because he is boundless and unlimited.

The first of these questions contains four points of inquiry:

1. Is God unlimited?
2. Is anything other than God unlimited in essence?
3. Can anything be unlimited in size?
4. Can there be an unlimited number of things?

Article 1: Is God unlimited?

1. It seems that God is not unlimited. For everything unlimited is imperfect because it has parts and matter, as Aristotle says.[1] But God is the very summit of perfection. So he is not unlimited.
2. Moreover, Aristotle says that to be limited or unlimited a thing must first be extended.[2] But God is not extended since he is not a body, as I have shown. So it does not belong to God to be unlimited.[3]
3. Moreover, if something is in one place and not in another, it is spatially limited. So to be one thing and not something else is to be limited as regards substance. But God is one thing and not another, for he is not stone or wood, for example. So God is limited in so far as he is a substance.

---

[1] *Physics* 3.6, 207a27.   [2] *Physics* 1.2, 185b2.   [3] 1a 3.1.

On the contrary, Damascene calls God 'limitless, eternal and unbounded'.[4]

Reply: Aristotle tells us that in ancient times all philosophers considered the first source to be unlimited[5] – and reasonably so since they saw no limit to the things deriving from the first source. But because they made a mistake about the nature of this source, they made a corresponding mistake about its limitlessness. They thought of the first source as matter, so they assigned a material limitlessness to it (saying that the first source of things was some limitless body).

We must therefore remember that anything not limited can be called limitless. But there is a sense in which matter is limited by form, and a sense in which form is limited by matter. Form limits matter because matter is potentially able to receive many forms before assuming a particular form. Then it is determined by the form assumed. Matter limits form because a form, as such, may be shared by many things, but, when acquired by matter, it becomes determinately the form of some particular thing. But a form in limiting matter perfects it, so that material limitlessness is imperfect in character: it is matter without form, so to say. Matter, however, does not perfect a form. Rather, it restricts its full scope, so that the limitlessness of a form undetermined by matter is perfect in character.

Now, the most formal thing of all is existence itself, as I have shown above.[6] So, since God's existence is not acquired by anything (since, as I have shown, God is his own subsistent existence)[7] God himself is clearly both limitless and perfect.

Hence:

1. The answer to the first difficulty is now plain.
2. The boundary of an extended thing is, so to speak, the form of its extension. The fact that setting bounds to extension produces shape, a sort of dimensional form, indicates this. So limitlessness of extension is the kind of limitlessness associated with matter, and such limitlessness is not to be ascribed to God, as I have said.
3. The very fact that God's existence itself subsists without being acquired by anything, and is, as such, limitless, distinguishes it from everything else and sets other things apart from it. In the same way, if

---

[4] *On the Orthodox Faith* 1.4. PG 94.800.   [5] *Physics* 3.4, 203b4.   [6] 1a 3.4; 4.3, *ad* 1.   [7] 1a 3.4.

whiteness subsisted of itself, the very fact that it was not the whiteness of something would distinguish it from all whiteness existing in a subject.

Article 2: Is anything other than God unlimited in essence?

1. It seems that something other than God can be essentially infinite. For a thing's power is commensurate with its essence. So, if God is essentially unlimited, he must also be unlimited in power. This means that he can produce an unlimited effect, for power is measured by the effects that it can produce.

2. Moreover, anything with unlimited power has an unlimited essence. Now, the powers of a created intellect are unlimited, for such an intellect perceives universal ideas capable of applying to an unlimited number of individuals. So, every created being endowed with intellect is unlimited.

3. Again, prime matter is something other than God, as I have shown.[8] But prime matter is unlimited. So, something other than God can be unlimited.

On the contrary, Aristotle says that what is unlimited cannot be derived from anything else.[9] But everything other than God derives primarily from him. So, nothing other than God is unlimited.

Reply: Things other than God can be unlimited in some, but not all, respects. For if we talk of the limitlessness associated with matter, then clearly everything that actually exists possesses form, and its matter is therefore determined by that form. But because matter determined by a substantial form is still potentially capable of receiving many accidental forms, that which simply speaking is limited may yet in some respect be called unlimited. Wood, for example, limited by its form, is yet in a certain respect unlimited, inasmuch as it is capable of an unlimited number of shapes.

If, however, we talk of the limitlessness associated with form, then clearly things composed of form and matter are limited in all respects and unlimited in none. Yet, if there exist created forms not assumed by

---

[8] 1a 3.8.   [9] *Physics* 3.4, 203b7.

matter but subsisting themselves, as some people say is the case with angels, then such forms will be in a certain respect unlimited (i.e. inasmuch as they are not contained or restricted by matter). But since such subsistent created forms acquire their existence and are not identical with it, that existence itself is of necessity contained and restricted by some specifying nature. So, subsistent created forms cannot be unlimited in all respects.

Hence:

1. The notion of something made whose essence is to exist is contradictory, for subsistent existence is uncreated existence. So, the notion of something both made and absolutely unlimited is contradictory. Therefore, although God's power is unlimited, he still cannot make an absolutely unlimited thing, no more than he can make an unmade thing (for this involves contradictories being true together).

2. That the extent of an intellect's powers is in some sense unlimited follows from the fact that intellect is a form that is not contained by matter. For either it is completely separate, as angelic substances are, or, in the case of an intellectual soul joined to a body, it is at least able to understand independently of bodily organs.

3. Prime matter does not exist by itself anywhere, for it is not an actually existing thing. It is only potentially existent. So, it is a product as a by-product of creation. Again, even the potentiality of prime matter is unlimited only in some respects, not all, for matter can assume only physical forms.

Article 3: Can anything be unlimited in size?

1. It seems that something can be actually unlimited in size. There is no falsity in mathematics. As Aristotle says, 'abstraction is not falsification'.[10] But mathematics employs the concept of unlimited size; for a geometer, when proving something, will say 'Let this line be infinite.' So, it is not impossible for there to be something of unlimited size.

2. Moreover, something may have any property that does not contradict its nature. But limitlessness does not contradict the nature of extension. Indeed, in order to be limited or unlimited, something must

[10] *Physics* 2.2, 193b35.

first, it seems, be extended. So, it is perfectly possible for there to be something unlimited in extent.

3. Moreover, extension is divisible without limit, for Aristotle defines the continuum as 'that which is infinitely divisible'.[11] But alternatives are substitutable one for the other, and the alternative to division and subtraction is addition and multiplication. So, it seems that extension can be multiplied without limit and that unlimited size is, therefore, possible.

4. Again, as Aristotle says, the continuity and extent of both movement and time derive from the spatial extension that movement must traverse.[12] Now, both time and movement could conceivably be endless, for any point that you choose in time or in circular movement is a beginning as well as an end. So, endless extension is also conceivable.

On the contrary, all bodies have surfaces, and any body having a surface is limited since surface is the boundary of bodies. So, all bodies are limited. The same argument applies to surfaces and lines. So, nothing extended can be unlimited.

Reply: To be unlimited in size is not the same thing as to be unlimited in essence. For even if there existed bodily things of unlimited size (fire or air, say), these would still be limited in essence: limited to a particular species by their form, and to a particular individual of the species by their matter. So, granted (from what I have said) that no creature is unlimited in essence,[13] we need to ask whether anything created can be unlimited in size.

We must therefore note that a body, which is a determinate magnitude, may be considered in two ways: mathematically when we consider only its size, and naturally when we consider its matter and form. It is clear that a body cannot actually exist naturally without limits, for all natural bodies have some determinate substantial form. But when a substantial form is determinate the accidents that follow on it must also be determinate, and size is one of these accidents. So every natural body has a determinate maximum and minimum size. It is therefore impossible for any natural body to be unlimited. We can see this by considering movement. Some movement comes naturally to any physical body. But no movement comes naturally to an unlimited body. Not rectilinear

---

[11] *Physics* 3.1, 200b20.   [12] *Physics* 4.11, 219a12.   [13] 1a 7.2.

movement, because things only move naturally in straight lines when not in their natural place (impossible in the case of an unlimited body, since it would fill all space, and one place would not be more natural to it than another). And an unlimited body cannot revolve either, for in movement like that one part of the body changes places with another part, and this would be impossible if the revolving body were unlimited in size. For if two lines are drawn from the centre of a body, the further they extend from the centre the further becomes the distance between them. In an unlimited body they would become infinitely distant from one another, and one line would never be able to reach the place of the other.

Things are no different for a mathematical body. For if we imagine such a body in actual existence, we shall have to imagine it with a form, since actuality requires form. But the form of anything extended as such is its shape, so the body will have to have a shape, and it will therefore be limited, because a shape must be contained within a boundary or boundaries.

Hence:

1. Geometers need not postulate lines that are actually infinite, but lines from which they can cut off whatever length they require, and such are the lines they call infinite.
2. Lack of limits may be compatible with the notion of magnitude in general, but it contradicts the notion of any specific magnitude (be it two feet, or a yard, or a circle or a triangle). Now things cannot exist in a genus without existing in some species of the genus. Because no species of magnitude can be limitless, all limitless magnitude is therefore impossible.
3. As I have said, the limitlessness of magnitude is the kind of limitlessness associated with matter.[14] But division breaks a whole down into its matter, for parts have the nature of material elements. And addition is a movement towards completion that has the nature of form. So, there can only be unlimited division of magnitude, not unlimited addition.
4. Movement and time do not exist all at once but bit by bit, so their actuality is shot through with potentiality. But magnitude exists all at

[14] 1a 7.1, *ad* 2.

once. Therefore, since potentiality characterizes matter, the extensive limitlessness associated with matter is incompatible with magnitude in its entirety, though compatible with time and movement in their entirety.

Article 4: Can there be an unlimited number of things?

1. It seems that there can be an unlimited number of things. For it is not impossible for something potential to be made actual. But it is possible to multiply number indefinitely. So, there can be an unlimited number of things.
2. Moreover, any type can be realized in some actual individual of the type. But there are unlimited types of geometrical figure. So, there can actually be an unlimited number of such figures.
3. Again, things not mutually conflicting do not rule each other out. Yet, given any large number of things, one can find another large number that does not conflict with the first, and can therefore coexist with it; and so on without limit. So, an unlimited number of things can actually exist.

On the contrary, we read in the book of Wisdom, 'You order all things by weight, number and measure.'[15]

Reply: On this point there have been two opinions. Some (e.g. Avicenna and Algazali) held that a number of things cannot actually be intrinsically unlimited, though there can exist a number of things that do happen to be unlimited.

We call a number of things 'intrinsically unlimited' when something requires for its existence that there be an unlimited number of things. But there can be no such thing, for something would then necessarily depend on an unlimited number of other things, and would, therefore, never come to exist, for nothing can traverse the infinite.

We say, however, that a number of things happens to be unlimited when nothing requires it to be unlimited and yet, in fact, it is so.

To make the distinction clear: a certain number of things are intrinsically necessary to carpentry (a hammer, a hand to wield it, and a mind with practical knowledge). If the number of such things were multiplied

---

[15] Wisdom 11:21.

indefinitely, the job of carpentry would never be finished, for it would depend on an unlimited number of causes. But if, in fact, a number of hammers are used, a new one being picked up when a previous one breaks, then there just happens to be a number of hammers. As it happens, many hammers are used for the work, but, if unlimited time is available for the work, it makes no difference whether one or two or more, or indeed an unlimited number are used. In the same way, then, the people to whom I am currently referring believed that a number of things that happens to be unlimited could actually exist.

This, however, is impossible. For any multitude of things one must specify what makes them a multitude. The relevant species for a multitude is the number of things in it. But no number is infinite, for number results from counting through a set in units. So, no multitude of things can actually be intrinsically unlimited, nor can it happen to be unlimited. Again, every set of things existing in the world has been created, and anything created falls under some definite purpose of its creator, for no agent acts to no purpose. So all created things must be subject to definite enumeration. Thus even a number of things that happens to be unlimited cannot actually exist.

But an unlimited number of things can exist potentially. For increase in number results from division of a continuum. The more one divides something, the greater number of things one obtains. Thus, just as there is potentially no limit to the division of a continuum (which is a break-down into matter, as I have previously shown)[16] so, and for the same reason, there is potentially no limit to numerical addition.

Hence:

1. Whatever potentially exists is brought into actual existence in accordance with its own way of existing. Thus days do not come into existence all at once, but one after another. Likewise, an unlimited number of things is not brought into existence all at once, but bit by bit: first a certain number, then an additional one, and so on without limit.

2. There are unlimited types of geometrical figures because number is unlimited, and the figures are typified as three-sided, four-sided, and so on. Therefore, just as an unlimited number of things cannot be

---

[16] 1a 7.3, *ad* 3.

brought into actual existence all at once, neither can a multitude of geometrical figures.

3. Although positing one set of things will not conflict with the positing of another set, positing an unlimited number will conflict with each specific number. We cannot, therefore, have an actually unlimited number of things.

Question 8
God's existence in things

Since it clearly belongs to something unlimited to exist everywhere in everything, I now consider whether this is so of God.

This question has four points of inquiry:

1. Is God in everything?
2. Is God everywhere?
3. Is God everywhere by his essence, power and presence?
4. Does being everywhere belong to God alone?

Article 1: Is God in everything?

1. It seems that God is not in everything. For nothing can be both in everything and above everything. But we read in the Psalms that God is above everything: 'The Lord is high above all nations, etc.'[1] So, he is not in everything.
2. Moreover, something is contained by what it is in. But God is not contained by things. He contains them. So, things are in God and God is not in things. This is why Augustine says that 'he is not in any place, but things are in him'.[2]
3. Moreover, the more powerful an efficient cause is, the more extended is its sphere of action. But God is the most powerful efficient cause. So, his action can reach to things distant from him, and he has no need to be in them.

---

[1] Psalms 112:4.   [2] *On Eighty-Three Varied Questions* 1.20. PL 40.15.

78

4. Again, devils are things of some kind. But God is not in devils, for 'light has no communion with darkness', as 2 Corinthians says.[3] So, God is not in everything.

On the contrary, a thing is present wherever it is active. But according to Isaiah, God is active in everything: 'You, Lord, have wrought all our works in us.'[4] So, God is in everything.

Reply: God is in everything; not indeed as part of their essence, or as an accident, but as an efficient cause is present to that in which its action is taking place. For every efficient cause must be connected with that upon which it acts and must touch it by its power (compare Aristotle's proof that for one thing to move another, the two must exist together).[5] Now, since it is God's essence to exist, created existence must be his proper effect, as burning is fire's proper effect. But God causes this effect in things not just when they begin to exist but all the time they are maintained in existence, just as the sun is lighting up the atmosphere all the time the atmosphere remains lit. During the whole period of a thing's existence, therefore, God must be present to it, and present in a way that accords with the way in which the thing possesses its existence. Now, existing is more intimately and profoundly interior to things than anything else, for existing (as is clear from what I have already said)[6] is formal with respect to all that really exists. So, God must be, and be intimately, in everything.

Hence:

1. The perfection of his nature places God above everything. But as causing their existence, he is also in everything, as I have been saying.
2. Although we say that bodily things are in something since something contains them, immaterial things contain that in which they exist, as the soul contains the body. So, God also contains things by being in them. However, we use the bodily metaphor and talk of everything being in God inasmuch as he contains them.
3. No matter how powerful an efficient cause is, its action can only reach to distant things by using intermediaries. Yet it belongs to God's great power that he acts in everything without intermediary causes. So, nothing is distant from him in the sense of him not being in it. Nevertheless we speak of things unlike God in nature or grace as

---

[3] 2 Corinthians 6:14.   [4] Isaiah 26:12.   [5] *Physics* 7.2, 243a4.   [6] 1a 3.4; 4.1, *ad* 3.

being distant from him, just as the perfection of his nature places him above everything.

4. When referring to devils, one may be thinking either of their nature, which comes from God, or of their disfigurement due to sin, which does not. So, we can only admit that God exists in devils if we add the qualification 'inasmuch as they, too, are things'. But we need no qualification when saying that God is present in things whose nature is not disfigured.

Article 2: Is God everywhere?

1. It seems that God is not everywhere. For this would mean that he is in every place. But it does not belong to God to be in every place, because it does not belong to him to be in any place at all. As Boethius says, 'incorporeal things are not in a place'.[7] So, God is not everywhere.

2. Moreover, place is related to what is permanent in the same way as time to successive things. But it is impossible for any indivisible instant of action or change to occur at more than one time. So, it is equally impossible for any indivisible permanent thing to exist in more than one place. Yet God's existing is permanent, not transient. So, he cannot exist in more than one place, and he cannot, therefore, be everywhere.

3. Moreover, if something is wholly in one place, a part of it is not somewhere else. But God exists wholly wherever he is, for he has no parts. So, none of him is anywhere else and he is, therefore, not everywhere.

On the contrary, we read in Jeremiah, 'I fill heaven and earth.'[8]

Reply: A place is a sort of thing, so there are two ways of understanding 'being in a place'. First, by analogy with other things, that is to say, in whatever way we understand 'being in' when talking of other things, and the attributes of any place are in the place in this sense. Second, in the way peculiar to places alone, namely, the way in which things occupying places are in those places. In both these ways there is a sense in which God is in every place (i.e. everywhere).

First, he is in every place by giving it existence and the power to be a place, just as he is in all things by giving them existence, power and

---

[7] *How Substances Are Good in Virtue of Their Existence without Being Substantial Goods* (*De Hebdomadibus*). PL 64.1311.
[8] Jeremiah 23:24.

activity. Second, just as anything occupying a place fills that place, so God fills all places, but not as bodies do. Bodies fill places by excluding other bodies from where they are, while God's presence in a place does not exclude the presence there of other things. Rather, God fills all places by giving existence to everything occupying them.

Hence:

1. Incorporeal things are not in a place because of contact between their surfaces, like bodies, but from a contact of power.
2. Indivisibility is twofold. In one sense it characterizes any point within a continuum, for example a point within a set of things that are fixed in relation to one another, and also a moment within things that are flowing. In any set of things that are fixed, such indivisible points have a set position, and so they cannot be in more than one place or part of a place. Similarly, in any action or change indivisible instants occur in a set order, and so cannot occur in more than one moment of time. But in another sense indivisibility characterizes things that are outside any kind of continuum, and in this sense we predicate indivisibility of substances like God, the soul and angels (none of which are bodies). Such indivisible things are related to a continuum, not as being part of it, but as being in causal contact with it. So, depending on whether their sphere of action is small or large, and comprehends one or more things, they are present in a small place or a large one, and in one place or more than one.
3. We call something a whole with respect to its parts, and there are two kinds of parts. First we have parts of an essence (as when we say that form and matter are parts of something composite, and as when we say that genus and difference are parts of a species). Then we have parts of something extended – the parts into which something extended is divided. So, what is wholly in a place to its whole extent cannot extend outside that place. For the extent of anything occupying place is measured by the extent of the place, and unless the place were the thing's whole place, the extent would not be the thing's whole extent. But we do not measure wholeness of essence by wholeness of place, and what is wholly in something according to its whole essence can therefore yet be in some manner outside it. This is clear even of accidents that happen to be extended. For if we are thinking of wholeness of essence, whiteness is wholly present everywhere on a

surface, and its full specific nature is realized in every part. But if we are thinking of the wholeness of the extent that it happens to possess, then whiteness is not wholly present everywhere on the surface. But the only wholeness that incorporeal things either inherently possess, or happen to possess, is the wholeness of their essential nature. Therefore, just as the soul exists wholly everywhere in the body, God exists wholly in each and every thing.

Article 3: Is God everywhere by his essence, power and presence?

1. To say that God exists in things by his essence, presence and power, hardly seems a satisfactory classification of the ways that God is in things. For to exist in something else by essence is to be in that thing essentially. But God is not in anything else essentially, for he does not belong to the essence of anything. So, we ought not to say that God exists in things by his essence, presence and power.

2. Moreover, being present in something is the same as not being absent from it. But God, precisely as existing in all things by his essence, is not absent from them. So, for him to exist in everything by his essence and by his presence are the same. It is therefore redundant to say that God exists in things by his essence, presence and power.

3. Moreover, just as God is the source of everything by his power, he is also such by his knowledge and will. But we do not say that God is in things by his knowledge and will. Neither, therefore, should we say that he is in them by his power.

4. Again, there are many perfections, like grace, added to the substance of things. So, if we say that God exists in some people in a special way by grace, it seems that we ought to acknowledge special ways in which he exists in things corresponding to each perfection.

On the contrary, Gregory tells us that 'God is in everything in a general way by his presence, power and substance, but we say that he is in some things in a more intimate way by grace.'[9]

---

[9] Actually quoted from the *Glossa ordinaria* on the Song of Songs 5:17 (one of the glosses on Scripture current in the Middle Ages), where it is attributed to Gregory, but without reference.

Reply: We say that God is in something in two ways. First, as an efficient cause, and in this way God is in everything he creates. Second, as an object aimed at by some activity within an acting subject, and this applies only to mental activities where the known is in a knower, and the desired is in one who desires. In this second way, therefore, God exists in a special fashion in those reasoning creatures that actually know and love him, or are disposed to do so. And since this is the result of a grace to the reasoning creature, as I shall show later,[10] we say that God is in this way in holy people by grace.

But to grasp the way in which he exists in other created things, we must draw an analogy from human affairs. Thus we say that a king is in the whole of his kingdom by his power, though he is not present everywhere. Again, in virtue of its presence, a thing exists in everything within its field of view, so we say that everything in a house is present even to a person not existing substantially in every part of that house. Finally, we say that something is substantially or essentially where its substance is.

In the past, certain people (called Manichees) declared that immaterial and imperishable things are subject to God's power while visible and perishable things are subject to some contrary power. As against this we must say that God is in everything by his power.

Yet other people believed everything to be subject to God's power while excluding things here below from his providence. The book of Job represents these people as saying, 'he walks around the poles of the heavens and does not take note of our doings'.[11] As against this we must say that God is in everything by his presence.

There were others again who said that God's providence oversees everything although God does not create everything without intermediate causes (that is, that he created only the first creatures, which then created others). As against this we must say that God is in everything by his essence.

So, God is in everything by his power (inasmuch as everything is subject to this), by his presence (inasmuch as everything is naked and open to his gaze), and by his essence (inasmuch as he exists in everything by causing its existence, as I have already said).[12]

---

[10] 1a 12; 43.3; 1a2ae 109.1; 109.3.　[11] Job 22:14.　[12] 1a 8.1.

Hence:

1. We say that God exists in all things by essence, not as being part of their essence but, as I have said, because his substance causes their existence.[13]

2. We can speak of something being present to people whenever it lies within their field of vision, even if it is far away from them in substance, as I have said. Hence the necessity of asserting the two ways in which God is in things: by essence and by presence.

3. It is of the nature of knowledge and will that what is known should exist in the knower and that what is willed should exist in the one willing. So, by his knowledge and will, things exist in God rather than God in things. But it is of the nature of power to initiate activity in something else. Hence, an efficient cause is brought into contact and relation with outside things by virtue of its power. This is why an efficient cause can be described as existing in something else by its power.

4. Grace is the only perfection added to the substance of things that makes God to be in them as a known and loved object. So, grace alone makes God exist in things in a unique way. But there is another unique way in which God is in something – by being one with a particular human being, as I shall explain in due course.[14]

Article 4: Does being everywhere belong to God alone?

1. It seems that being everywhere does not belong to God alone. For Aristotle says that universals exist everywhere and always.[15] And prime matter, being in all bodies, is also everywhere. Now, I have already made it clear that neither of these is God.[16] So, being everywhere does not belong to God alone.

2. Moreover, there is number in all numbered things. But the book of Wisdom declares the whole world to have been created as numbered.[17] So, it is some number that exists in the whole world – that is to say, everywhere.

---

[13] 1a 8.1.
[14] Aquinas is here referring to what he says about Christ later in the *Summa Theologiae* and in texts not included in the present volume.
[15] *Posterior Analytics* 1.31, 87b33.   [16] 1a 3.5 and 8.   [17] Wisdom 11:21.

3. Moreover, as Aristotle says, the whole world is a sort of whole and perfect body.[18] But the whole world is everywhere, for there is no place outside it. So, it is not only God that is everywhere.

4. Moreover, there would be no place outside an unlimited body, if such existed. So it would be everywhere. So, it seems that being everywhere need not belong to God alone.

5. Moreover, souls, as Augustine says, are 'wholly in the whole and wholly in every part of the whole'.[19] If, then, nothing existed in the world but one animal, its soul would be everywhere. So, being everywhere need not belong to God alone.

6. Again, as Augustine also says, 'wherever the soul sees it perceives, and it lives wherever it perceives, and it exists wherever it lives'.[20] But the soul, in a sense, sees everywhere, for bit by bit it sees the whole heavens. So, the soul is everywhere.

On the contrary, Ambrose asks 'who would dare to give the name "creature" to the Holy Spirit, who exists always, everywhere, and in everything; for this without doubt is something belonging only to God?'[21]

Reply: Being everywhere primarily and essentially belongs to God alone. By 'being everywhere primarily' I mean 'being everywhere as a whole'. For to exist everywhere, but with a different part in different places, is not to be everywhere primarily, for no property of a part belongs primarily to the whole: thus the whiteness of a man with white teeth belongs primarily to the teeth, not to the man. By 'being everywhere essentially' I mean not just happening to be everywhere in certain circumstances, as a grain of wheat would be everywhere if no other bodies existed. Something exists everywhere essentially when it is such that it would exist everywhere in any circumstances. But only God exists in this way. For no matter how many places one may think up, even infinitely more than now exist, he would necessarily exist in all of them, since nothing can exist unless he causes it to do so.

So, to be everywhere primarily and essentially belongs to God, and only to God, for, no matter how many places one may think up, he (and not just parts of him) will necessarily exist in them.

---

[18] *On the Heavens* 1.1, 268b8.   [19] *On the Trinity* 6.6. *PL* 42.929.   [20] Letter 137.2. *PL* 33.518.
[21] *On the Holy Spirit* 1.7. *PL* 16.723.

Hence:

1. Universals[22] and prime matter are indeed everywhere, but not with one and the same existence.

2. Number, being an accident, is not essentially in a place but only happens to be there. Nor is it complete in each numbered thing. Rather, it partly exists in each. We cannot therefore conclude that number is primarily and essentially everywhere.

3. The whole body of the world is everywhere piece by piece, not whole in every place, and therefore not everywhere at once. Nor is it essentially everywhere, for if there were other places it would not be in them.

4. An unlimited body, if it existed, would exist everywhere, but only piece by piece.

5. If only one animal existed, then its soul would indeed exist every-where primarily. But it would do so only accidentally.

6. We can understand the phrase 'wherever the soul sees' in two ways. First, we can take the adverb 'wherever' as determining the object of the seeing. In this sense it is true that, when the soul is seeing the heavens, it is seeing in the heavens and thus perceiving in the heavens. But it does not follow that it lives or exists in the heavens because these two verbs do not name actions going out to external objects. Second, we can take 'wherever' as determining the position of the one seeing. And in this sense it is true that the soul lives and exists where it sees and perceives. But then it does not follow that it exists everywhere.

---

[22] Attributes that can exist in many things at once.

Question 9
God's unchangeableness

As a next step I turn to God's unchangeableness and consequent eternity.

For this question about unchangeableness there are two points of inquiry:

1. Is God altogether unchangeable?
2. Is only God unchangeable?

Article 1: Is God altogether unchangeable?

1. It seems that God is not altogether unchangeable. For anything that moves itself is changeable in some way. As Augustine says, however, 'the creating spirit moves himself, though not in space and time'.[1] So, God is changeable in some way.

2. Moreover, the book of Wisdom describes wisdom as being 'more mobile than any moving thing'.[2] But God is wisdom itself. So, God is changeable.

3. Again, 'drawing near' and 'drawing away' are descriptions of movements. But Scripture applies them to God: 'draw close to God and he will draw close to you'.[3] So, God is changeable.

On the contrary, we read in Malachi, 'I am God, and I do not change.'[4]

Reply: What I have said so far proves God to be altogether unchangeable.

---

[1] *On the Literal Interpretation of 'Genesis'* 8.20. PL 34.388. [2] Wisdom 7:24. [3] James 4:8.
[4] Malachi 3:6.

87

First, because I have proved that there must be some first existent, whom we call God, absolutely actual and with no potentiality at all, since actuality, simply speaking, precedes potentiality.[5] But anything undergoing change, whatever the change, is somehow potential. So, it clearly follows that God cannot change in any way.

Second, anything undergoing change changes in some way but remains the same in another. Something changing from white to black, for example, stays the same with respect to substance. Things that change are, therefore, always composite. But God, as I have shown, is entirely simple and in no way composite.[6] So, he clearly cannot change.

Third, because anything that changes acquires something through its change by attaining something previously not attained. But God, being limitless, and embracing within himself the whole fullness of perfection of all existence, cannot acquire anything. Nor can he move out towards something previously not attained. So, change does not belong to him at all.

And this is why some ancient thinkers, compelled by truth itself, so to speak, held that the first source of things is unchangeable.

Hence:

1. Augustine is here using a Platonic way of speaking, according to which the first source of movement is said to move itself (meaning by 'movement' any operation at all, even understanding, willing and loving). So, since God understands and loves himself, the Platonists said that God moves himself, but they were not referring, as I now am, to the movement and change of something potential.

2. To call wisdom mobile is a metaphorical way of saying that wisdom spreads its own likeness throughout the length and breadth of things. For nothing can exist unless it is a sort of reflection that derives from God's wisdom as from its primary operative and formal cause (just as works of handicraft derive from craftsmanship). Inasmuch, then, as this likeness to divine wisdom is transmitted step by step from the highest things (which share the likeness most) to the lowest (which share it least), we talk of God's wisdom sallying forth, as it were, and moving into things. It is as though we talked of the sun sallying forth on earth when its light rays touch earth. This is the explanation that

---

[5] 1a 2.3; 3.1.   [6] 1a 3.7.

Dionysius gives when he says that 'every going forth of the divine majesty comes to us set in motion by the Father of lights'.[7]

3. Scripture is here talking of God in metaphors. For just as we say that the sun enters or departs from a house by touching the house with its rays, so we say that God draws near to us when we receive an influx of his goodness, or draws away from us when we fail him.

Article 2: Is only God unchangeable?

1. It seems that not only God is unchangeable. For Aristotle says that anything changing contains matter.[8] But there are people who believe that certain created substances (e.g. souls and angels) exist without matter. So, not only God is unchangeable.

2. Moreover, all change has a goal in view. So, things that have already achieved their ultimate goal will not change. But some creatures (e.g. the blessed in heaven) have already achieved their ultimate goal. So, some creatures are unchangeable.

3. Again, changeable things can vary. But forms are invariable. As the *Book of the Six Principles* says, 'form is that which subsists with simple and invariable being'.[9] So, to be unchangeable is not exclusively true of God.

On the contrary, Augustine says, 'God alone is unchangeable; while the things that God made are made from nothing and are therefore changeable.'[10]

Reply: Only God is altogether unchangeable. Creatures can all change in some way or other.

For one must realize that there are two possible grounds for calling something changeable: its own power, and that of something else. Before creatures existed, their existence was possible not because of any created power, since nothing created exists eternally, but simply because God had the power to bring them into existence. Now, bringing things into existence depends on God's will, and the same goes for preserving them in existence. For God preserves them in existence only by perpetually giving existence to them, and were he to withdraw his activity from them,

---

[7] *The Celestial Hierarchy* 1.1. *PG* 3.120. [8] *Metaphysics* 2.2, 994b25.
[9] *Book of Six Principles* 1. *PL* 188.1257. The reputed work of Gilbert de La Porrée (d. 1154).
[10] *On the Nature of the Good* 1. *PL* 42.551.

all things would fall back into nothingness, as Augustine makes clear.[11] So, just as before things existed on their own it was in the creator's power for them to exist, now that they exist on their own it is in the creator's power for them not to exist. So, they are changeable because of power present in another – God, who was able to bring them into existence out of nothing and is able to reduce them again from existence to nothingness.

Even if we think about changeableness in things as due to their own power, it remains that every creature is still changeable in some way. For we must distinguish in creatures both active and passive power. I call 'passive power' the capacity of a thing to be perfected, either in being or by attaining the goal of its action. So, if we consider the changeableness consequent upon a thing's power with respect to being, not everything is changeable, but only those things in which possibilities can exist without being realized. Thus bodies here on earth can change substantially in being (for the matter in them can exist without assuming the form of those particular substances). They can also change in such accidental modes of being as the subject can do without (as people can change from being white to being some other colour because they, as subjects, can do without whiteness). If, however, the accidental mode of being derives from what a subject is essentially, the subject cannot do without it, and cannot therefore change with respect to it. Thus, for example, snow cannot become black. In heavenly bodies, on the other hand, the potentiality of the matter is wholly realized by the form so that the matter cannot exist without that form; and such bodies cannot, therefore, change substantially in being, although they can change place, for a subject can exist without being in this or that particular place. Again, substances that are not bodies but forms subsisting in themselves cannot do without existence, even though they are related to that existence as potentialities to some actualization; for existence follows immediately upon form, and something can perish only by losing its form. In a pure form, then, there is no potentiality of non-existence. So, such substances are unable to change or vary in being. And this is what Dionysius means when he says that 'created intellectual substances are free from generation and from all variation, being neither bodies nor material'.[12] Such substances can, however, change in two ways. First, because of their potentiality with respect to some goal, they can (as Damascene says) change their minds

---

[11] *On the Literal Interpretation of 'Genesis'* 4.12. *PL* 34.305. [12] *The Divine Names* 4.1. *PG* 3.693.

and choose evil rather than good.[13] Second, they can change place, because, their power being limited, they can bring it to bear on places not previously touched by it. This cannot be said of God, who in his limitlessness, fills all places, as I have said.[14]

In all creatures, then, there exists potentiality for change, either substantially (as with perishable bodies), or in place (as with the heavenly bodies), or in being ordered to a goal and by the application of power to different things (as with angels). There is also a changeableness common to the whole universe of creatures, for whether they exist or not is subject to the creator's power. So, because God cannot change in any of these ways, only he is completely unchangeable.

Hence:

1. This argument holds for changeableness in being (either substantial or accidental), for that is the kind of change with which philosophers dealt.
2. In addition to the immutability that belongs to them by nature, good angels are endowed by God's power with unchangeable choice. But they can still change as regards place.
3. We speak of forms as invariable because they themselves cannot be subjects of variation. But they still take part in variation inasmuch as a subject may have now this and now that form. Clearly, then, they vary in exactly the same way as they exist. For we say that they are beings, not because they are subjects that exist, but because things have existence through them.

---

[13] *On the Orthodox Faith* 2.3. PG 94.868.   [14] 1a 8.2.

Question 10
God's eternity

I turn now to the topic of eternity.

For this question there are six points of inquiry:

1. What is eternity?
2. Is God eternal?
3. Does eternity belong only to God?
4. Is eternity different from time?
5. Is aeviternity different from time?
6. Is there only one aeviternity, as there is only one time and one eternity?

Article 1: What is eternity?

1. It seems that Boethius's definition of eternity is unsuitable. He says that 'eternity is the complete and instantaneously whole perfect possession of interminable life'.[1] But 'interminable' is a negative term (such as belongs only in the definition of something defective). But eternity is not defective. So 'interminable' should not occur in a definition of eternity.

2. Moreover, 'eternity' means a sort of duration. But duration is connected with existence rather than with life. So we should use 'existence' rather than 'life' when defining eternity.

3. Moreover, we use 'whole' when referring to something with parts. But eternity is simple and, therefore, has no parts. So we should not describe it as 'whole'.

[1] *The Consolation of Philosophy* 5, prosa 6. *PL* 63.858.

4. Moreover, several days or several times cannot occur instantaneously. But in speaking of eternity we use 'day' and 'time' in the plural. For example, the prophet Micah says 'his going forth is from the beginning, from the *days* of eternity'.[2] And in Romans we read, 'according to the revelation of the mystery kept secret through eternal *times*'.[3] So eternity is not instantaneously whole.

5. Again, 'whole' means the same as 'complete'. So, given that eternity is whole, it is redundant to add that it is complete.

6. Again, possession is unconnected with duration. But eternity is a sort of duration. So it is not 'possession'.

Reply: Just as we can only come to know simple things by way of composite ones, we can only come to know eternity by way of time, which is merely the 'numbering of before and after in change'. For in any change there is successiveness, one part coming after another. And we arrive at the notion of time by numbering the antecedent and consequent parts of change – time simply being this numberedness of before and after in change. But something lacking change and never varying its mode of existence will not display a before and after. So, just as numbering the antecedent and the consequent in change produces the notion of time, awareness of invariability in something altogether free from change produces the notion of eternity. Again, as Aristotle points out, we say that time measures things that begin and end in time,[4] and this is because we can assign a beginning and an end to any changing thing. But things that are altogether unchangeable cannot have a beginning any more than they can display successiveness.

So, two things characterize eternity. First, anything existing in eternity is *unending* – that is, it lacks both beginning and end (for both may be regarded as limits). Second, eternity itself exists as an *instantaneous whole* lacking successiveness.

Hence:

1. We often use negations to define simple things (as when we say that a point has no parts). This is not because negation is part of their essence, but because our mind first of all grasps composite things and cannot come to know simple things except by denying composition to them.

---

[2] Micah 5:2.   [3] Romans 16:25.   [4] *Physics* 4.12. 221b28.

2. Something truly eternal is not only existent but living. Yet 'to live' signifies a kind of activity, while 'to be' does not. And a flow of duration is more apparent in activity than in existence. Time, for example, is a numbering of change.

3. We speak of eternity as a 'whole', not because it has parts, but because nothing is lacking to it.

4. Just as Scripture describes God metaphorically in bodily terms (although he is not a body), so it describes eternity in temporal and successive terms (even though eternity exists instantaneously).

5. We need to note two things about time: that time itself is successive, and that an instant of time is incomplete. Boethius uses 'instantaneously whole' to deny that eternity is time, and he uses 'complete' to exclude the 'now' of time.

6. To possess something is to hold it firmly and restfully. So we use the word 'possession' to signify the unchangeableness and constancy of eternity.

Article 2: Is God eternal?

1. It seems that God is not eternal. For we cannot say that God is something produced. But eternity is produced. Boethius says that 'the flowing instant produces time and the abiding instant eternity'.[5] Augustine says that 'God is the source of eternity.'[6] So, God is not eternal.

2. Moreover, eternity cannot measure what exists before and after eternity. But according to the *Book of Causes*, God exists before eternity.[7] And according to Exodus, where we read that 'the Lord will reign to eternity and beyond',[8] he also exists after eternity. So, eternity does not belong to God.

3. Moreover, eternity is a sort of measure. But we cannot measure God. So, we cannot ascribe eternity to him.

4. Again, present, past and future do not exist in eternity, which, as I have said, is instantaneously whole.[9] But Scripture uses verbs in the present, past and future tenses when it talks of God. So, God is not eternal.

[5] *On the Trinity* 4. PL 64.1253. [6] *On Eighty-Three Varied questions* 1.23. PL 40.16.
[7] *Book of Causes* 2. [8] Exodus 15:18. [9] 1a 10.1.

On the contrary, the *Athanasian Creed* proclaims, 'Eternal the Father, eternal the Son, eternal the Holy Spirit.'[10]

Reply: I have already shown that the nature of eternity follows from unchangeableness as the nature of time follows from change.[11] So, eternity belongs principally to God, who is utterly unchangeable. Not only that, but God is his own eternity, whereas other things, not being their own existence, are not their own duration. God, however, is his own uniform existence. So, God is his own eternity just as he is his own essence.

Hence:

1. We speak of the abiding instant as producing eternity according to our way of conceiving the situation. For just as we become aware of time by becoming aware of the flowing 'now', we grasp the idea of eternity by grasping the idea of an abiding 'now'. We should take Augustine's statement that 'God is the source of eternity' to refer to eternity as shared. For, just as God shares his unchangeableness with other things, he also shares his eternity.

2. And this gives us the key to the second difficulty. For God exists before the eternity shared by immaterial substances. Hence it is that in the same passage we read that 'intelligence is coextensive with eternity'. As to the statement in Exodus that 'the Lord will reign to eternity and beyond', we should realize that 'eternity' here is a synonym for 'ages' (the word used in another translation). So, we say that God reigns beyond eternity because he outlasts all ages – outlasts, that is to say, any given period of duration, for, as Aristotle says, an age is nothing more than the period of something's duration.[12] Or we can also say that God reigns beyond eternity because, even if something else were to exist for ever (as certain philosophers believed the rotation of the heavens to do), the Lord would still reign beyond it since his reign is instantaneously whole.

3. Eternity and God are the same thing. So, calling God eternal does not imply his being measured by something extrinsic. The notion of measurement arises only in our way of conceiving the situation.

---

[10] Early Christian creed named after St Athanasius (296–373) but composed by an unknown author sometime between 380 and 430.
[11] 1a 10.1.   [12] *On the Heavens* 1.9, 279a23.

4. We use tensed verbs when we speak of God not so as to imply that he lives through a present, past and future, but because his eternity comprehends all phases of time.

Article 3: Does eternity belong only to God?

1. It seems that eternity does not belong only to God. For Daniel prophesies that 'those who instruct many in righteousness shall be as stars in perpetual eternities'.[13] But if only God were eternal there could be only one eternity. So, not only God is eternal.
2. Moreover, we read in Matthew, 'Depart, you cursed, into eternal fire.'[14] So, not only God is eternal.
3. Again, what is necessarily so is eternally so. But there are many necessary things: the first principles of demonstration, for example, and all propositions employed in demonstrations. So, not only God is eternal.

On the contrary, Jerome tells Marcella that 'God alone has no beginning.'[15] But whatever has a beginning is not eternal. So, only God is eternal.

Reply: Eternity, in the true and proper sense, belongs only to God, for eternity follows upon unchangeableness, as I have made clear.[16] And, as I have also shown, God alone is altogether unchangeable.[17] Certain things, however, receive a share in his unchangeableness from God, and to that extent they share in his eternity.

The unchangeableness that some things obtain from God amounts to them never ceasing to exist. So the earth, as we read in Ecclesiastes, 'abides eternally'.[18] Other things, although perishable, are called in the Scriptures 'eternal' because they endure for a long time – so the psalm sings of 'eternal mountains'[19] and Deuteronomy refers to 'the fruits of the eternal hills'.[20]

Yet others share eternity still more fully, by possessing unchangeableness of existence and even of activity. Such are the angels and saints enjoying sight of the divine Word. For, as Augustine says, 'changing thoughts' have no part in the saints' vision of the Word.[21] And this is why

[13] Daniel 12:3. [14] Matthew 25:41. [15] Letter 15. *PL* 22.357. [16] 1a 10.1. [17] 1a 9.2.
[18] Ecclesiastes 1:4. [19] Psalms 75:5. [20] Deuteronomy 33:15.
[21] *On the Trinity* 15.16. *PL* 42.1079.

we say that those who see God have eternal life, as in John: 'this is eternal life to know you, etc.'²²

Hence:

1. We speak of there being many eternities because many things share God's eternity by contemplating him.
2. We call the fire of hell eternal only because it is unending. But the pains of hell include change, for we read in Job that 'they shall pass from waters of snow to excessive heat'.²³ In hell, then, there is no true eternity, but rather time; as the psalm says 'their time shall last for ever'.²⁴
3. Necessity is a mode of truth. Now, truth, according to Aristotle, resides in the mind.²⁵ So, necessary truths are eternal only if they exist in the eternal mind, which is nothing other than God's mind. So, it does not follow that anything other than God is eternal.

Article 4: Is eternity different from time?

1. It seems that eternity is no different from time. For two measures of duration can only be simultaneous if one is part of the other; thus two days or hours cannot occur simultaneously, but an hour and a day can, for an hour is part of a day. But eternity and time both signify some sort of measure of duration and thus both exist together. So, since eternity is not part of time but exceeds and includes it, it seems that time is part of eternity, not something different from it.
2. Moreover, according to Aristotle, the 'now' persists unchanged throughout time.²⁶ But the nature of eternity seems to consist precisely in remaining indivisibly the same throughout the whole course of time. So, eternity is identical with the 'now' of time, and since the 'now' of time is not substantially different from time itself, neither is eternity.
3. Again, since the measure of the most fundamental change measures all change (as Aristotle says),²⁷ it seems that the measure of the most fundamental existence should measure all existence. But eternity measures divine existence (the most fundamental existence). So, it

---

²² John 17:3.   ²³ Job 24:19.   ²⁴ Psalms 80:16.   ²⁵ *Metaphysics* 6.4, 1027b27.
²⁶ *Physics* 4.11, 219b11; 13, 222a15.   ²⁷ *Physics* 4.14, 223b18.

measures all existence. Yet the existence of perishable things is measured by time. So, time is either eternity or part of eternity.

On the contrary, eternity is an instantaneous whole, while in time there is before and after. So, time and eternity differ.

Reply: Time and eternity clearly differ. Some people construe the difference as residing in the fact that time has a beginning and an end while eternity has neither. But this difference is accidental, not essential. For even if time has always existed and will always exist (as those hold who think the heavens will rotate for ever), there will still remain the difference that Boethius points out between time and eternity: that eternity is an instantaneous whole while time is not;[28] eternity measures permanent existence and time measures change.

If, however, the suggested difference applies to the things measured rather than to the measures themselves, there is some ground for it. For, as Aristotle says, time measures only things beginning and ending in time.[29] So, even if the heavens rotated for ever, time would measure not the whole duration of the movement, since the infinite is immeasurable, but each revolution separately as it begins and ends in time.

Or again, if we think in terms of potential beginnings and ends, the suggested difference could validly apply to the measures themselves. For even if time lasted for ever, it would be possible to mark off beginnings and ends in it by dividing it into parts. And so, in fact, we talk of the beginning and end of a day or year, which cannot occur in eternity.

These differences, however, are all consequent upon the primary and essential difference: that eternity exists as an instantaneous whole, whereas time does not.

Hence:

1. This would be a valid argument if time and eternity were measures of the same type, which they clearly are not if one considers the different things that they measure.

2. The 'now' remains unchanged as the point of perspective for a given subject over a certain period of time, but it is constantly different in what it refers to, because just as time corresponds to movement, so the 'now' corresponds to something whose referent is changeable. But something moving remains the same individual throughout the course

---

[28] *On the Consolation of Philosophy* 5, prosa 6. PL 63.859.   [29] *Physics* 4.12, 221b28.

of time, even though it differs in position, being first here and then there; its movement consists in a change of position. Similarly, time consists in the flow of the 'now' whose referent is being altered. But eternity remains unchanged both in substance and form. So, eternity differs from the 'now' of time.

3. Just as eternity is properly the measure of existing as such, so time is properly the measure of change. So, in so far as anything falls short of permanence in its existing and is subject to change, it will fall short of eternity and be subject to time. Since they are changeable, therefore, the existing of perishable things is measured by time and not by eternity. For time measures not only the actually changing but also the changeable. So, it measures not only movement but also rest, the state of the movable when not moving.

Article 5: Is aeviternity different from time?

1. 'Aeviternity'[30] seems to be just another name for time. For Augustine speaks of 'God moving immaterial creatures through time'.[31] But we define 'aeviternity' as 'the measure of immaterial substances'. So, time and aeviternity do not differ from each other.

2. As I have said, the nature of time is such that it involves a before and after, while eternity is instantaneously whole. But aeviternity is not eternity, for according to Ecclesiasticus the eternal 'wisdom precedes aeviternity'.[32] So, aeviternity is not instantaneously whole but possesses a before and an after, which makes it the same as time.

3. Moreover, were aeviternity to lack a before and an after, then, for things measured by aeviternity, existing in the present or past would be the same as existing in the future. Such things, consequently, since they cannot not have existed in the past, would not be able not to exist in the future. And this is false, for they can be annihilated by God.

4. Again, the duration of aeviternal things is infinite when it comes to the past. But if aeviternity is a simultaneous whole, it would follow that

---

[30] As time measures the careers of material things and eternity the life of God, aeviternity measures the lives of angels. Angels are in a sense midway between material things and God, like material things in being created, unlike them in being immaterial. So being aeviternal is supposed to be in some way midway between being eternal and being temporal.
[31] *On the Literal Interpretation of 'Genesis'* 8.20 and 22. *PL* 34.388–9. [32] Ecclesiasticus 1:1.

something created is actually infinite, which is impossible. So, aeviternity is no different from time.

On the contrary, Boethius writes of 'he who orders time to go from aeviternity'.[33]

Reply: Aeviternity is neither time nor eternity. It lies somewhere between the two.

Certain people express the difference by saying that eternity has neither beginning nor end, that aeviternity has a beginning but no end, and that time has both a beginning and an end. But this, as we have seen, is an accidental difference.[34] For even if aeviternal things have always existed and always will exist (as some hold), or even if God were to bring them to an end sometime (as he is able to do), aeviternity would still be distinguishable from both eternity and time.

Others express the difference between the three measures by saying that eternity does not have a before and after, that time has a before and after (together with newness and oldness), and that aeviternity has a before and after, but no newness or oldness. But this is self-contradictory. If it is newness and oldness of the measure itself that is meant, the contradiction is obvious. For the before and after of duration cannot be simultaneous. So, if aeviternity has a before and after, an after-part must become newly present as each fore-part moves away, and there will be newness in aeviternity just as there is in time. If the newness and oldness of the things measured is meant, an inconsistency still arises. For it is due to their changeable existence that temporal things age with time and, as Aristotle shows, the before and after of time derives from this changeableness in the thing measured.[35] So, if aeviternal things cannot be new or old, this will be because their existence is unchangeable. And in that case the measure itself will have no before and after.

We therefore say that as eternity is the measure of abiding existence, the further a thing falls short of abiding existence, the further it falls short of eternity. Now, some things fall far enough short of abiding existence to have an existence consisting in or subject to change, and time measures such things: all movements, for example, and, in the case of perishable things, even their existence. Other things do not fall so far short of

[33] *On the Consolation of Philosophy* 3, metra 9. PL 63.758.
[34] 1a 10.4.   [35] *Physics* 4.12, 221a31 and 220b9.

abiding existence that their existence consists in or is subject to change. But it is still accompanied by some actual or potential change. Take, for example, the heavenly bodies. While existing unchanged in substance, they undergo change of place. For another example, consider angels, who combine unchangeable existence with changeability of choice at the natural level, and with changeability of thoughts, affections and, in their own fashion, places. So, aeviternity measures these sorts of thing, and it therefore lies somewhere between eternity and time. Eternity itself measures any existing which is both unchangeable and unaccompanied by changeableness.

In short: time has a before and an after; aeviternity has no before nor after in itself but can be accompanied by it; eternity possesses neither a before nor an after, and is incompatible with them.

Hence:

1. Inasmuch as their thoughts and affections display successiveness, immaterial creatures are measured by time. So, Augustine says in the same passage that to be moved through time is to be moved in affections. But, as regards their natural way of existing, they are measured by aeviternity, and, inasmuch as they contemplate God's glory, they share in eternity.
2. Though aeviternity is instantaneously whole, it differs from eternity in being able to coexist with before and after.
3. There is no difference of past and future in an angel's existence as such, but only one consequent upon accompanying changes. But we distinguish between angels that exist, have existed, or will exist in the future, because we talk in the way we think, and we think of the existence of angels by relating it to different periods of time. Now, in talking of angels as existing or having existed, we incorporate a supposition such that the opposite of what we say is no longer within God's power. But in talking of them as existing in the future, we as yet make no such supposition. Absolutely speaking, that angels should or should not exist is within God's power. So, God can cause an angel not to exist in future, even if he cannot cause it not to exist while it exists, or not to have existed when it already has.
4. The duration of aeviternity is unlimited in the sense of not being limited by time. But it is possible for something created to be unlimited – if we think of it as not limited by some other creature.

Article 6: Is there only one aeviternity?

1. It would seem that more than one aeviternity exists. For we read in the apocryphal books of Ezra that 'the majesty and power of aeviternities is with you, Lord'.[36]

2. Moreover, different genera have different measures. Now, some things measured by aeviternity are bodies (like the heavenly bodies), and some (like angels) are immaterial substances. So, there is more than one aeviternity.

3. Moreover, if aeviternity is a kind of duration, everything having one aeviternity will have the same duration. But not all things measured by aeviternity have the same duration, for some come into existence later than others (the clearest case is that of human souls). So, there is not only one aeviternity.

4. Again, things which do not depend on each other do not seem to have the same measure of duration. Thus, one time measures everything temporal, it seems, because time measures first the most fundamental process in the world, and this process is in a way the cause of everything else. But aeviternal things do not depend on each other. So, there is more than one aeviternity.

On the contrary, aeviternity is simpler than time, and nearer to eternity. But only one time exists. Still more, then, is there only one aeviternity.

Reply: There are two opinions on this point – some people saying that there is only one aeviternity, some saying that there are many. And to decide which is nearer the truth we must ask ourselves why time is one, for we come to understand the immaterial through the material.

Some derive the unity of time in all temporal things from the unity of a number in numbered things – time being, as Aristotle says, 'a numbering'.[37] But this line of thinking is not good enough, for time is not a number abstracted from the things that it numbers. It is a number that exists in the thing that is numbered (otherwise it would lack continuity, just as the continuity of ten units of cloth derives not from the number but from the thing numbered). But the number in numbered things differs in different things and is not the same for all.

---

[36] 3 Ezra 4:40.   [37] *Physics* 4.12, 220b8.

So others derive the unity of time from the unity of eternity, the source of all duration. All duration, they say, is one at source, though multiplied according to the differing things that receive duration from this primary source. Others again derive the unity of time from the unity of prime matter, the fundamental subject of the changes that time measures. Neither derivation seems adequate, however.

For things that are one in source or in subject, especially when they are distant sources and subjects, are not one simply speaking, but only one in certain respects.

The true ground of time's unity is therefore the unity of the most fundamental motion in the world, by which (since it is the simplest) all other motions are measured, as Aristotle says.[38] Time is not only the measure of this motion, but also an accident of it, and so receives unity from it. But time is merely a measure of other motions, and so is not diversified by their diversity. For one measure, when independently existent, can measure many things.

Given this foundation, we must note two opinions concerning immaterial substances. Certain people have held with Origen that they all came from God as equal in the same way, or (as others have said) as equal in different ways. Other people have held that all immaterial substances came from God in a certain order and hierarchy, and this seems to be Dionysius's opinion. He says that, when it comes to immaterial substances, some are first, some are intermediate, and others are last, even within one order of angels.[39] So, holders of the first opinion must confess more than one aeviternity, corresponding to the many equally primary substances measured by aeviternity. Holders of the second opinion, however, must confess only one aeviternity, for Aristotle says that the simplest thing in a genus measures the other things,[40] so that the simpler existence of the primary aeviternal thing (simpler because more primary) will measure the existence of everything aeviternal, and because, as I shall later show, the second opinion is nearer to the truth,[41] I shall here admit only one aeviternity.

Hence:

1. 'Aeviternity' sometimes means 'age' (i.e. the period of a thing's duration); and in this sense we talk of many aeviternities, as of many ages.

---

[38] *Metaphysics* 10.1, 1053a8.   [39] *On the Celestial Hierarchy* 10.2. *PG* 3.273.
[40] *Metaphysics* 10.1, 1052b33.   [41] 1a 47.2; 50.4.

2. Although the heavenly bodies differ in nature from immaterial things, both kinds of thing agree in existing unchangeably. And they are, as such, both measured by aeviternity.

3. Not all temporal things come into existence together. But they are all measured by one and the same time as the primary temporal thing. In the same way, all aeviternal things are measured by the same aeviternity as the first, even if they do not come into existence together.

4. In order for one thing to measure others, it does not have to cause them all, but only to be simpler than them all.

Question 11

God's oneness

I must now follow what I have so far said with a treatment of God's oneness.

This question has four points of inquiry:

1. Does one add anything to being?
2. Is 'one' the opposite of 'many'?
3. Is there only one God?
4. Is God supremely one?

Article 1: Does one add anything to being?

1. It seems that one does add something to being. For everything that is in a determinate genus has something added to it by something that is common to all genera. But one is in a determinate genus since it is the source of number, which is a species of quantity. So, one adds something to being.
2. Moreover, whatever divides some common reality does so by being added to it. But we subdivide beings into one and many. So, one adds something to being.
3. Moreover, if one added nothing to being, the words 'one' and 'being' would be synonymous. But it is trifling to say that whatever exists exists. In that case, however, it would be trifling to say that whatever exists is one – and this is not so. So, one must add something to being.

On the contrary, Dionysius says that 'nothing exists without being somehow one'. But if being one added something to existing, it would narrow its application, and Dionysius would be wrong.[1] So, one adds nothing to being.

Reply: Oneness adds nothing real to any existent thing. It simply denies division of it. For to be one is just to be undivided, and from this it is clear that to be is to be one. For every being is either simple or composite. But simple things are neither actually nor potentially divided, while composite things do not exist as long as their constituent parts are divided (they exist only after these parts have come together to compose the thing). Clearly, then, everything's existence is grounded in indivision. And this is why things guard their unity as they do their existence. Hence:

1. Two opposing positions have been adopted by those who identify the one that is convertible with being and the one that initiates number. Pythagoras and Plato, seeing that the one that is convertible with being adds nothing to being but simply signifies the undivided substance of a being, thought this is also true of the one that initiates number. Since number is composed of unities, they believed number to be the substance of all things. Avicenna, on the other hand, seeing that the one initiating number adds something to substance (for otherwise number composed of unities would not be a species of quantity), believed that the one convertible with being adds something to the substance of a being, as whiteness adds something to a human being. But this is clearly false, for everything is one of its very substance. If it were one by something else, that something else, being itself one, would be one by something else again, and so on and so on. Better not to embark on such a course and to say, therefore, that the one convertible with being adds nothing to being, and that the one that initiates number adds something belonging to the genus of quantity.

2. There is nothing to stop things from being divided in one way and undivided in another (numerically divided, for example, yet undivided in kind), and they will then be in one way one, and in another way many. If something is (simply speaking) undivided, either because it is undivided essentially, though divided in what does not pertain to its essence (e.g. one substance having many accidents), or

[1] *The Divine Names* 13.2. PG 3.977–80.

because it is actually undivided, although potentially divided (e.g. a whole having many parts), then such a thing will be simply speaking one, and it will be many only in a certain respect. On the other hand, if things are, simply speaking, divided, though in a certain respect undivided (like things divided in substance, though undivided in species or in causal origin), then they will be, simply speaking, many, and one only in a certain respect (as things many in number can be of one species or origin). Now we subdivide being into one and being many (taking 'one' simply speaking, and 'many' in a certain respect). For we cannot say that the many, as such, exist except in so far as they have a certain unity. Thus, Dionysius says that no 'manifold exists without being somehow one: for many parts are one whole, many accidents one in subject, many things one in species, many species one in genus, and many processes one in origin'.[2]

3. It is not trifling to say that what exists is one. For unity adds to existence conceptually.

Article 2: Is one the opposite of many?

1. It seems that one is not the opposite of many. For we cannot predicate an opposite of its opposite. Yet the many are always in a certain respect one, as I have said.[3] So, one is not opposed to many.

2. Moreover, nothing is composed of its opposite. But the many is composed of unities. So, unity is not opposed to the many.

3. Moreover, one thing has only one opposite. But few is the opposite of many. So, one is not the opposite of many.

4. Again, if one and many are opposed, it must be as indivision and division are (i.e. as lack to possession). But this does not seem right, for unity would then be subsequent as an idea to the many, and defined in terms of it. In fact, though, we define the many in terms of unity, and we are not here offering a circular definition. So, one and many are not opposites.

On the contrary, things are opposed if their definitions are opposed. But indivision defines unity while division enters into the definition of the many. So, one and many are opposites.

---

[2] *The Divine Names* 13.2. *PG* 3.980. [3] 1a 11.1, *ad* 2.

Reply: One is the opposite of many, but in differing ways. The one that is the beginning of enumeration is different from the many, which can be numbered, as a measure differs from what it measures, for one is by definition the fundamental unit of measure, and number is the many actually measured in terms of these units, as Aristotle says.[4] The one that is convertible with being, however, differs from the many in the way that indivision is contrasted with division (i.e. by lacking division).

Hence:

1. A privation is not a denial of existence altogether, for Aristotle defines privation as non-existence of something in some subject.[5] It is a denial of existence in some respect. So, within a being, considered as a whole, it can happen that there is a privation of being that is grounded in the being itself. This is the case when there is a privation of some special attribute like sight, whiteness, or something similar. And what is true of being is true of the one and the good, for they are convertible with being. For the privation of the good is grounded in the presence of a good, and absence of unity is grounded in something that is. So, the many turn out to be somehow one, the bad thing turns out to be a sort of good, and the non-existent turns out to be a kind of existent. But we are not predicating an opposite of its opposite here. For we should understand one term simply speaking, and we should understand the other only relatively. For what is existent in a certain respect is non-existent simply speaking (as the potentially existent does not actually exist), and what is existent simply speaking does not exist in a certain respect (as a substance will lack certain accidents). Similarly, therefore, what is good in a certain respect is bad simply speaking, or vice versa. And what is one simply speaking is many in a certain respect, or vice versa.

2. A whole can be homogeneous, if composed of similar parts, or heterogeneous, if composed of dissimilar parts. In homogeneous wholes the component parts share the form of the whole – as every bit of water is water. And this is how a continuum is made up of its parts. But in heterogeneous wholes the parts lack the form of the whole. Thus, no part of a house is itself a house, and no part of a human being is a human being, and the many amounts to this second kind of whole. So,

---

[4] *Metaphysics* 10.1, 1052b18; 6, 1057a3.   [5] *Metaphysics* 4.2, 1004a15.

108

because no part of the many has the form of the many, the many is composed of unities, like a house from things not houses. But these unities compose the many inasmuch as they exist, not inasmuch as they are undivided and opposed to the many (as the parts of a house make up the house because they are bodies of a certain sort, not because they are not houses).

3. We can understand 'many' in two ways. Taken absolutely, it is opposed to oneness. But it can also be understood as signifying a certain excess. In this sense, 'many' is opposed to 'few'. In the first sense two are many, but not in the second.

4. The one is opposed to the many because it lacks the division possessed by the many. So, division must precede unity as an idea in our minds, though not without qualification. For we grasp simple things by way of composite ones, as when we define a point as something without parts, or as the beginning of a line. Even in our minds, however, the many is subsequent to the one, for we conceive divided things as many only by ascribing unity to each of them. So, oneness enters the definition of the many, but the many does not enter the definition of oneness. But division arises in the mind simply by negating existence. So, the first idea to arise in the mind is that of the existent, then that this existent is not that existent (and thus we apprehend division). Finally, we arrive at the notion of oneness and that of the many.

Article 3: Is there only one God?

1. It seems that God is not one. For St Paul says 'there are indeed many gods and many lords'.[6]

2. Moreover, we cannot predicate of God the unity with which number begins since we cannot predicate quantity of him. Nor can we predicate of God the oneness convertible with being, for this implies privation, and privation implies imperfection, which cannot belong to God. So, we should not say that there is only one God.

On the contrary, Deuteronomy proclaims: 'Hear, O Israel, the Lord our God is one God.'[7]

Reply: We can show that there is only one God in three ways.

---

[6] 1 Corinthians 8:5.   [7] Deuteronomy 6:4.

First, with reference to God's simplicity. For clearly no individual can share with others its very singularity. Socrates can share what makes him human with many others, but what makes him this human being can belong only to one human being. So, if Socrates were *this* human being just by being a human being, there could no more be many human beings than there could be many Socrates. But this is also true of God. For, as I have shown, God is his own nature.[8] So, to be God is to be this God. And it is therefore impossible for there to be many Gods.

Second, with reference to God's unlimited perfection. For God, as I have shown, embraces in himself the whole perfection of existing.[9] But many Gods, if they existed, would have to differ. Something belonging to one would not belong to the other. If this were a privation, one God would not be altogether perfect, while, if it were a perfection, the other God would lack it. So, there cannot be more than one God. This is why philosophers in ancient times, compelled by truth itself, so to speak, held that if the source of things is unlimited it cannot be many.

Third, with reference to the oneness of the world: for we find all existing things to be in mutual order, some of them subordinate to others. But different things combine in a single order only where there is a single cause of order. For unity and order is introduced into a plurality of things more perfectly by a single cause than by many, for unity produces unity intrinsically, while the many produce unity only incidentally and in so far as they are also somehow one. So, the primary source of unity and order in the universe, namely, God, must himself be one, for the primary is always essentially, not incidentally, most perfect.

Hence:

1. St Paul's phrase 'many gods' alludes to the mistaken beliefs of those who worshipped many gods – thinking the planets, other stars, and even particular parts of the world, to be divine. So, he continues, 'yet there is for us one God and Father, etc.'
2. We do not predicate of God the unity with which number begins. We predicate this only of material things. For the unity with which number begins belongs to the genus of mathematical entities, which exist in matter but are defined without reference to matter. The one that is convertible with being, on the other hand, is a sort of

---

[8] 1a 3.3.   [9] 1a 4.2.

metaphysical entity that does not depend on matter. Although there is no privation in God, because of our ways of understanding things, we can only know him if we conceive him as lacking or excluding certain attributes. So, there is nothing wrong with describing God as lacking things (being without a body, for example, or without limits). In the same way we call God one.

Article 4: Is God supremely one?

1. It seems that God is not supremely one. But we speak of unity as an absence of division. However, it is impossible for something to be more or less absent. So, we cannot say that God is more one than other things that are one.
2. Moreover, nothing seems more indivisible than things like points and units, which are indivisible both actually and potentially. But the degree of unity we ascribe to something depends on its degree of indivisibility. So, God is not more one than points and units.
3. Again, just as what is essentially good is supremely good, what is essentially one is supremely one. As Aristotle tells us, however, every being is essentially one.[10] So, everything is supremely one, and God is therefore no more one than anything else.

On the contrary, Bernard says that 'among all the things that we say are one, the unity of the divine Trinity takes pride of place'.[11]

Reply: Since to be one is to exist undivided, anything supremely one must be both supremely existing and supremely undivided. But God is both of these things. He exists supremely since he has not acquired an existence which his nature has then determined. God is subsistent existence itself and is not determined in any way. He is also supremely undivided since, as I have shown, he is altogether simple, not divided in any way, either actually or potentially.[12] So, God is clearly supremely one. Hence:

1. Although there cannot be more or less privation as such, we can speak of something as having more or less of a lack inasmuch as it has more

---

[10] *Metaphysics* 4.2, 1003b32.
[11] St Bernard of Clairvaux (1090–1135), *On Consideration* 5.8. *PL* 182.799.   [12] 1a 3.7.

or less of a given attribute. So, we can call something really one more or less, inasmuch as it is divided (or divisible) less or more or not at all.

2. The point and numerical unity are not really beings, since they only exist as accidents in a subject. So, neither of them is really one. For just as no subject is really one because subject and accident are distinct, so neither is an accident.

3. Though everything that exists is one in substance, not every substance has the same relation to unity. For certain substances have many component parts, and some do not.

Question 12

How God's creatures know him

Having considered what God is in himself, I turn now to consider what our minds can make of him – how his creatures know him. Here there are thirteen points of inquiry:

1. Can a created mind see God's essence?
2. Does a mind see God's essence by means of any created species?
3. Can God's essence be seen with bodily eyes?
4. Can a created mind see God's essence by its own natural powers?
5. Does a created mind need a created light in order to see God's essence?
6. Is God's essence seen more perfectly by one than by another?
7. Can a created mind comprehend God's essence?
8. Does a created mind see all things in seeing God's essence?
9. Is it by means of any likeness that it knows what it sees there?
10. Does it see all that it sees in God at one and the same time?
11. Can anyone in this life see God's essence?
12. Can we know God through our natural reason in this life?
13. Besides the knowledge we have of God by natural reason, is there in this life a knowledge that we have through grace?

Article 1: Can a created mind see God's essence?

1. It seems that no created mind can see God's essence. For commenting on St John's words, 'No one has ever seen God', Chrysostom says: 'It is not only the prophets who have never seen what God is; neither the angels nor the archangels have seen him either, for how could created

nature see the uncreated?'[1] And Dionysius says: 'Sense cannot reach him, nor imagination, nor opinion, nor reasoning, nor knowledge.'[2]

2. Moreover, the unlimited is, as such, unknowable. But I have already shown that God is unlimited.[3] So, he must in himself be unknown.

3. Moreover, a created mind only knows what is there to be known, for the first thing the mind grasps of anything is that it is something or other. But God is not there. As Dionysius says, he is beyond what is there.[4] So, he is not intelligible. Rather, he is beyond understanding.

4. Again, since in knowledge the thing known is some sort of perfection of the knower, it cannot be altogether out of proportion to the knower. But there is no proportion whatever between a created mind and God. They are infinitely distant from each other. So, such a mind cannot see God's essence.

On the contrary, we read in 1 John, 'We shall see him just as he is.'[5]

Reply: Something is knowable in so far as it is actual. But God is wholly actual. And so, in himself, God is supremely knowable. Yet what is in itself supremely knowable may so far exceed the power of a particular mind as to be beyond its understanding – rather as the sun is invisible to bats because it is too bright for them. With this in mind some have said that no created mind can see God's essence.

This view, however, is wrong. For our ultimate happiness consists in our highest activity, which is the exercise of our mind, and if a created mind were never able to see God's essence, either it would never attain happiness, or its happiness would consist in something other than God. This is contrary to faith, for the ultimate perfection of the rational creature lies in the source of its being. For everything achieves its perfection by rising as high as its source.

The view just mentioned is also philosophically untenable. For it belongs to human nature to look for the causes of things. That is how intellectual problems arise. But this natural tendency could not be fulfilled if the mind of a rational creature were incapable of arriving at the first cause of things. So, we must grant without reservation that the blessed see God's essence.

---

[1] *Homilies on John* 15. PG 59.98.   [2] *The Divine Names* 1. PG 3.593.   [3] 1a 7.1.
[4] *The Divine Names* 4. PG 3.697.   [5] 1 John 3:2.

Hence:

1. Both of these authorities are speaking not simply of seeing God's essence but of comprehending it. Thus Dionysius introduces the words quoted by saying, 'All find it completely impossible to comprehend him, for sense cannot attain to him, etc.'[6] And Chrysostom, soon after the passage quoted says, 'By vision is meant contemplation of the Father and perfect comprehension of him such as the Father has of the Son.'[7]

2. The unlimited in the sense of matter not perfected by form, is, as such, unknowable because it is through form that anything is known. But the unlimited in the sense of a form not confined by matter, is, in itself, supremely knowable. It is in this latter sense that God is unlimited or infinite, not in the first sense, as is clear from what I have already said.[8]

3. We do not say that God is 'not there' so as to mean that he does not exist at all. We mean that, being his own existence, God transcends all that is there. It follows from this not that he cannot be known but that he is beyond all that can be known of him (this is what is meant by saying that he cannot be comprehended).

4. When we say one thing is in proportion to another we can either mean that they are quantitatively related (in this sense double, triple and equal are kinds of proportion), or else we can be thinking only of any kind of relation that one thing may have to another. It is in this latter sense that we speak of a proportion between creatures and God, in that they are related to him as effects to cause and as the partially realized to the absolutely real. In this sense it is not altogether disproportionate to the created mind to know God.

Article 2: Does a mind see God's essence by means of any created species?

1. It seems that a created mind sees God's essence by means of a likeness. For we read in 1 John, 'We know that when he appears we shall be like him, and we shall know him just as he is.'[9]

---

[6] *The Divine Names* 4. PG 3.697. [7] *Homilies on John* 15. PG 59.99. [8] 1a 7.1. [9] 1 John 3:2.

2. Moreover, Augustine says, 'A likeness of God comes to be in us when we know him.'[10]

3. Again, actual thought is the realized intelligibility of what is known, just as actual sensation is the realized sensibleness of what is known. But this occurs only when sense is formed by a likeness of something sensible, or the mind by a likeness of something intelligible. So, if God is actually seen by the created mind, he must be seen through some likeness.

On the contrary, Augustine says that St Paul's words, 'we see now in a mirror and obscurely', refer 'to any likeness that may help us to understand God'.[11] But to see God in his essence is not to see him 'obscurely in a mirror'. On the contrary. So, God's essence is not seen through any likeness.

Reply: In order to see, whether with the senses or the mind, two things are needed: there must be a power of sight, and the thing to be seen must come into sight. For we do not see unless the thing seen is somehow in us.

Now, corporeal things are obviously not in those who see them by essence but only by image. We see a stone, for example, not because the stone itself is in our eyes but because its image is. But if one and the same thing were both the thing seen and the source of the power of sight, then the one who sees would receive from that thing both the power of sight and the form by which it sees.

Now it is clear that God is the author of the power of understanding and can also be an object of understanding. The power of understanding in a creature (since it is not itself God's essence) must, therefore, be a sharing by likeness in the one who is the primordial intelligence. We therefore call it a sort of intelligible light derived from the primordial light, and we say this both of the natural power of understanding or of any additional power that comes from grace or glory. In order to be capable of seeing God at all, therefore, the power of sight needs to receive a certain likeness of him.

When, however, we consider God's essence as an object of sight, it is impossible that it should be united with the power of sight by any created image.

---

[10] *On the Trinity* 9.11. PL 42.969. [11] *On the Trinity* 15.9. PL 42.1069.

First, because (as Dionysius says)[12] things of a higher order cannot be known through likenesses of an inferior order. We cannot even know the essences of incorporeal things through bodily likenesses; much less could we see God's essence through any kind of created likeness.

Second, because, as I have said, God's essence is to exist,[13] and since this could not be the case with any created form, no such form could represent God's essence to the understanding.

Third, God's essence is unfathomable, containing to a transcendent degree whatever can be signified or understood by the created mind. This could not be represented by any created likeness since every created form is determinately this rather than that, whether it be wisdom, power, existence itself or anything else. So, to say that God is seen by means of a likeness is to say that his essence is not seen, which is false.

Accordingly we should say that for seeing God's essence some likeness is required on the part of the power of sight, namely the light of divine glory strengthening the mind, of which the psalm speaks, 'In your light we shall see light.'[14] It is not that God's essence can be seen by means of any created likeness representing him as he is.

Hence:

1. This authoritative text is speaking of the likeness which comes through sharing in the light of glory.
2. Augustine is here speaking of the knowledge we can have of God in the present life.
3. God's essence is existence itself. So, as other intelligible forms, which are not identical with their existence, are united to the mind by means of a sort of mental existence by which they inform and actualize the mind, the divine essence is united to a created mind so as to be what is actually understood, and through its very self it causes the mind actually to understand.

Article 3: Can God's essence be seen with bodily eyes?

1. It seems that God's essence can be seen with bodily eyes. For Job says, 'In my flesh I shall see God', and, 'I have heard you with the hearing of the ear, but now my eye sees you.'[15]

---

[12] *The Divine Names* 4. PG 3.588.   [13] 1a 3.4.   [14] Psalms 35:10.   [15] Job 19:26; 42:5.

2. Moreover, Augustine says, 'The eyes [of the blessed] will have a greater power of sight, not in the sense that they will become more piercing than those of eagles or serpents – for however acutely these beasts see, they see nothing but material things – but in the sense that they will see incorporeal things.'[16] Whatever can see incorporeal things can, however, be raised up to see God. So, the eyes of a glorified body can see God.

3. Again, someone can see God in the imagination, for we read in Isaiah, 'I saw the Lord seated on his throne.'[17] But what we imagine has its origin in the senses, for the imagination, according to Aristotle, is 'a change brought about by the activity of the senses'.[18] So, God can be seen by bodily vision.

On the contrary, Augustine says, 'Nobody has ever seen God as he is, whether in this present life or in the angelic life, in the way that our bodily eyes see visible things.'[19]

Reply: It is impossible to see God by the power of sight or by any other sense or sensitive power. As I shall later show, any power of this kind is the proper activity of some corporeal organ,[20] and such activity must belong to the same order as that of which it is the activity. So, no such power could extend beyond corporeal things. But God is not corporeal, as I have shown.[21] So, he cannot be seen by sense or imagination but only by the mind.

Hence:

1. 'In my flesh I shall see God' does not mean that I shall see God by means of the bodily eye, but that I shall see him when I am in the flesh, that is, after the resurrection. 'Now my eye sees you' refers to the eye of the mind, as when St Paul says, 'May he grant you a spirit of wisdom in knowing him; may he enlighten the eyes of your mind.'[22]

2. Augustine is here merely making a suggestion, not committing himself to a definite position. This is clear from what he says immediately afterwards: 'They (the eyes of the glorified body) would have to have an altogether different power if they were to see incorporeal things.' Later he finds his own solution saying, 'It is

---

[16] *The City of God* 22.29. *PL* 41.799.   [17] Isaiah 6:1.   [18] *On the Soul* 3.3, 429a1.
[19] Letter 147.11. *PL* 33.609.   [20] 1a 12.4; 78.1.   [21] 1a 3.1.   [22] Ephesians 1:17.

extremely likely that we shall then see the bodies that make up the new heaven and the new earth in such a way as to see God present everywhere in them, governing everything, even material things. We shall not merely see him as we now do when "the invisible things of God are made known to us by the things he has made" but rather as we now see the life of the living breathing people we meet. The fact that they are alive is not something we come to believe in but something we see.'[23] So, it is evident that our glorified eyes will see God as they now see the life of another. For we do not see life by bodily eyesight, as though it were visible in itself as a proper object of sight. It is not itself perceived by sense, but known by another cognitive power in conjunction directly with sensation. That God's presence is known immediately by the mind once it sees those bodies results from two causes: from the mind's own penetrating clearness, and from the reflection of divine brightness in our renewed bodies.

3. God's essence is not seen in the imagination. What appears there is an image representing God according to some likeness, as the divine Scriptures describe God metaphorically by means of material things.

Article 4: Can a created mind see God's essence by its own natural powers?

1. It seems that a created mind might see God's essence by its own natural powers. For Dionysius says that an angel is 'a pure and most clear mirror, reflecting, if one may dare to say it, the whole beauty of God'.[24] But to see something in a mirror is really to see it. So, since an angel understands itself by means of its own natural powers, it would seem that it must also understand the divine essence by these powers.

2. Moreover, what is supremely visible becomes less visible to us only through some defect in our vision, whether physical or intellectual. But an angel's mind does not suffer from any defect. Therefore, since God is supremely intelligible in himself, he must be supremely intelligible to an angel. For if an angel can understand less intelligible things by its own powers, much more will it be able to understand God.

3. Again, the reason why bodily senses cannot be raised up to understand incorporeal being is that it is beyond their natural scope. So, if

[23] *The City of God* 22.29. *PL* 41.800.   [24] *The Divine Names* 4. *PG* 3.724.

seeing God's essence were beyond the natural scope of a created mind, it would seem that no such mind could attain to it. But, as is clear from what I said above,[25] this is not so. So, it seems that it must be natural to a created mind to see God.

On the contrary, we read in Romans, 'The grace of God is eternal life.'[26] But eternal life, as we know from John, consists in seeing God's essence: 'This is eternal life, their knowing you, the only true God.'[27] So, to know God's essence belongs to a created mind by grace and not by nature.

Reply: It is impossible for a created mind to see God's essence by its own natural powers. Something is known by being present in the knower. But how it is present is determined by the knower's way of being. So, the way something knows depends on the way it exists, and if the way of being of the thing to be known is beyond that of a knower, knowledge of that thing is beyond the knower's natural power.

Now, there are different ways in which things have ways of being. Some have natures that cannot exist except as instantiated in individual matter. All bodies are of this kind. There are other things whose natures subsist independently and not by being in matter. These have existence simply by being the natures that they are. Yet existence is still something they have; it is not what they are. The incorporeal beings we call angels are of this kind. Finally, there is the way of being that belongs only to God, for his existence is what he is.

Knowledge of things that exist in the first way is connatural to us, for the human soul, through which we know, is itself the form of some matter. There are two ways in which we know such things: by sensing them, and by understanding them. Sensing consists in the proper activity of certain bodily organs, and it is connatural to this power to know things precisely in so far as they are in individual matter; thus by sense we know only individual things. The power of understanding does not consist in the activity of corporeal organs; so, although the natures that it connaturally knows cannot exist except in individual matter, it knows them not merely as they are in such matter, but as made abstract by the operation of the mind. Thus by understanding we can know things universally, which is beyond the scope of the senses.

---

[25] 1a 12.1.   [26] Romans 6:23.   [27] John 17:3.

Knowledge of things that exist in the second way is connatural to an angel's mind, which can know natures that are not in matter. But this is beyond the natural scope of human understanding in this life while the soul is united to the body.

Finally, only to the divine intellect is it connatural to know subsistent existence itself. This is beyond the scope of any created understanding, for no creature is its existence. It only has a share in existence. So, no created mind can see God's essence unless he, by his grace, joins himself to that mind as something intelligible to it.

Hence:

1. It is indeed connatural to an angel to know God by his likeness shining forth in the angel itself. But, as I have shown, to know God by any kind of created likeness is not to know his essence.[28] So, it does not follow that an angel knows God's essence by its natural powers.

2. An angel's mind has no defect, if by 'defect' we mean a privation, a lack of what should be present. But if we take 'defect' to mean simply the absence of some perfection, then all creatures are defective by comparison with God. For none of them has all the excellence found in God.

3. Since eyesight is completely corporeal it cannot be raised to what is immaterial. But the human or angelic mind by its nature already transcends the material to some extent. So, it can be raised by grace beyond its nature to something higher than the material. An indication of this is that bodily sight is confined to knowing a nature as it is in a particular concrete thing. It cannot in any way come to know it in abstraction. The mind, on the other hand, can consider in abstraction what it knows in the concrete. For though we know things that have their forms in matter, our minds can yet untie the two and consider their forms as such. Similarly, although it is connatural to an angel's mind to know existence as concrete in a particular nature, it can still so far distinguish the two as to know that the thing and its existence are not identical. Therefore, since a created mind has the capacity by nature to see the concrete form or concrete act of existence in abstraction by analysis, it can, by grace, be raised so that it may know separate subsisting being and separate subsisting existence.

---

[28] 1a 12.2.

Article 5: Does a created mind need a created light in order to see God's essence?

1. It seems that a created mind does not need a created light in order to see God's essence. For among sensible things what is luminous of itself does not need any extra light in order to be visible. Neither therefore should this be the case with intelligible things. But God is intelligible light. So, he is not seen by any created light.

2. Moreover, when God is seen through some medium he is not seen in his essence. But if he were seen by some created light, he would be seen through a medium, and his essence would not be seen.

3. Again, whatever is itself a creature could belong to some creature by nature. So, if there is a created light through which God's essence is seen, this light could belong by nature to some creature and such a creature at least would not need any additional light in order to see God. This, however, is impossible. So, it is not necessary that every creature should require additional light in order to see God.

On the contrary, we read in the psalm, 'In your light we shall see light.'[29]

Reply: Whatever is raised beyond its own nature must be made apt for this by a disposition beyond its own nature – as air, if it is to receive the form of fire, needs to be predisposed to it. But, when a created intellect sees God's essence, that very essence becomes the form through which the intellect understands. So, there must be some supernatural disposition given to the understanding beyond its own nature in order for it to be raised to such sublimity. Since, as I have shown,[30] the natural power of the intellect is not sufficient to see God's essence, this power of understanding must come to it by divine grace. We call this increase in the power of understanding 'illumination' of the mind, and we speak of the intelligible form as 'light'. This is the light spoken of in the Apocalypse, 'The brightness of God will illuminate her'[31] – that is, the community of the blessed enjoying the vision of God. By this light we are made deiform (like God), as John says, 'When he appears we shall be like him, and we shall see him just as he is.'[32]

---

[29] Psalms 35:10.   [30] 1a 12.4.   [31] Apocalypse 21:23.   [32] 1 John 3:2.

Hence:

1. The function of a created light is not to make God's essence intelligible, for it is intelligible of itself. Its purpose is to strengthen our minds in understanding, rather as a skill increases the effectiveness of any of our powers, and as light in bodily vision makes the medium actually transparent so that it can be altered by colour.
2. This light is not needed as a likeness in which God's essence may be seen, but to perfect the mind and strengthen it so that it may see God. It is not the medium *in* which God is seen, but the means *by* which he is seen. So, it makes the vision of God no less immediate.
3. A disposition to the form of fire can belong by nature only to something that has that form. So, the light of glory can be natural to a creature only if that creature is naturally divine, which is impossible. It is by this light that a creature becomes godlike or deiform, as I have already said.[33]

Article 6: Is God's essence seen more perfectly by one than by another?

1. It seems that, of those who see God's essence, one does not see it more perfectly than another. We read in 1 John, 'We shall see him just as he is',[34] but he *is* in only one way. So, he will only be seen in one way – not, therefore more by some and less by others.
2. Moreover, Augustine says that the 'same thing cannot be better understood by one than by another'.[35] But all who see God's essence understand it, for it is by our minds that we see God, not by our senses, as I have already noted.[36] So, no individual sees better than another when seeing God's essence.
3. Again, when something is seen more perfectly, that is either because of something to do with the thing seen or because of something to do with the power of sight. In the former case it might be that the object is more perfectly present to the one who sees – present in a more perfect likeness. But this has no relevance to the present discussion, for God is present to the mind not by a likeness but by his own

---

[33] See the body of the present article.   [34] 1 John 3:2.
[35] *On Eighty-Three Varied Questions* 1.32. PL 40.22.   [36] 1a 12.3.

essence. So, if someone sees God more perfectly than someone else, that can only be because of a difference in the power of understanding, from which it follows that someone of high intelligence sees God more clearly than someone whose intelligence is lower. But this cannot be right since, in beatitude, we are all promised equality with angels.

On the contrary, eternal life consists in the vision of God, as we know from John: 'This is eternal life, that they might know you, the only true God.'[37] So, if all saw God's essence equally, all would be equal in eternal life, which is contrary to what St Paul says: 'Star differs from star in brightness.'[38]

Reply: Among those who see God's essence, some will see him more perfectly than others. This is not because of a likeness of God which is more perfect in some than in others, for, as I have shown, the vision of God is not through any likeness.[39] It is because some minds have a greater power or ability to see God than others. This ability to see God does not belong to a mind by its own nature but by the light of glory, which renders a mind in some sense like God, as I have said.[40]

So, a mind that has a greater share in the light of glory will see God more perfectly. Those share more in the light of glory who have more charity, for greater charity implies greater desire, and this itself in some way predisposes people and fits them to get what they desire. So, someone with greater charity will see God more perfectly and will be more blessed.

Hence:

1. The adverbial 'just as' in 'We shall see him just as he is' refers not to the manner in which we shall see him but to what we shall see. The sentence means that we shall see God's existence, which is his essence. It does not mean that the manner in which we shall see him is as perfect as the manner in which he is.

2. The same solution applies to the second objection. 'A thing cannot be thought better by one than by another without error' is true if 'better' refers to the thing thought, for one is wrong if one thinks of a thing as being better or worse than it actually is. But the statement is false if taken as referring to the mode of knowing. For, even though it

---

[37] John 17:3. [38] 1 Corinthians 15:41. [39] 1a 12.2. [40] 1a 12.5.

is not positively erroneous, the thinking of one person can be worse than the thinking of another.

3. The differences between those who see God have nothing to do with what is seen, for this (God's essence) is the same for all. Nor are they differences in likeness through which the object is seen. They are due to differences of intellectual capacity, which is not inborn, but given by the light of glory, as I have said.[41]

Article 7: Can a created mind comprehend God's essence?

1. It seems that those who see God's essence comprehend him. For St Paul says, 'I press on, seeking to comprehend.'[42] He does not do this in vain, for he says elsewhere, 'I do not run as one uncertain of my goal.'[43] In the same place he invites others to do the same, '. . . so run that you may comprehend'.

2. Moreover, Augustine says, 'We say that something is comprehended when the whole of it is so visible that nothing of it is hidden.'[44] But when God is seen in his essence the whole of him is seen and nothing is hidden, for God is simple. So, whoever sees God's essence comprehends him.

3. It might be argued 'Yes, we see the totality of God but we do not see him totally.' But this will not do, for 'totally' here is meant to apply either to him or to the seeing. But it is him in his totality that we see, for 'we shall see him just as he is', as I have said.[45] We see him totally, for the mind sees God with its whole power. So, whoever sees God in his essence sees him totally and, therefore, comprehends him.

On the contrary, Jeremiah writes 'most powerful, great and strong, Lord of armies is your name, mighty in your designs, incomprehensible in your thoughts.'[46]

Reply: Augustine says that for a mind to attain God in any way is a great happiness, but it is impossible for any created mind to comprehend him.[47] To comprehend is to understand perfectly, and we understand something perfectly when we understand it as well as it can be

---

[41] See the body of the present article.   [42] Philippians 3:12.   [43] 1 Corinthians 9:26.
[44] Letter 147.9. *PL* 33.606.   [45] 1a 12.6, *ad* 1.   [46] Jeremiah 32:18.
[47] Sermons 117.9. *PL* 38.663.

understood. So, we do not comprehend a proposition that could be known by demonstration if all we have is a probable opinion about it. Someone who can prove that the angles of a triangle equal two right angles may be said to comprehend this fact. But people who are merely of the opinion that it is so because the learned say so, or because it is commonly agreed that it is so, do not comprehend it because they have not reached the most perfect sort of understanding available in this case.

Now, no created mind can attain the perfect sort of understanding of God's essence that is intrinsically possible. This is clear as follows: each thing can be understood to the extent that it is actually realized. God, therefore, whose actual being is infinite, as noted above,[48] can be infinitely understood. But a created mind understands God more or less perfectly according to the degree of the light of glory that floods it. Since the created light of glory cannot be infinite, no matter what mind it is received in, it is impossible for a created mind to understand God infinitely; it is impossible, therefore, to comprehend him.

Hence:

1. 'To comprehend' means two things. Strictly and properly it means to contain something, and in this sense God cannot be comprehended either by the mind or by anything else. The infinite cannot be contained in the finite. God exists infinitely and nothing finite can grasp him infinitely. It is of comprehension in this sense that I am now speaking.

   In a broader sense, however, comprehending is the opposite of pursuit. We say that anyone who reaches someone by laying hold comprehends that person. In this sense the blessed do comprehend God: 'I held him and will not let him go.'[49] It is in this sense that St Paul's authoritative texts use the word. So comprehension is one of the three endowments of the soul, corresponding to hope as vision does to faith, and as fruition or enjoyment does to charity. In this life not everything in our vision is in our grasp, for we see some things in the distance and we see things that are not in our power. We do not enjoy all we grasp – either because it does not please us or because it is not what we are ultimately seeking (the satisfaction and calming of all our desires). But the blessed have this triple gift in God, for they see him, and seeing him they possess him, holding him for ever in their sight;

[48] 1a 7.1. [49] Song of Songs 3:4.

and holding him they enjoy him as their ultimate goal fulfilling all their desires.

2. When we say that God is incomprehensible we do not mean that there is something about him that is not seen, but that he cannot be seen as perfectly as he is in himself visible. When people have only a probable opinion about a proposition that can be proved, no part of the proposition is hidden from them. They understand both subject and predicate, and the fact that these are conjoined. But they do not understand the proposition as well as it can be understood. Hence Augustine, defining comprehension, says that a whole 'is totally comprehended when it is so seen that no part of it is hidden, or so that all its limits can be seen',[50] for we reach all the limits of something when we reach the limit in our way of knowing it.

3. The word 'totally' applies to the object. But it is not that we do not know of the whole way of being of the thing. Rather, our way of knowing does not measure up to this. Whoever sees God in his essence sees something that exists infinitely and sees it to be infinitely intelligible – but without understanding it infinitely. It is as though one might be of the opinion that a certain proposition can be proved without being able to prove it oneself.

Article 8: Does a created mind see all things in seeing God's essence?

1. It seems that those who see God in his essence see all things in him. Gregory says, 'What is it that they do not see who see the one who sees all things?'[51] But God sees all things. So, those who see God see all things.

2. Moreover, whoever sees a mirror sees what is reflected in it. But everything that is or could be is reflected in God as in a mirror, for he knows all things in himself. So, whoever sees God sees all that is or could be.

3. Moreover, someone who understands the greater can understand the lesser, as Aristotle says.[52] But everything that God makes or can make is something less than his essence. So, whoever understands God can understand all that God has made or can make.

---

[50] Sermons 117.9. *PL* 38.663.   [51] *Dialogues* 4.33. *PL* 77.376.   [52] *On the Soul* 3.4, 429b3.

4. Again, a rational creature naturally wishes to know everything. So if it were not to know all things in knowing God, its desires would not be satisfied, and it would not be happy in seeing God, which seems paradoxical. In seeing God, therefore, a rational creature sees all things.

On the contrary, angels see God's essence but do not know everything. According to Dionysius lesser angels are purified of their unknowing by greater ones.[53] And angels do not know future contingents or the secrets of the heart, for knowledge of these belong only to God. So, it cannot be that whoever knows God's essence knows all things.

Reply: A created mind seeing the divine essence does not see in it all that God does or can do. It is obvious that some things are seen in God in so far as they exist in him by nature. But all other things are in God in the way that an effect exists virtually in its cause, so these are seen in God as effects in their cause. Now, the more perfectly we see a cause, the more of its effects we see in it. Sharply intelligent people who grasp a principle can immediately grasp its implications, whereas people who are less bright have to have each conclusion explained to them. Only someone who wholly comprehends a cause will see all its effects in it, and everything about them. But no created mind can wholly comprehend God, as I have shown.[54] So, no created mind seeing God sees all that God makes or can make, for this would be to comprehend his power. Yet the more perfectly God is seen the more of what he makes or can make is seen in him.

Hence:

1. Gregory is thinking of sufficiency from the viewpoint of what is seen (i.e. God), and God sufficiently contains and shows forth all things. But it does not follow from this that those who see God see all things, for they do not perfectly comprehend him.

2. People who see a mirror do not necessarily see everything that is in it if they do not see it perfectly.

3. Although it is a greater thing to see God than to see all other things, it is a greater thing to see God in such a way that all other things are seen in him than to see him in such a way that only a certain amount

---

[53] *The Celestial Hierarchy* 7. PG 3.208.   [54] 1a 12.7.

is seen in him. I have already shown that the amount we see in God depends on how perfectly we see him.[55]

4. A rational creature's natural desire is to know all that belongs to the perfection of the mind, namely the species and genera of things, and their natures. Anyone who sees God's essence sees these. But to know other singulars, together with their thoughts and deeds, does not of itself belong to the perfection of a created mind, and such a mind does not naturally seek after it. Nor does it seek to know what has not yet happened but can be brought about by God. But if God alone were seen (since he is the fount and source of all being and truth), he would so satisfy a creature's desire for knowledge that it would seek nothing further by way of happiness. As Augustine says, 'Unhappy are those who know all [creatures] but do not know you: blessed are those who know you even though they do not know them. And those who know both you and them are not the happier because of them but are happy simply because of you.'[56]

Article 9: Is it by means of any likeness that those who see God's essence see what they do in it?

1. It seems that what is seen in God by those who see the divine essence is seen through a likeness. For knowledge comes about through the assimilation of the knower to the known. The mind in its realization becomes the realized intelligibility of the thing to be known, and sight in its realization becomes the realized visibility of the thing to be seen. This happens because the knowing power is formed by a likeness of the thing known, as the pupil of an eye is formed by the likeness of colour. So, if the minds of those who see God in his essence are to understand other creatures in God, they must be formed by the likenesses of those creatures.

2. Moreover, people remember what they have previously seen. But St Paul, who according to Augustine[57] saw God's essence when he was rapt in his ecstasy, remembered many things he saw in rapture after he ceased to see them; for he said, 'I have heard secret words which it is not given to people to speak.'[58] So, some likenesses of the things he

---

[55] See the body of the present article.   [56] *Confessions* 5.
[57] *On the Literal Interpretation of 'Genesis'* 12.28. PL 34.478.   [58] 2 Corinthians 12:4.

remembered must have remained in his mind, and these likenesses or semblances must have been there when he was actually seeing God's essence.

On the contrary, it is with one view that we see a mirror and what is in it. But we see everything in God as in a sort of intelligible mirror. So, if God himself is not seen through any likeness, but by his essence, neither are the things seen in him seen by any likeness or semblance.

Reply: Those who see God's essence do not see it through a likeness but through God's essence united to their minds. For everything is known in so far as its likeness is in the knower. This happens in two ways since, as things that resemble something else also resemble each other, the power of knowing can be conformed to the thing known in two ways. It can be formed directly by the likeness of the known thing, and then the thing is known in itself. Alternatively, it can be formed by the likeness of something which is itself like the known thing, and then the thing is known not in itself but in a likeness. After all, it is one thing to know people themselves, and another to know those people on the basis of a picture. So, to know things through their own likenesses in the mind is to know them in themselves, or in their own natures. But to know them through their likenesses pre-existing in God is to see them in God. These two kinds of knowledge are different. When things are known in God by those who see his essence, therefore, they are not seen through any likeness but in the same way that God himself is known, just by God's essence being present in the mind.

Hence:

1. The mind of one who sees God is assimilated to what it sees in God by being joined to the divine essence, in which the likenesses of all things pre-exist.

2. There are some powers of knowing which from likenesses first conceived can form others – as when we imaginatively form the image of a golden mountain from the images of gold and a mountain, or as when we form the notion of a species from the ideas of a genus and a difference. In a similar way, we can form a likeness of something from a picture of it. This is how St Paul, or anyone else who sees God's essence, can form, from a vision of the divine essence, the likenesses of the things seen there, which in St Paul's case remained after the vision itself had ceased. But to see things through

likenesses formed in this way is not to see them as they are seen in God.

Article 10: Do those who see God's essence see all that they see in it at the same time?

1. It seems that those who see God's essence do not see all that they see in it at the same time. For Aristotle says that, though we may know many things, we understand only one thing at a time.[59] But what is seen in God is understood since we see God by our understanding. So, those who see God cannot see many things in him all at once.
2. Moreover, Augustine says, 'God moves spiritual creatures in time'[60] – that is, he moves them to know and love. But an angel is a spiritual creature who sees God. So, since time implies succession, those who see God know and love things successively.

On the contrary, Augustine says, 'Our thoughts will not fly back and forth, first to one thing then to another, but we shall see all our knowledge in a single simultaneous view.'[61]

Reply: The things that are seen in the Word are not seen successively but together. The reason why we cannot think of many things at once is that we need many likenesses in the mind in order to think of them, and one mind cannot be formed by many likenesses at once (just as a body cannot assume many shapes at once). When many things can be thought of through one likeness (as with the parts of a whole) they can be thought of together, but when each thing requires a different likeness they can be thought of only successively. Now, if all things were to be thought of through one likeness of them all, they could all be thought of together. I have already shown that all the things seen in God are seen not each by its own likeness but by the one essence of God.[62] So, they are seen together and not successively.

Hence:

1. We understand one thing at a time in that we understand through one concept at a time. But many things can be understood at once if they are understood through the same concept – as we understand

---

[59] *Topics* 2.10, 114b34.   [60] *On the Literal Interpretation of 'Genesis'* 8.20. *PL* 34.388.
[61] *On the Trinity* 15.16. *PL* 42.1079.   [62] 1a 12.9.

that a human being is both animal and rational when we understand what a human being is, and as we see in a flash that a house has both walls and a roof.

2. Angels in their natural knowledge (in which they know things through different concepts implanted in them) do not know everything at once. In this sense their minds are moved through time. But, in so far as they see things in God, they see them all at once.

Article 11: Can anyone in this life see God's essence?

1. It seems that someone in this life could see God's essence. For Jacob says, 'I saw God face to face.'[63] But we know from 1 Corinthians that to see God face to face is to see his essence: 'Now we see in a mirror by dull reflections, but then we shall see face to face.'[64] So, it is possible in this life to see God's essence.

2. Moreover the Lord said of Moses, 'I speak to him mouth to mouth; he sees God clearly, not through enigmas and figures.'[65] But this is to see God in his essence. So, someone in this life can see God in his essence.

3. Moreover, that in which we know all other things, and by which we judge them, must be something we know through itself. But we already know all things in God, for Augustine says, 'If we both see that what you say is true, and we both see that what I say is true, where do we see this? Neither I in you nor you in me, but both of us in the unvariable truth itself above our minds.'[66] Again he says that 'we judge all things according to divine truth'.[67] He also says that 'the business of reason is to judge these corporeal things by incorporeal and eternal standards, which must be beyond the mind if they are to be unvariable'.[68] So, we see God himself even in this life.

4. Again, Augustine says that by our intellectual vision we see what is in the soul by its essence.[69] But intellectual vision does not see intelligible things by any likeness but by their essences, as he also says in the same place. So, since God is in our souls by his essence, it must be in his essence that we see him.

[63] Genesis 32:30.   [64] 1 Corinthians 13:12.   [65] Numbers 4:8.
[66] *Confessions* 12.25. *PL* 32.840.   [67] *On True Religion* 30.31. *PL* 34.146–7.
[68] *On the Trinity* 12.2. *PL* 42.999.
[69] *On the Literal Interpretation of 'Genesis'* 12.24 and 31. *PL* 34.474 and 479.

On the contrary, Exodus says, 'No human being shall see me and live.'[70] And the Gloss adds, 'As long as we live in this mortal life we can see God by certain images, but we cannot see him by the likeness which is his very nature.'[71]

Reply: Something that is nothing other than human cannot see God's essence unless it is removed from this mortal life. For the way in which a thing knows depends on the way it has its being, as I have said.[72] As long as we are in this life our souls have their being in corporeal matter. So they cannot by nature know anything except what has its form in matter or what can be known through such things. But the divine essence obviously cannot be known through the natures of material things, for I have shown that any knowledge of God that we have through a created likeness is not a knowledge of his essence.[73] So it is impossible for the human soul, as it is in this life, to see God's essence. An indication of this is that the more the soul is abstracted from material things the greater is its capacity for understanding abstract intelligible things – which is why divine revelations and visions of the future come more often during dreams and ecstasies. So, it is impossible for a soul, while it lives normally on earth, to be raised to an understanding of that which is most intelligible of all – God's essence.

Hence:

1. As Dionysius says, the Scriptures speak of us seeing God when we form certain images of the divine, whether sensible or imaginary.[74] When he says 'I saw God face to face', Jacob refers not to God's essence but to an image representing it. It belongs to an especially high form of prophecy to see God represented as something speaking, even though it is only in a vision of the imagination, as I shall later show.[75] An alternative explanation would be that Jacob refers to a high and extraordinary degree of contemplation.

2. God can work miracles with minds as well as bodies, in either case raising them beyond the normal order of things to a supernatural level. Thus he may raise up certain minds to see his essence in this life, but not by making use of their bodily senses. Augustine says that

[70] Exodus 33:20.   [71] *Glossa ordinaria. PL* 76.91.   [72] 1a 12.4.   [73] 1a 12.2.
[74] *The Celestial Hierarchy* 4. *PG* 3.180.   [75] 1a2ae 174.3.

this is what happened to Moses, the teacher of the Jews, and to St Paul, the teacher of the Gentiles.[76]

3. We say that we see everything in God and judge everything by him in so far as by sharing in his light we are able to see and judge, for the natural light of reason is a sort of sharing in divine light. In the same way we say that we see and judge all sensible things in the sun – that is, by the light of the sun. Augustine therefore says, 'The lessons of instruction can only be seen as it were by their own sun',[77] namely God. Just as we can see sensible things without seeing the essence of the sun, we can see things intellectually without seeing God's essence.

4. By intellectual vision we see what is in the soul as a thought in the mind. God is in the souls of the blessed in this way but not in ours. He is in us by presence, essence and power.

Article 12: Can we know God by our natural reason in this life?

1. It seems that we cannot know God by our natural reason in this life. For Boethius says, 'reason cannot grasp simple forms'.[78] But God, as I have shown, is a supremely simple form.[79] So, we cannot gain knowledge of him by natural reason.

2. Moreover, according to Aristotle the soul understands nothing by natural reason without images.[80] But since God is incorporeal our imagination can have no image of him. So, we cannot know him by natural reason.

3. Both good and bad people have natural reason since they each have a human nature. But only the good have knowledge of God. As Augustine says, 'The weak eye of the human mind is not fixed on that excellent light unless purified by the justice of faith.'[81] So, we cannot know God by natural reason.

On the contrary, St Paul says, 'What is known about God [i.e. what can be known about him by natural reason] is manifest in them.'[82]

---

[76] *On the Literal Interpretation of 'Genesis'* 12.26–8. *PL* 34.476–82.   [77] *Soliloquies* 1.8. *PL* 32.877.
[78] *The Consolation of Philosophy* 5, prosa 4. *PL* 63.847.   [79] 1a 3.7.
[80] *On the Soul* 3.7, 431a16.   [81] *On the Trinity* 1.2. *PL* 42.822.   [82] Romans 1:19.

Reply: The knowledge that is natural to us has its source in our senses and therefore extends just so far as it can be led by sensible things. But our understanding cannot reach to a vision of God's essence from these, for sensible creatures are effects of God which are unequal to the power of their cause. So, knowing them does not lead us to understand the whole power of God, and we do not thereby see his essence. Yet they are effects which are causally dependent, so we can at least be led from them to know of God that he exists and that he has whatever must belong to him as the first cause of all things, a cause that surpasses all that he causes.

So, we know about God's relation to creatures (that he is the cause of them all), and about the difference between him and them (that he is not a part of what he has caused). We also know that the difference between God and his effects is not due to any deficiency in him but to the fact that he vastly surpasses them all.

Hence:

1. By reason we can know *that* a simple form is, even though we cannot succeed in understanding *what* it is.
2. God is known to natural reason through the images of his effects.
3. Knowledge of God through his essence belongs only to the good since it is a gift of grace. But the knowledge we have by natural reason belongs to both good and bad. Augustine says in his *Reconsiderations*, 'I now disapprove of what I said in a certain prayer, "O God who wants only the clean of heart to know truth . . .", for one could reply that many who are unclean know many truths' (i.e. by natural reason).[83]

Article 13: Besides the knowledge we have of God by natural reason, is there in this life a deeper knowledge that we have through grace?

1. It seems that by grace we do not have a deeper knowledge of God than we have by natural reason. For Dionysius says that those best united to God in this life are united to him as to something utterly unknown.[84] He says this even of Moses, who received great graces of knowledge. But we can come to be joined to God by natural reason

---

[83] *Reconsiderations* 1.4. *PL* 32.589.   [84] *Mystical Theology* 1. *PG* 3.1001.

> without knowing what he is. So, grace gives us no greater knowledge of God than natural reason does.

2. Moreover, by natural reason we only come to know God through images in the imagination. Yet the same is true of the knowledge we have through grace, for Dionysius says: 'It is impossible for the divine ray to shine upon us except as screened round about by the many-coloured sacred veils.'[85] So, by grace we have no fuller knowledge of God than we have by natural reason.

3. Again, our minds adhere to God by the grace of faith. But faith does not seem to be knowledge, for Gregory says we have 'faith and not knowledge of the unseen'.[86] So, grace adds nothing to our knowledge of God.

On the contrary, St Paul says, 'God has revealed to us through his Spirit' a wisdom which 'none of this world's rulers knew'[87] – and a gloss says that this refers to philosophers.[88]

Reply: We have a more perfect knowledge of God by grace than we have by natural reason. The latter depends on two things: images derived from the sensible world, and the natural intellectual light by which we make abstract intelligible concepts from these images. But human knowledge is helped by the revelation of grace when it comes to both of these. The light of grace strengthens the intellectual light. As is clear in the case of prophetic visions, God gives us images better suited to express divine things than those we receive naturally from the sensible world. Moreover, God sometimes gives us sensible signs and spoken words to show us something of the divine – as at the baptism of Christ, when the Holy Spirit appeared in the form of a dove and the voice of the Father was heard saying, 'This is my beloved Son.'[89]

Hence:

1. Although in this life revelation does not tell us what God is and so joins us to him as if to an unknown, nevertheless it helps us to know him better in that it shows us more and greater works of his and teaches us things about him that we can never arrive at by natural reason, as for instance that God is both three and one.

---

[85] *The Celestial Hierarchy* I. *PG* 3.121.   [86] *Homily 26 on the Gospel. PL* 76.1202.
[87] I Corinthians 2:8, 10.   [88] Interlinear gloss from St Jerome. *PL* 30.752.   [89] Matthew 3.17.

2. The stronger our intellectual light, the deeper the understanding we derive from images, whether these are received in a natural way, from the senses, or formed in the imagination by divine power. Revelation provides us with a divine light which enables us to attain a more profound understanding from these images.

3. Faith is a sort of knowledge in that it makes the mind assent to something knowable. Yet the assent here is not due to the vision of the believer but to the vision of the one who is believed. So, in so far as it lacks the element of seeing, faith fails to be knowledge in a strict sense of the term, for such knowledge causes the mind to assent through what is seen and through an understanding of first principles.

Question 13
Talking about God

Having considered how we know God, I now turn to consider how we speak of him, for we speak of things as we know them. Here there are twelve points of inquiry:

1. Can we use any words to refer to God?
2. Do we predicate of God substantially?[1]
3. Do we predicate of God literally, or must we always do so metaphorically?
4. Are the many terms we predicate of God synonyms?
5. Are words we use both of God and of creatures used univocally or equivocally?
6. Given that we actually use them analogically, do we predicate them primarily of God or of creatures?
7. In speaking of God, can we use words that imply temporal succession?
8. Is 'God' the name of a nature or of a certain activity?
9. Is the name 'God' peculiar to God or not?
10. When it is used of God, of what shares in divinity, and of what is merely supposed to do so, is it used univocally or equivocally?
11. Is 'The One who Is' the most appropriate name for God?
12. Can we formulate affirmative propositions about God?

---

[1] I.e. do words in the category of substance express God's nature when used to describe him?

Article 1: Are any words suitable for talking about God?

1. It seems that no words are suitable for talking about God. For Dionysius says, 'of him there is no naming nor any opinion',[2] and we read in Proverbs, 'What is his name or the name of his son if you know?'[3]

2. Moreover, nouns are either abstract or concrete. But concrete nouns are inappropriate to God because he is altogether simple; and we can rule out abstract nouns because they do not signify a complete subsistent thing. So, we can predicate no term of God.

3. Again, a noun signifies something as coming under some description; verbs and participles signify it as enduring in time; pronouns signify it as being pointed out or as being in some relationship. None of these is appropriate to God: he has no qualities or accidental attributes; he is non-temporal; and he cannot be pointed to because he is not available to the senses; moreover he cannot be referred to by relative pronouns since the use of these depends on the previous use of some other referring term such as a noun, participle or demonstrative pronoun. So, there is no way of referring to God.

On the contrary, in Exodus we read, 'The Lord is a great warrior; His name is Almighty.'[4]

Reply: Aristotle says that spoken words are signs for thoughts, and thoughts are likenesses of things.[5] So, words refer to things indirectly through thoughts. We can therefore designate something in so far as we can know it intellectually. Now, I have already shown that we cannot see God's essence in this life.[6] We only know him from creatures. We think of him as their source, and then as surpassing them all and as lacking anything that is merely creaturely. So, we can designate God from creatures, though the words we use do not express the divine essence as it is in itself. In this they differ from a term like 'human being', which is intended to express by its meaning the essence of human being as it is – for the meaning of 'human being' is given by a definition of human being which expresses its essence, for the nature that a name signifies is the definition.

[2] *The Divine Names* 1. PG 3.593.   [3] Proverbs 30:4.   [4] Exodus 15:3.
[5] *On Interpretation* 1.1, 16a3.   [6] 1a 12.4.

Hence:

1. We say that God has no name, or is beyond naming, because his essence is beyond what we understand of him and the meaning of the names we use.

2. Since we come to know God from creatures, and since this is how we come to refer to him, the expressions we use to name him signify in a way that is appropriate to the material creatures we ordinarily know. Among such creatures the complete subsistent thing is always a concrete union of form and matter; for the form itself is not a subsistent thing, but that by which something subsists. Because of this the words we use to signify complete subsistent things are concrete nouns which are appropriate to composite subjects. When, on the other hand, we want to speak of the form itself we use abstract nouns which do not signify something as subsistent, but as that by which something is: 'whiteness', for example, signifies that by which something is white.

   Now God is both simple, like a form, and subsistent, like something concrete. So, we sometimes refer to him by abstract nouns (to indicate his simplicity) while at other times we refer to him by concrete nouns (to indicate his subsistence and completeness) – though neither way of speaking measures up to his way of being, for in this life we do not know him as he is in himself.

3. To signify something as coming under some description is to signify it as subsisting in a certain nature or definite form. I have already said that the reason we use concrete nouns for God is to indicate his subsistence and completeness;[7] it is for the same reason that we use nouns signifying a thing under some description. Although they imply temporal succession, we can use verbs and participles of him because his eternity includes all time. Just as we can understand what is both simple and subsistent only as though it were composite, so we can understand and speak of the simplicity of eternity only after the manner of temporal things. It is composite and temporal things that we ordinarily and naturally understand. We can use demonstrative pronouns of God in so far as they point, not to something seen, but to something understood, for so long as we know something, in whatever

---

[7] See the reply to objection 2 in the present article.

way, we can point it out. So, just as nouns and participles and demonstrative pronouns can signify God, so can relative pronouns.

Article 2: Do we predicate any term of God substantially?

1. It seems that we predicate no term of God substantially. For John Damascene says, 'The words used of God must signify not what he is substantially but what he is not, or his relationship to something else, or something that follows from his nature or activity.'[8]
2. Moreover, Dionysius says, 'You will find a chorus of holy teachers seeking to distinguish clearly and laudably the divine processions in the naming of God.'[9] This means that the words which the holy teachers use in praising God differ according to his different causal acts. But to speak of something's causal activity is not to speak of its essence. So, such words are not predicated of God substantially.
3. Again, we designate things to the extent that we understand them. But in this life we do not understand God's substance (what God is). So, we cannot predicate anything of him substantially (we cannot say what he is).

On the contrary, Augustine says, 'To be God is to be strong, to be wise, or whatever else we say of his simplicity in order to signify his substance.'[10] So, all such terms signify God's substance.

Reply: It is clear that the problem does not arise for negative terms or for words which express the relationship of God to creatures. These obviously do not express what he is but rather what he is not or how he is related to something else – or, better, how something else is related to him. The question is concerned with words like 'good' and 'wise' which are neither negative nor relational terms, and about these there are several opinions.

Some have said that sentences like 'God is good', though they sound like affirmations, are in fact used to deny something of God rather than to assert anything. Thus, for example, when we say that God is living we mean that he is not like something inanimate, and likewise for all such propositions. This was the view of the Rabbi Moses.[11]

---

[8] *On the Orthodox Faith* 1.9. PG 94.835. [9] *The Divine Names* 1. PG 3.589.
[10] *On the Trinity* 6.4. PL 42.927.
[11] Moses Maimonides (1138–1204), *Guide for the Perplexed* 1.58.

Others said that such sentences are used to signify the relation of God to creatures, so that when we say 'God is good' we mean that God is the cause of goodness in things, and likewise in other such propositions.

Neither of these views seems plausible, however, for three reasons.

First, on neither view can there be any reason why we should use some words about God rather than others. God is just as much the cause of bodies as he is of goodness in things. So, if 'God is good' means no more than that God is the cause of goodness in things, why not say 'God is a body' since he is the cause of bodies? Likewise, we could also say 'God is a body' because we want to deny that he is merely potential being like prime matter.

Second it would follow that everything we say of God is true only in a secondary sense, as when we say that medicine is 'healthy', meaning merely that it causes health in the one who takes it. But it is the living body that we call healthy in a primary sense.

Third, this is not what people want to say when they talk about God. When people speak of the 'living God' they do not simply want to say that God is the cause of our life, or that he differs from a lifeless body.

So, we must find some other solution to the problem: that such words do say what God is (they are predicated of him in the category of substance),[12] but they fail adequately to represent what he is. The reason for this is that we speak of God as we know him, and since we know him from creatures we can only speak of him as they represent him. Any creature, in so far as it possesses any perfection, represents God and is like him, for he, being simply and universally perfect, has pre-existing in himself the perfections of all his creatures, as I have already noted.[13] But a creature is not like God as it is like another member of its species or genus. It resembles him as an effect may in some way resemble a transcendent cause although failing to reproduce perfectly the form of the cause – as in a certain way the forms of inferior bodies imitate the power of the sun. I explained this earlier when I was dealing with God's perfection.[14] So, words like 'good' and 'wise' when used of God do signify something that God really is, but they signify it imperfectly because creatures represent God imperfectly.

So, 'God is good' does not mean the same as 'God is the cause of goodness' or 'God is not evil'. It means that what we call 'goodness' in

---

[12] They express his nature.   [13] 1a 4.2.   [14] 1a 4.3.

creatures pre-exists in God in a higher way. Thus God is not good because he causes goodness. Rather, goodness flows from him because he is good. As Augustine says, 'Because he is good, we exist.'[15]

Hence:

1. Damascene is saying that these words do not signify what God is since none of them express completely what he is; but each signifies imperfectly something that he is, just as creatures represent him imperfectly.

2. Sometimes the reason why a word comes to be used is quite different from the meaning of the word. Take, for example, the Latin word *lapis* (stone). Speakers of Latin derive the word from *laedens pedem* (what hurts a foot). However, it is not used to mean 'what hurts a foot', but to refer to a particular kind of physical object. Otherwise everything that hurts a foot would be a stone. In the case of words used of God we may say that the reason they came to be used derives from his causal activity, for our understanding of him, and our language about him, depends on the different perfections in creatures which represent him, however imperfectly, in his various causal acts. Nevertheless, we do not use these words to signify his causal acts. 'Living' in 'God is living' does not mean the same as 'causes life'. We use the sentence to say that life pre-exists in the source of all things, though in a higher way than we can understand or signify.

3. In this life we cannot understand God's essence as it is in itself. But we can do so in so far as the perfections of his creatures represent it. And this is how the words we use can signify it.

Article 3: Can we say anything literally about God?

1. It seems that we cannot use any word literally of God. For, as I have said, we take every word we use when talking about God from our speech about creatures.[16] But we use such words metaphorically of God, as when we call him a 'rock' or a 'lion'. So, we only speak metaphorically when talking about God.

2. Moreover, we do not use a word literally of something if it would be more accurate not to use it than to use it. But according to Dionysius

---

[15] *On Christian Doctrine* 1.32. *PL* 34.32.   [16] 1a 13.1.

it would be truer to say that God is not good or wise or any such thing than to say that he is.[17] So, we say none of these things literally of God.

3. Again, we apply the names of bodily things to God only metaphorically, for he is incorporeal. But all such names imply corporeal conditions, for they signify temporal succession and composition of matter and form, which belong to the material world. So, we use such words only metaphorically of God.

On the contrary, Ambrose says, 'Some names clearly show forth what is proper to divinity, and some express the luminous truth of the divine majesty, but there are others which we predicate of God metaphorically and through a certain likeness.'[18] So, we do not use all words of God metaphorically. We use some of them literally.

Reply: As I have said, we know God from the perfections that flow from him to creatures,[19] and these perfections certainly exist in him in a more excellent way than they do in them. Yet we understand such perfections as we find them in creatures, and as we understand them so we use words to speak of them. Thus we have to consider two things in the words we use to attribute perfections to God: first, the perfections themselves that are signified (goodness, life, and the like); second, the way in which they are signified. As far as the perfections signified are concerned, we use the words literally of God, and in fact more appropriately than we use them of creatures, for these perfections belong primarily to God and only secondarily to other things. But so far as the way of signifying these perfections is concerned, we use the words inappropriately, for they have a way of signifying that is appropriate to creatures.

Hence:

1. Some words that signify what has come forth from God to creatures do so in such a way that part of the meaning of the word is the imperfect way in which creatures share in God's perfection. Thus it is part of the meaning of 'stone' that it is a material thing. We can use such words of God only metaphorically. There are other words, however, that simply mean certain perfections without any indication of how these perfections are possessed – words, for

---

[17] *The Celestial Hierarchy* 2. PG 3.41.   [18] *On Faith* 2, prol. PL 16.583.   [19] 1a 13.2.

example, like 'being', 'good', 'living', and so on, and we can use words like these literally of God.

2. The reason why Dionysius says that such words are better denied of God is that what they signify does not belong to God in the way that they signify it, but in a higher way. In the same passage he therefore says that God is beyond every substance and life.[20]

3. These words imply bodily conditions not in what they mean but in the way in which they signify it. But the ones that are used metaphorically have bodily conditions as part of what they mean.

Article 4: Are all the words we predicate of God synonymous?

1. It seems that all the words we apply to God are synonymous. For synonyms are words that mean exactly the same thing. But whatever words we apply to God refer to exactly the same reality in God, for his goodness, and his wisdom, and such-like are identical with his essence. So, all these expressions are synonyms.

2. Moreover, if someone should argue that, although they signify the same thing, they do so from different points of view, there is an answer we can give: that it is useless to have different points of view which do not correspond to any difference in the thing viewed.

3. Again, something that can only be described in one way is more perfectly one than something that can be described in many ways. But God is supremely one. So, he is not describable in many ways, and the many things we say about him all have the same meaning: they are synonymous.

On the contrary, piling up synonyms adds nothing to the meaning: 'clothing garments' are just the same as 'garments'. So, if everything we say about God is synonymous it would be inappropriate to speak of 'the good God' or anything of the kind. Yet Jeremiah says, 'Most strong, mighty and powerful, your name is Lord of armies.'[21]

Reply: The words we use to speak of God are not synonymous. This is clear enough in the case of words we use to deny something of him, or to speak of his causal relation to creatures. Such words differ in meaning

---

[20] *The Celestial Hierarchy* 2. *PG* 3.41. [21] Jeremiah 32:18.

according to the different things we wish to deny of him, or the different effects to which we are referring. But it should be clear from what I have previously said[22] that even the words that signify what God is (though they do it imperfectly) also have distinct meanings.[23]

What we mean by a word is the concept we form of what the word signifies. Since we know God from creatures, we understand him through concepts appropriate to the perfections that creatures receive from him. What pre-exists in God in a simple and unified way is divided among creatures as many and varied perfections. The many perfections of creatures correspond to one single source which they represent in varied and complex ways. Thus the different and complex concepts that we have in mind correspond to something altogether simple which they enable us imperfectly to understand. Thus the words we use for the perfections we attribute to God, though they signify what is one, are not synonymous, for they signify it from many different points of view.

Hence:

1. So, the solution to the first objection is clear. Synonyms signify the same thing from the same point of view. Words that signify the same thing that is thought of in different ways do not, properly speaking, signify the same, for words only signify things by way of thoughts, as I noted above.[24]

2. The many different points of view are not baseless and pointless, for they all correspond to a single reality which each represents imperfectly in a different way.

3. It belongs to the perfection of God's unity that what is many and diverse in others should in him be unified and simple. That is why he is one thing described in many ways, for our minds learn of him in the many ways in which he is represented by creatures.

Article 5: Do we use words univocally or equivocally of God and creatures?

1. It seems that words used both of God and of creatures are used univocally. The equivocal is based on the univocal as the many is based on the one. A word such as 'dog' may be used equivocally of

---

[22] 1a 13.2.   [23] 1a 13.1 and 2.   [24] 1a 13.1.

the animals that bark and of something in the sea [i.e. dogfish], but only because it is first used univocally (of the things that bark); otherwise there would be nowhere to start from and we should go back for ever. Now some causes are univocal because their effects have the same name and description as themselves – what is generated by human beings, for example, is also a human being. But some causes are equivocal, as is the sun when it causes heat, for the sun itself is only equivocally hot. Since, therefore, the equivocal is based on the univocal it seems that the first agent upon which all others are based must be a univocal one. So, we univocally predicate the terms that we use of God and of creatures.

2. Moreover, there is no resemblance between things that are only equivocally the same. But according to Genesis there is a resemblance between creatures and God: 'Let us make human beings in our own image and likeness.'[25] So, it seems we can say something univocally of God and creatures.

3. Again, as Aristotle says, the measure must be of the same order as the thing measured.[26] But God is the first measure of all beings, as Aristotle also says. So, God is of the same order as creatures and something can therefore be said univocally of both.

On the contrary, the same word when used with different meanings is used equivocally. But no word when used of God means the same as when it is used of a creature. 'Wisdom', for example, means a quality when it is used of creatures, but not when it is applied to God. So, it must have a different meaning, for we have here a difference in the genus which is part of the definition. The same applies to other words. So, we must use all of them equivocally when we apply them to both God and creatures.

Furthermore, God is more distant from any creature than any two creatures are from each other. Now there are some creatures so different that we can say nothing univocally of them (when they differ in genus, for example). Much less, therefore, can we say anything univocally of creatures and God. Everything we say of them we must say equivocally.

---

[25] Genesis 1:26.   [26] *Metaphysics* 10.1, 1053a24.

Reply: It is impossible to predicate anything univocally of God and creatures. Every effect that falls short of the power of its agent cause represents it inadequately, for it is not the same kind of thing as its agent cause. Thus what exists simply and in a unified way in the cause will be divided up and take various different forms in such effects – as the simple power of the sun produces many different effects in things on earth. In the same way, as I said earlier, all the perfections which in creatures are many and various pre-exist in God as one.[27]

The words denoting perfections that we use in speaking of creatures all differ in meaning and each one signifies a perfection as something distinct from all others. Thus when we say that a man is wise, we signify his wisdom as something distinct from the other things about him – his essence, for example, his powers, or his existence. But when we use 'wise' when talking about God we do not intend to signify something distinct from his essence, power or existence. When we predicate 'wise' of a human being we, so to speak, circumscribe and define the limits of the aspect of human beings that it signifies. But this is not so when we predicate 'wise' of God. What it signifies in him is not confined by the meaning of our word but goes beyond it. So, it is clear that we do not use 'wise' in the same sense of God and people, and the same goes for all other words. So, we cannot use them univocally of God and creatures.

Yet although we never use words in exactly the same sense of creatures and of God, we are not merely equivocating when we use the same word, as some have said, for if this were so we could never argue from statements about creatures to statements about God – any such argument would be invalidated by the Fallacy of Equivocation.[28] That this does not happen we know not merely from the teachings of the philosophers who prove many things about God but also from the teaching of St Paul, for he says, 'The invisible things of God are made known by those things that are made.'[29]

So, we must say that words are used of God and of creatures in an analogical way, in accordance with a certain order between them. We can

[27] 1a 13.4.
[28] The following argument commits this fallacy – all pigs are kept in pens, pens are something to write with, therefore all pigs are kept in something to write with. The premises do not imply the conclusion – that is, the argument is invalid – because 'pen' has a different sense in its two occurrences.
[29] Romans 1:20.

distinguish two kinds of analogical or proportional uses of language. First, there is the case of one word being used of two things because each of them has some order or relation to a third thing. Thus we use the word 'healthy' of both medicine and urine because each of these has some relation to health in animals, the former as a cause, the latter as a symptom of it. Second, there is the case of the same word used of two things because of some relation that one has to the other – as 'healthy' is used of medicine and animals because the former is the cause of health in the latter.

In this way some words are used neither univocally nor purely equivocally of God and creatures, but analogically, for we cannot speak of God at all except in the language we use of creatures, as I have said. So, whatever we say of both God and creatures we say in virtue of the order that creatures have to God as to their source and cause, in which all the perfections of things pre-exist most excellently.

This way of using words lies somewhere between pure equivocation and simple univocity, for the word is neither used in the same sense, as with univocal usage, nor in totally different senses, as with equivocation. The several senses of a word used analogically signify different relations to some one thing, as 'healthy', said of urine, indicates health in an animal, and as when it signifies a cause of that health when predicated of medicine.

Hence:

1. Even if it were the case that equivocal predications are based on the univocal, the same cannot be true when it comes to agent causation. A non-univocal efficient cause is causal with respect to an entire species – as the sun accounts for there being any people. A univocal cause, on the other hand, cannot be the universal cause of the whole species (otherwise it would be the cause of itself, since it is a member of that same species) but is the particular cause that this or that individual should be a member of the species. So, a universal cause, which must be prior to a particular cause, is non-univocal. Such a cause, however, is not wholly equivocal even though it is not univocal, for then there would be absolutely no resemblance between it and its effects. We could call it an analogical cause, and this would be parallel to the case of speech, for all univocal predications are based on one non-univocal, analogical predicate, that of being.

2. The resemblance of creatures to God is an imperfect one, for as I have said, they do not even share a common genus.[30]

3. God is not a measure proportionate to what is measured. So, it does not follow that he and his creatures belong to the same order.

The two arguments in the contrary sense do show that words are not used univocally of God and creatures. But they do not show that they are used equivocally.

Article 6: Do we predicate words primarily of God or of creatures?

1. It seems that the words we use of God apply primarily to creatures. For we speak of things as we know them since, as Aristotle says, words are signs for things as understood.[31] But we know creatures before we know God. So, our words apply to creatures before they apply to God.

2. Dionysius says that 'the language we use about God is derived from what we say about creatures'.[32] But when a word such as 'lion' or 'rock' is transferred from a creature to God it is used first of the creature. So, such words apply primarily to a creature.

3. Words used of both God and creatures are used of him in that he is the cause of all things, as Dionysius says.[33] But what we say of something in a causal sense applies to it only secondarily – as 'healthy' applies primarily to a living animal and only secondarily to the medicine that causes its health. So, we apply such words primarily to creatures.

On the contrary, we read in Ephesians, 'I bend my knees to the Father of our Lord Jesus, from whom all fatherhood in heaven and on earth is named';[34] and the same seems to apply to other words used of God and creatures. So, we use these words primarily of God.

Reply: Whenever a word is used analogically of many things, it is used of them because of some order or relation they have to some central thing.[35] In order to explain an extended or analogical use of a word it is necessary to mention this central thing. Thus you cannot explain what you mean by 'healthy' medicine without mentioning the health of the animal of which it is the cause. Similarly you must understand 'healthy' as applied to an

---

[30] 1a 4.3.   [31] *On Interpretation* 1.1, 16a3.   [32] *The Divine Names* 1. PG 3.596.
[33] *Mystical Theology* 1. PG 3.1000.   [34] Ephesians 3:14–15.   [35] *Metaphysics* 4.7, 1012a23.

animal before you can understand what is meant by 'healthy urine', which is a symptom of that health. The primary application of the word is to the central thing that has to be understood first. Other applications will be more or less secondary in so far as they approximate to this use.

Thus all words used metaphorically of God apply primarily to creatures and secondarily to God. When we use them of God they signify merely a certain likeness between God and a creature. When we speak metaphorically of a meadow as 'smiling' we only mean that it shows at its best when it flowers, just as people show at their best when they smile: there is a likeness between them. In the same way, if we speak of God as a 'lion', we only mean that, like a lion, he is mighty in his deeds. It is obvious that the meaning of such a word as applied to God depends on and is secondary to the meaning it has when used of creatures.

This would be the case for non-metaphorical words too if they were only used to express God's causality, as some have supposed. If, for example, 'God is good' meant the same as 'God is the cause of goodness in creatures' the word 'good' as applied to God must be defined in terms of what it means when applied to creatures; and hence 'good' would apply primarily to creatures and secondarily to God.

But I have already shown that words of this sort do not only say how God is a cause.[36] They also say what he is essentially. When we say that he is good or wise we do not simply mean that he causes wisdom or goodness, but that he possesses these perfections eminently. So, we should conclude that from the point of view of what the words mean they are used primarily of God and derivatively of creatures, for what the words mean (the perfections they signify) flows from God to creatures. But from the point of view of our use of the words we apply them first to creatures because we know them first. That is why, as I have mentioned already, they have a way of signifying that is appropriate to creatures.[37]

Hence:

1. This is valid so far as our first application of the words is concerned.
2. Words used of God metaphorically are not in the same case as the others, as I have said.[38]

---

[36] 1a 13.2.   [37] 1a 13.3.   [38] See the body of the present article.

3. This objection would be valid if all words were used to express God's causality and not to say what he is, as 'healthy' expresses the causality of a medicine and not what it consists in.

Article 7: In speaking of God, do we use words that imply temporal succession?

1. It seems that we do not apply to God words that imply temporal succession, even when we are speaking of his relation to creatures. It is generally agreed that such words signify what God is in himself. Thus Ambrose says that 'Lord' indicates his power,[39] but this is the divine substance, and 'creation' indicates his action, but this is his essence. God, however, is not temporal but eternal. So, we do not apply these words to him in a temporal sense but as applicable from eternity.

2. Moreover, whatever is true of something in a temporal sense can be said to be made (as, for example, what is white has been made white). But nothing in God is made. So, we say nothing of him in a temporal sense.

3. Moreover, if the reason why we use words of God in a temporal sense were that such words imply a relation to creatures, then the same would be true of every word that implied such a relation. But we apply some of these as from eternity. We say, for example, that God knew and loved creatures from eternity – 'I have loved you with an everlasting love.'[40] So, all other words, such as 'Lord' or 'Creator', are applicable from eternity.

4. Moreover, these words signify a relation, and this must therefore be a reality in God or in the creature alone. It cannot, however, be only in the creature, for if this were so, we would call God 'Lord' in virtue of the opposite relation existing in the creature. But we name nothing from its opposite. The relation, therefore, must be something real in God. Yet, since he is beyond time, it cannot be temporal. So, it seems that we do not use such words of God in a temporal sense.

5. Moreover, we call something relative in virtue of some relationship it has. For instance, we refer to someone as 'lord' because of the lordship he has, just as we call something white because of its whiteness. If, therefore, the relation of lordship were something that God did not

[39] *On Faith* 1.1. *PL* 16.553.   [40] Jeremiah 31:3.

really have but were merely a way of thinking of him, it would follow that God is not truly Lord, which is clearly false.

6. Again, when the two terms of a relationship are not of the same order, one may exist without the other – for example, the knowable can exist without knowledge, as we read in the *Categories*.[41] But in the case of relations between God and creatures, the two terms are not of the same order, and so something could be said relatively of God even though creatures did not exist. In this way words like 'Lord' and 'Creator' can apply to God from eternity and are not used in a temporal sense.

On the contrary, Augustine says that the relative term 'Lord' is applicable to God in a temporal sense.[42]

Reply: Some words that imply a relation to creatures are said of God in a temporal sense and not as applicable from eternity.

In order to explain this we must first say something about relations.

Some have said that being related to something is never a reality in nature – that it is something created by our way of thinking about things. But this is false because some things do have a natural order or relation to others. Since, whenever we can say of *x* that it is related to *y*, we can also say of *y* that it is related to *x*, there are three possibilities here.

Sometimes both what we say of *x* and what we say of *y* is true of them not because of any reality in them, but because they are being thought of in a particular way. When, for instance, we say that something is identical with itself, the two terms of the relation only exist because the mind takes one thing and thinks of it twice, thus treating it as though it has a relation to itself. Similarly, any relation between a thing and nothing is set up by the mind treating 'nothing' as though it were a term. The same is generally true of all relations that are set up as part of our thinking – the relation of *being a species of a certain genus*, for instance.

In the second case both what we say of *x* and what we say of *y* is true of them because of some reality in *x* and *y*. They are related because of something that belongs to both – quantity, for example, as with the relations of *being bigger than* and *being smaller than*, *being double* and *being half*, and so forth. It is the same with the relations that result

---

[41] *Categories* 7, 7b30.   [42] *On the Trinity* 5.16. PL 42.922.

from causal activity as *being what is changed by* and *being what changes*, *being father of* and *being son of*, and so forth.

In the third case the truth about *x* that it is related to *y* is due to something real in *x*, but the truth about *y* that it is related to *x* is not due to anything real in *y*. This happens when *x* and *y* are not of the same order. Take, for example, the relation of *being knowable by* and *knowing* (whether we mean knowledge by the senses or by the mind). When *x* is knowable by *y*, *x* is not in and by itself something knowable. In so far as it exists in its own right it lies outside the order of knowledge. So, while the relation of *knowing x* is a reality in the senses or mind of *y* – for knowing is what makes a real difference to these – *being knowable by y* is not a reality in *x*. Thus Aristotle says that we call some things relative not because they are related to others but because others are related to them.[43] We say that one side of a column is the right side because it is on the right side of some animal; the relation of *being on the right of* is real in the animal but not in the column.

Now, since God is altogether outside the order of creatures (because they are ordered to him but not he to them), it is clear that being related to God is a reality in creatures, but being related to creatures is not a reality in God. We say it about him because of the real relation in creatures. So it is that when we speak of his relation to creatures we can apply words implying temporal sequence and change, not because of any change in him but because of a change in the creatures; just as we can say that a column has changed from being on my left to being on my right, not through any alteration in the column, but simply because I have turned around.

Hence:

1. Some relative words signify a relationship, others signify that on account of which there is a relationship. Thus 'lord' says nothing more about a lord except that he stands in some relationship. To be a lord precisely is to be related to a servant – the same is true of words like 'father', 'son', and so forth. Other relative words, however, such as 'mover' and 'moved', 'head' and 'being headed', signify something on account of which there is a relationship. Some of the words we use of God are of the first kind and some of the second. 'Lord', for

---

[43] *Metaphysics* 5.15, 1021a29.

instance, signifies nothing but a relation to creatures, though it pre-supposes something about what God is, for he could not be lord without his power, which is his essence. Others such as 'Saviour' or 'Creator' which refer directly to God's activity, which is his essence, are of the second kind and signify something on account of which God has a relationship. But we use both sorts of word of him in a temporal sense in so far as they convey expressly or by implication a relation to creatures. We do not predicate them temporally in so far as they signify directly or indirectly the divine essence.

2. Relations that we attribute to God in a temporal sense are not real in him but belong to him as a way of speaking of him and with no real change in him. The same is true of any becoming that we attribute to him – as when we say, 'Lord, you have become a refuge for us.'[44]

3. Thinking is not something we do to other things, but remains within us; and the same is true of willing. So, we apply from eternity expressions signifying relations that ensue from God's thinking and willing. When, however, they signify relations that ensue from acts which, according to our way of thinking about God, proceed from him to external effects, they can be used of him in a temporal sense. This is the case with words like 'Creator' and 'Saviour'.

4. God's temporal relations to creatures are in him only because of our way of thinking of him, but the opposite relations of creatures to him are realities in the creatures. It is quite admissible to attribute a relation to God because of something that takes place in a creature, for we cannot express a reality in creatures without talking as though there were also matching relations in God. So, we say that God is related to a creature because the creature is related to him – just as, according to Aristotle, we say that the knowable is related to know-ledge because knowledge is related to it.[45]

5. God is related to creatures in so far as creatures are related to him. Since the relation of subjection to God is really in the creature, God is really Lord. It is the relationship of lordship in him that is supplied by our minds, not the fact of his being the Lord.

6. When we ask whether the terms of a relation are of the same order or not, we are not asking about the things that are said to be related but about the meaning of the relative words used. If one entails the other,

---

[44] Psalms 89:1.   [45] *Metaphysics* 5.15, 1021a30.

and vice versa, then they are of the same order – as with *being double* and *being half of* or with *being father of* and *being son of*. If, however, one entails the other, but not vice versa, then they are not of the same order. This is the case with *knowing* and *being knowable by*. For *x* to be knowable by *y* it is not necessary that *y* should be knowing *x*; it is sufficient that it should have the power to know *x*. Thus 'being knowable' signifies intelligibility as something prior to actual knowledge. If, however, we take 'being knowable' to mean being actually here and now intelligible, then it coincides with the actual exercise of knowledge, for a thing cannot be so known unless someone is knowing it. In a parallel way, although God is prior to creatures (as being knowable is prior to knowing) since '*x* is lord of *y*' and '*y* is subject to *x*' entail each other, *being lord of* and *being subject to* are of the same order. So, God was not lord until he had a creature subject to him.

Article 8: Is 'God' the name of a nature?

1. It seems that 'God' is not the name of a nature. For Damascene says that 'God' (θεός) is derived from θέειν, which means 'to take care of' or 'to foster all things'; or else from αἴθειν, which means 'to burn' – for our God is a fire burning up all wickedness; or from θεᾶσθαι, which means 'to consider all things'.[46] All the verbs mentioned here signify activity. So, 'God' signifies an activity, not a nature.
2. Moreover, we name things in so far as we know them. But we do not know God's nature. So, the term 'God' cannot signify what that is.

On the contrary, Ambrose says that 'God' is the name of a nature.[47]

Reply: The reason why we use a word to mean something is not always what the word is used to mean. We come to understand what a thing is from its properties or activities, and we often derive our name for the sort of thing something is from some property or activity of it. For example, speakers of Latin derive the word 'rock' (*lapis*) from something it does – hurting the foot (*laedens pedem*). Yet the word 'rock' signifies what a rock is in itself, not what it does. On the other hand, though, we do not name things we know in themselves (e.g. cold, heat, whiteness, and so

---

[46] *On the Orthodox Faith* 1.9. PG 94.835, 838.   [47] *On Faith* 1.1. PL 16.553.

on) from anything else. In their cases the reason why we use the word to mean something is the same as what it is used to mean.

Now, God is not known to us in his own nature, but through his activity or effects; so, as I have said, we can we derive the language we use in speaking of him from these.[48] 'God' is therefore the name of an activity, for it is an activity of God that leads us to use it – the word is derived from his universal providence: everyone who uses the word 'God' has in mind one who cares for all things. Thus Dionysius says, 'the Deity is what watches over all things in perfect providence and goodness'.[49] But, although derived from this activity, the word 'God' is used to signify the divine nature.

Hence:

1. Everything John Damascene says here refers to divine Providence, which is what makes us use the word 'God' in the first place.
2. The meaning of the name we give to something depends on how much of its nature we understand from its properties and effects. Since from its properties we can understand what a stone is in itself, the word 'stone' signifies the nature of the stone as it is in itself. Its meaning is the definition of a stone, in knowing which we know what a stone is; for 'what a word means is the definition'.[50] But from God's effects we do not come to understand what God's nature is in itself, so we do not know what God is. We know him, as I have noted, only as being excellent, as being causal, and as lacking in anything merely creaturely.[51] It is in this way that the word 'God' signifies the divine nature: it is used to mean something that is above all that is, and that is the source of all things and is distinct from them all. This is how those that use it mean it to be used.

Article 9: Is the name 'God' peculiar to God alone?

1. It seems that 'God' is not peculiar to God, but can be used of other things. For whatever shares in what a name signifies can share in the name. But I have just said that 'God' signifies the divine nature,[52] which, according to 2 Peter, is something that can be communicated

---

[48] 1a 13.1.   [49] *The Divine Names* 12. PG 3.969.   [50] *Metaphysics* 4.7, 1012a23.   [51] 1a 12.12.
[52] 1a 13.8.

to others: 'He has bestowed upon us precious and very great promises ... that by this we may become partakers of God's nature.'[53] So, 'God' may be applied to others besides God.

2. Furthermore, only proper names are altogether incommunicable. But 'God' is a common noun, not a proper name, as is clear from the fact that it can be used in the plural, as in the psalm: 'I have said that you are gods.'[54] So, 'God' is applicable to many things.

3. Again, as I have said, the name 'God' is applied to God because of an activity.[55] But other words that we use of God because of his activities (e.g. 'good', 'wise', and the like) are all applicable to many things. So, 'God' is as well.

On the contrary, we read in Wisdom, 'They gave the incommunicable name to sticks and stones',[56] and the reference is to God's name. So, the name 'God' is incommunicable.

Reply: A name may be used of many things in two ways, either properly or by metaphor. It is properly used of many when the whole of what it means belongs to each of them; it is used metaphorically when some part of what it means belongs to each. The word 'lion', for example, properly speaking, applies only to the things that have the nature it signifies, but it is also applied metaphorically to other things that have something of the lion about them. The courageous or the strong can be spoken of in this way as 'lions'.

To understand which names, properly speaking, apply to many things we must first recognize that every form that is instantiated by an individual either is or at least can be thought of as being common to many. Human nature can be thought of, and in fact is, common to many in this way. The nature of the sun, on the other hand, can be thought of as being, but in fact is not, common to many. The reason for this is that the mind understands such natures in abstraction from individual instances; hence whether it be in one individual or in many is irrelevant to our understanding of the nature itself. Given that we understand a nature we can always think of it as being in many instances.

An individual, however, from the very fact of being individual, is divided from all others. Hence a word that is used precisely to signify an individual cannot be applicable to many in fact, nor can it be thought of as applicable to many. It is impossible to think that there could be

---

[53] 2 Peter 1:4.   [54] Psalms 81:6.   [55] 1a 13.8.   [56] Wisdom 14:21.

many of some particular individual. Hence no proper name is properly speaking communicable to many, though it may be communicable through some resemblance – as a man may metaphorically be called 'an Achilles' because he has the bravery of Achilles.

But consider the case of forms which are instantiated not by being the form of an individual, but by themselves (inasmuch as they are subsistent forms). If we understood these as they are in themselves, it would be clear that they are not common to many in fact and also cannot be thought of as being common to many – except perhaps by some sort of resemblance as with individuals. In fact, however, we do not understand such simple self-subsistent forms as they are in themselves. We have to think of them on the model of the composite things that have their forms in matter. For this reason, as I said earlier, we apply to them concrete nouns that signify a nature as instantiated in an individual.[57] Thus the nouns we use to signify simple subsistent natures are grammatically the same as those we use to signify the natures of composite things.

Now, as I have said, we use 'God' to signify the divine nature,[58] and, since this nature cannot have more than one instance,[59] it follows that, from the point of view of what is in fact signified, the word cannot be used of many, though it can mistakenly be thought of as applying to many – rather as someone who mistakenly thought there were many suns would think of 'sun' as applying to many things. Thus we read in Galatians, 'You were slaves to gods who by nature were not gods',[60] and a gloss says, 'not gods by nature but according to the opinion of human beings'.[61]

Nevertheless the word 'God' does have several applications, though not in its full meaning. It is applied metaphorically to things that share something of what it means. Thus 'gods' can mean those who by resembling God share in some way in the divine, as in the psalm: 'I say you shall be gods.'[62]

If, however, a name were given to God, not as signifying his nature but referring to him as something distinct, regarding him as an individual, such a proper name would be altogether incommunicable and in no way applicable to others – perhaps the Tetragrammaton[63] was used in this way among the Hebrews: it would be as though someone were to use the word 'Sun' as a proper name designating this individual.

---

[57] 1a 13.1, *ad* 2.   [58] 1a 13.8.   [59] 1a 11.3.   [60] Galatians 4:8.   [61] Interlinear gloss. *PL* 192.139.
[62] Psalms 81:6.   [63] The four Hebrew letters that spell out God's personal name.

Hence:

1. God's nature can be communicated to others only in the sense that they can share in God's likeness.
2. 'God' is a common noun and not a proper name because it signifies the divine nature in the concrete, though God himself is neither universal nor particular. We do not, however, name things as they are in themselves but as they are to our minds. In fact, the name 'God' is incommunicable, rather as I said of 'Sun'.[64]
3. We apply words like 'good' and 'wise' to God because of the perfections that flow from God to creatures. They do not signify God's nature; rather, they signify these perfections absolutely speaking. So, not only can we think of them as applicable to many things; they actually are so. But we apply the word 'God' to him because of the activity peculiar to him which we constantly experience, and we use it to signify his nature.

Article 10: Is the name 'God' used in the same sense of God, of what shares in divinity and of what is merely supposed to do so?

1. It seems for three reasons that 'God' is used univocally of what has the divine nature, what shares in this nature, and what is supposed to have it. For when we do not have the same meaning for the same word we cannot contradict each other. Equivocation eliminates contradiction. But when Catholics say 'The idol is not God', they contradict pagans who say 'The idol is God.' So, 'God' is being used univocally by both.
2. Furthermore, an idol is supposed to be God, but is not so in fact, just as the enjoyment of the delights of the flesh is supposed to be felicity, but is not so in fact. But the word 'happiness' is used univocally of this supposed happiness and of true happiness. So, 'God' must also be used univocally of the supposed and the real God.
3. Again, words are used univocally if they have the same meaning. But when Catholics say there is one God they understand by 'God' something almighty, to be revered above all things. But pagans

---

[64] See the body of the present article.

mean the same when they say that their idol is God. So, the word is used univocally in the two cases.

On the contrary, what is in the mind is a sort of picture of what is in reality, as *On Interpretation* says.[65] But when we say 'That is an animal', both of a real animal and of one in a picture, we are using the word equivocally. So, 'God' used of the real God and of what is thought to be God is used equivocally. Furthermore, we cannot mean what we do not understand. But pagans do not understand the divine nature. So, when they say, 'The idol is God', they do not mean true divinity. Yet when Catholics say that there is only one God they mean this. So, Catholics and pagans do not use the term 'God' univocally. They predicate it equivocally of the true God and of what is supposed to be God.

Reply: In the three meanings listed above, 'God' is used neither univocally nor equivocally but analogically. When a word is used univocally it has exactly the same meaning in each application. When it is used equivocally it has an entirely different meaning in each case. But when it is used analogically its meaning in one sense is to be explained by reference to its meaning in another sense. Thus to understand why we call accidents 'beings' we have to understand why we call substances beings. Likewise, we need to know what it means for animals to be healthy before we can understand what expressions like 'healthy urine' or 'healthy medicine' mean. For healthy urine indicates a state of health, and healthy medicine makes animals healthy.

It is the same with the case I am now considering. For we have to refer to the use of 'God' as meaning the true God in order to explain its use as applied to things that share in divinity or which are supposed to be gods. When we say that something is a 'god' by sharing in divinity we mean that it shares in the nature of the true God. Similarly, when we say that an idol is a god, we take 'god' to mean something that people suppose to be the true God. So, it is clear that while 'God' is used with different meanings, one of these meanings is involved in all the others and the word is therefore used analogically.

Hence:

1. We say that a word has different uses not because we can use it in different statements but because it has different meanings. Thus 'man'

[65] *On Interpretation* 1, 16a5.

has one meaning and one use whatever it is predicated of, whether truly or falsely. It would be said to have several uses if we meant it to signify different things – if, for instance, one speaker used it to signify a man and another to signify a stone or something else. Thus it is clear that Catholics,[66] when they say that an idol is not God, are contradicting pagans who affirm that it is God, for both are using 'God' to signify the true God. When pagans say 'The idol is God' they are not using 'God' to mean that which is merely supposed to be God. If they were, they would be speaking truly, as Catholics do when they sometimes use the word in that way (cf. 'All the gods of the pagans are demons').[67]

2, 3. We can make the same reply to the second and third objections. For these have to do with the different statements we can make with a word, not with a difference in meaning.

4. As to the fourth argument which takes the opposite point of view: the word 'animal' is not used wholly equivocally of a real animal and an animal in a picture. Aristotle uses the word 'equivocal' in a broad sense to include the analogical;[68] thus he sometimes says that 'being', which is used analogically, is used equivocally of the different categories.

5. Neither Catholics nor pagans understand the nature of God as he is in himself, but both know him as in some way causing creatures, as surpassing them and as set apart from them, as I have said.[69] In this way when pagans say 'The idol is God' they can mean by 'God' just what Catholics mean when they declare, 'The idol is not God.' People who knew nothing whatever about God would not be able to use 'God' at all, except as a word whose meaning they did not know.

Article 11: Is 'The One who Is' the most appropriate name for God?

1. It seems that 'The One who Is' is not the most appropriate name for God. For the name 'God' cannot be shared, as I have said.[70] But 'The One who Is' is a name that can be shared. So, it is not the most appropriate name for God.

---

[66] Aquinas used this to refer to all Western Christians, and in this particular use it might simply refer to Christians.
[67] Psalms 95:5.   [68] *Categories* 1, 1a1.   [69] 1a 12.12.   [70] 1a 13.9.

2. Dionysius says, 'To call God good is to show forth all that flows from him.'[71] But what is supremely characteristic of God is to be the source of all things. So, the most appropriate name for God is 'The Good' rather than 'The One who Is'.

3. Every name of God seems to imply a relation to creatures – for we only know God from creatures. But 'The One who Is' implies no such relation. So, it is not the most appropriate name for God.

On the contrary, we read in Exodus that when Moses asked, 'If they ask me, "What is his name?" what shall I say to them?', the Lord replied, 'Say this to them, "The One who Is has sent me to you."'[72] So, 'The One who Is' is the most appropriate name for God.

Reply: There are three reasons for regarding 'The One who Is' as the most appropriate name for God.

First, because of its meaning; for it does not signify any particular form, but existence itself. Since the existence of God is his essence, and since this is true of nothing else (as I have shown),[73] it is clear that this name is especially fitting for God, for we name everything by its form.

Second, because of its universality. All other names are either less general or, if not, they at least add some nuance of meaning which restricts and determines the original sense. In this life our minds cannot grasp what God is in himself; whatever way we have of thinking of him is a way of failing to understand him as he really is. So, the less determinate our names are, and the more general and simple they are, the more appropriately do we apply them to God. That is why Damascene says, 'The first of all names used of God is "The One who Is", for he comprehends all in himself, he has his existence as an ocean of being, infinite and unlimited.'[74] Any other name selects some particular aspect of the being of the thing, but 'The One who Is' fixes on no aspect of being but stands open to all and refers to God as to an infinite ocean of being.

Third, 'The One who Is' is the best name for God because of its tense. For it signifies being in the present, and it is especially appropriate to predicate this of God – for his being knows neither past nor future, as Augustine says.[75]

---

[71] *The Divine Names* 3. *PG* 3.680.   [72] Exodus 3:13 and 14.   [73] 1a 3.4.
[74] *On the Orthodox Faith* 1.9. *PG* 94.836.   [75] *On the Trinity* 5.2. *PL* 42.912.

Hence:

1. 'The One who Is' is more appropriate than 'God' because of what makes us use the name in the first place, that is, his existence, because of the unrestricted way in which it signifies him, and because of its tense, as I have just said.[76] But when we consider what we use the word to mean, we must admit that 'God' is more appropriate, for we use this to signify the divine nature. Even more appropriate is the Tetragrammaton which is used to signify the incommunicable and, if we could say such a thing, the individual substance of God.

2. 'The Good' is a more fundamental name for God in so far as he is a cause. But it is not more fundamental simply speaking, for to be comes before being a cause.

3. God's names need not necessarily imply a relation to creatures. It is enough that they should come to be used because of the perfections that flow from God to creatures, and of these the primary one is existence itself, from which we get the name 'The One who Is'.

Article 12: Can we formulate affirmative propositions about God?

1. It seems that we cannot formulate affirmative propositions about God. For Dionysius says, 'Negative propositions about God are true, but affirmative ones are vague.'[77]

2. Moreover, Boethius says, 'A simple form cannot be a subject.'[78] But God is a simple form to the highest degree, as I have already shown.[79] So, he cannot be a subject. But affirmative propositions are about their subjects. So, we cannot formulate such propositions about God.

3. Again, we fall into error when we understand something as different from the way it is. Now God is altogether without composition in his being, as I have proved.[80] So, since every affirmative act of the intellect understands an object as composite, it would seem that we cannot truly formulate affirmative propositions about God.

On the contrary, what is of faith cannot be false. But some affirmative propositions are matters of faith, as, for example, that God is three and

---

[76] See the body of the present article.   [77] *The Celestial Hierarchy* 2. PG 3.140.
[78] *On the Trinity* 2. PL 64.1250.   [79] 1a 3.7.   [80] 1a 3.7.

one, and that he is almighty. So, we can formulate true affirmative propositions about God.

Reply: In every true affirmative proposition, although the subject and predicate signify what is in fact in some way the same thing, they do so from different points of view. This is so both in propositions that express an accidental predication and in those that express an essential predication. After all, in 'The man is a white thing' it is clear that 'man' and 'white thing' refer to the same object but differ in meaning, since what it is to be a man is not the same as what it is to be a white thing. But it is also true for a statement such as 'human beings are animals'. That which is human is truly an animal: in one and the same thing we find the sensitive nature because of which we call it an animal and the rational nature because of which we call it a human being.

There is even a difference in point of view between subject and predicate when they have the same meaning, for when we put a term in the subject place we think of it as referring to something, whereas in the predicate place we think of it as saying something about the thing, in accordance with the saying 'we understand predicates formally (as meaning a form), and we understand subjects materially (as referring to what has the form)'.

The difference between subject and predicate represents two ways of looking at a thing, while the fact that they are put together affirmatively indicates that it is one thing that is being looked at. Now, God, considered in himself, is altogether one and simple, yet we think of him through a number of different concepts because we cannot see him as he is in himself.

But although we think of him in these different ways we also know that to each corresponds a single simplicity that is one and the same for all. We represent the different ways of thinking of God in the difference of subject and predicate. We represent his unity by bringing them together in an affirmative statement.

Hence:

1. Dionysius says that what we assert of God is vague (or, according to another translation, 'incongruous') because no word used of God is appropriate to him in its way of signifying, as I have observed.[81]

---

[81] 1a 13.6.

2. Our minds cannot understand subsisting simple forms as they are in themselves. We understand them in the way that we understand composite things, in which there is the subject of a form and something that exists in that subject. And so we apprehend a simple form as if it were a subject, and we attribute something to it.

3. In the sentence, 'We fall into error when we understand something as different from the way it is', 'different from' can refer either to the thing understood or the way of understanding. Taken in the former sense the proposition means that we are mistaken when we understand something to be different from what it is. That is true, but it is irrelevant when it comes to our present concern, for when we formulate propositions about God we do not say that he has any composition. We understand him to be simple. But if we take 'different from' to apply to the way of understanding, then the proposition is false, for the way of understanding is always different from the way the thing understood is. It is clear, for example, that our minds non-materially understand material things inferior to them; not that they understand them to be non-material, but that we have a non-material way of understanding. Similarly when our minds understand simple things superior to them we understand them in our own way, that is on the model of composite things; not that we understand the simple things to be composite, but that composition is involved in our way of understanding them. So, the fact that our statements about God are composite does not make them false.

Question 14

God's knowledge

Foreword

Having considered God's substance, I next need to consider its operations. Now, there are two kinds of operation: one that remains in an agent, and another that goes out to produce an external effect. So, I shall first begin by treating of God's knowledge and will – for knowing is in the person who knows, and willing in the person who wills. Then I shall deal with God's power, which I consider to be the principle of divine operation going out to produce an external effect. Since knowing is a kind of living, after considering God's knowledge I shall have to consider God's life. Since knowledge is of what is true, I shall also need to treat of truth and falsity. Again, since all that is known is in the knower, and since the intelligible natures of things as they exist in God's knowledge are called Ideas, my treatment of God's knowledge will also need to include a consideration of God's Ideas.

There are sixteen points of inquiry concerning God's knowledge:

1. Is there knowledge in God?
2. Does God understand himself?
3. Does God have comprehensive knowledge of himself?
4. Is God's very understanding his substance?
5. Does he know things other than himself?
6. Does he know such things specifically?
7. Is God's knowledge discursive?
8. Is God's knowledge the cause of things?
9. Does God know non-existent things?

10. Does he know evils?
11. Does his knowledge extend to individuals?
12. Does he know infinites?
13. Does he know contingent future events?
14. Does he know propositions?
15. Is his knowledge changeable?
16. Is his knowledge of things theoretical or practical?

Article 1: Is there knowledge in God?

1. It would seem that there is no knowledge in God. For knowledge is a disposition, which God cannot have since a disposition is intermediate between potentiality and actuality. So, there is no knowledge in God.
2. Moreover, since knowledge is of conclusions, it is a kind of cognition caused by something else, namely from knowing principles. But in God there is nothing caused. So, there is no knowledge in God.
3. Again, all knowledge is either universal or particular. But in God there is no universal and particular, as is clear from what I said above.[1] So, there is no knowledge in God.

On the contrary, St Paul says, 'O the depth of the riches of the wisdom and knowledge of God.'[2]

Reply: God has knowledge in the most perfect way. This will become evident if we note that the difference between knowing and non-knowing subjects is that the latter have nothing but their own form, whereas a knowing subject is one whose nature it is to have in addition the form of something else; for a species[3] of the thing known is in the knower. Thus, clearly, the nature of a non-knowing subject is more confined and limited by comparison with knowing subjects. The latter have a greater scope and extension. Hence Aristotle says that 'the soul is in a manner all things'.[4] Now, form is limited by matter, which is why I said above that the freer forms are from matter the more they approach to a kind of

---

[1] 1a 13.9, *ad* 2.   [2] Romans 11:33.
[3] Representation. Aquinas speaks as if having a representation of a thing's form in one's mind amounts to having that form itself in one's mind.
[4] *On the Soul* 3.8, 431b21.

infinity.[5] So, it is clear that something's freedom from matter is the reason why it is able to know, and the capacity to know is in proportion to the degree of freedom from matter. Thus we say that plants have no knowledge because of their materiality.[6] But the senses can know because they can receive the species of things without the matter. Intellect is still more capable of knowing because it is freer from matter and unmixed, as we read in Aristotle.[7] So, since God is immaterial in the highest degree, as is clear from what I have said,[8] it follows that he has knowledge in the highest degree.

Hence:

1. As I have said, the perfections which go out from God into creatures are in God in a higher way.[9] So, whenever we attribute to God a description taken from any perfection of a creature we must eliminate from its meaning all that pertains to the imperfect way in which we find it in the creature. So, knowledge in God is not a quality, nor an habitual capacity, but substance and pure actuality.

2. As I have said, what exists in creatures divided and multiplied exists in God as undivided and unified.[10] Now, in people different objects of knowledge imply different kinds of knowledge: in knowing principles we speak of ourselves having 'understanding', in knowing conclusions 'science', in knowing the highest cause 'wisdom', in knowing human actions 'counsel' or 'prudence'. But God knows all these things by one simple cognition, as I shall show later.[11] So, we can call God's simple knowledge by all these names, provided that in using any of them of God we exclude from their meaning all that implies imperfection and retain only what implies perfection. Hence we read: 'With him is wisdom and strength; he has counsel and understanding.'[12]

3. Knowledge depends on the capacity of knowers; for what is known is in knowers according to the measure of their capacity. Now, since God's nature exists in a manner higher than that by which creatures exist, his knowledge does not exist in him in the manner of created knowledge, so as to be universal or particular, or to be habitual or potential, or to be similarly qualified.

---

[5] 1a 7.1 and 2.   [6] *On the Soul* 2.12, 424a32.   [7] *On the Soul* 3.4, 429a18.   [8] 1a 7.1.   [9] 1a 4.2.
[10] 1a 13.4.   [11] 1a 14.7.   [12] Job 12:13.

Article 2: Does God understand himself?

1. It seems that God does not understand himself. For the *Book of Causes* says that 'all knowers who know their own essence are in the condition of returning on their essence by a complete returning'.[13] But God does not go forth outside his essence, nor is he moved in any way. It is therefore impossible for him to return to his essence. So, he does not understand himself.

2. Moreover, to understand is a kind of passivity and movement, as Aristotle states,[14] and knowledge is an assimilation to the thing known. Also, something as known is a perfecting of the knower. But nothing is moved or is passive or is perfected under its own agency. As Hilary says, 'something is not its own likeness'.[15] So, God does not know himself.

3. Again, our likeness to God is chiefly in our intellect. As Augustine says, it is in our mind that we are made in God's image.[16] But, as we read in Aristotle, our intellect does not understand itself except as it understands other things.[17] So, God does not understand himself – except, perhaps, in understanding other things.

On the contrary, St Paul says, 'Only the Spirit of God knows the things of God.'[18]

Reply: God knows himself through himself. This will become evident if we note that whereas in activities which produce an external effect the object of the activity (its end or terminus) is something outside the agent, in activities which take place in an agent the object which is the end of the activity lies in the agent itself. The object in the agent is the activity actually taking place. Thus we find Aristotle saying that the actualization of what is sensible is the senses while they are active, and the actualization of what is intelligible is the intellect while it is active.[19] We have actual sensation or actual knowledge because our intellect or senses are informed by the species of a sensible or intelligible object. Sense or intellect is different from the sensible or intelligible only to the extent that the latter are in a state of potentiality.

---

[13] *Book of Causes* 15.   [14] *On the Soul* 3.4, 429b24; 3.7, 431a6.   [15] *On the Trinity* 3.23. *PL* 10.92.
[16] *On the Literal Interpretation of 'Genesis'* 6.12. *PL* 34.348; *On the Trinity* 15.1. *PL* 42.1057.
[17] *On the Soul* 3.4, 430a2.   [18] 1 Corinthians 2:2.   [19] *On the Soul* 3.2, 426a16; 3.4, 430a16.

So, since God has no potentiality, but is pure actuality, intellect and what is known must be identical in every way in him. He would therefore never lack an intelligible species, as our intellect does when it is only potentially knowing. Nor would an intelligible species be different in him from the substance of his intellect, though in us the intelligible species is different from the substance of our intellect when we are actually knowing. In God, though, the intelligible species is God's very intellect. So, he understands himself through himself.

Hence:

1. For a thing to 'return on its own essence' is simply for it to be self-subsistent. A form, when it perfects matter by giving it existence, in a certain sense spreads itself out over the matter. But in so far as it has existence in itself, it returns on itself. So, those powers of knowing which are not subsistent but are the acts of certain organs, do not know themselves, as is clear in the case of each of the senses. But powers of knowing which are subsistent do know themselves. Hence the statement in the *Book of Causes* that 'knowers who know their own essence return upon their own essence'. But to be self-subsistent belongs to God in the highest degree. So, if we use that manner of speaking, he 'returns to his own essence' and knows himself, in the highest degree.

2. When we call the act of understanding a kind of movement or passivity, we use the expressions 'to move' and 'to be passive' equivocally, as Aristotle says.[20] For the act of knowing is not a movement in the sense of an actualization of something incompletely actualized and passing from one subject to another. It is the act of something completely actualized, taking place within the agent itself. Similarly, for an intellect to be perfected by what is intelligible, or assimilated to it, is proper to an intellect which is at some time in a state of potentiality. For in being potential itself, it differs from the intelligible, and is assimilated to it by the intelligible species which is the likeness of the thing known, and the intellect is completed by it as a potency that is actualized. But God's intellect, which is in no way potential, is not completed by the intelligible, nor assimilated to it. It is its own completeness and its own intelligible object.

---

[20] *On the Soul* 3.4, 429b24; 3.7, 431a6.

3. Existence in nature does not belong to prime matter, which of itself is potential, except in so far as it is brought to actuality by a form. Now, our passive intellect has, in the order of knowing, the same condition as that of prime matter in the order of natural things. It is potentially able to receive intelligible forms as prime matter is potentially able to receive natural forms. So, our passive intellect can have an activity which it can know only when it is perfected by the intelligible species of something. In that way it knows itself through an intelligible species, as it does other things: for in knowing the intelligible it obviously knows its own act of knowing, and knows the power of knowing through the act of knowing. But God's condition is that of pure actuality, both in the order of existence and in that of knowledge. So, he knows himself through himself.

Article 3: Does God have comprehensive knowledge of himself?

1. It seems that God does not have comprehensive knowledge of himself. For Augustine says that 'that which comprehends itself is finite to itself'.[21] But God is in all ways infinite. So, God does not have comprehensive knowledge of himself.
2. Moreover, if someone were to say that God is infinite to us but finite to himself, we could reply that everything is truer with God than it is with us. So, if God is finite to himself but infinite to us, it is truer to say that God is finite than that he is infinite, which is contrary to what I have already said.[22] So, God does not have comprehensive knowledge of himself.

On the contrary, we have Augustine's words in the same work: 'Everything that knows itself comprehends itself.'[23] But God knows himself. So, he comprehends himself.

Reply: God comprehends himself perfectly, as the following line of thought makes clear. We say that we comprehend something when our knowledge of it can go no further, that is, when we know it as completely as it is knowable. For example, we comprehensively know a demonstrable

---

[21] *On Eighty-Three Varied Questions* 1.15. PL 40.14. [22] 1a 7.1.
[23] *On Eighty-Three Varied Questions* 1.15. PL 40.14.

proposition when we know it through demonstration, but not when we know it through some merely probable reason. Now, it is evident that God knows himself as fully as he is fully knowable. But something is knowable in proportion to its actuality. As we read in the *Metaphysics*, something is known as actual, not as potential.[24] But God's power to know is equal to his actuality in existence. For his power to know comes from his actuality, his freedom from all matter and potentiality, as I have shown.[25] Clearly, then, God knows himself to the extent to which he is knowable. So, he comprehends himself perfectly.

Hence:

1. Strictly speaking, 'to comprehend' means 'to hold or enclose something else'. Taken in that sense, all that is comprehended must be finite, as all that is enclosed must be. Yet in saying that God is comprehended by himself we do not mean that his intellect is other than himself, and holds or encloses himself. We should explain such expressions negatively. Thus we say that God is 'in himself' because he is not contained by anything outside himself. Similarly, we say that he is comprehended by himself because there is no part of himself that escapes him. We may quote Augustine: 'The whole is comprehended by vision when it is seen in such a way that no part of it escapes the one who sees.'[26]

2. We should understand 'God is finite to himself' by a proportional comparison. Just as something finite does not exceed a finite intellect, so God does not exceed his intellect. But we do not say that God is 'finite to himself' so as to mean that he knows that he is finite.

Article 4: Is God's very understanding his substance?

1. It seems that God's very understanding is not his substance. For understanding is an activity of some sort. But an activity is something proceeding *from* an agent. So, God's very understanding is not his very substance.

2. Moreover, to know that one knows is not to understand anything important or anything which counts as a primary object of knowledge. It is to understand something secondary and accessory. So, if God is

---

[24] *Metaphysics* 9.9, 1051a31.   [25] 1a 14.1.   [26] Letter 147.9. *PL* 33.605.

his understanding, this understanding will be the same as it is in ourselves when we understand ourselves and will not, therefore, be something important.

3. Again, all understanding is the understanding of something. So, when God understands himself, and if he is identical with his understanding, he understands himself understanding himself understanding, and so on without end. So, God's understanding is not his substance.

On the contrary, Augustine says, 'To be and to be wise are the same in God.'[27] But to be wise is the same as to understand. Therefore, to be and to understand are the same in God. But God's being is his substance, as I have shown.[28] So, God's understanding is his substance.

Reply: We must hold that God's understanding is his substance. For, as Aristotle says, if it were other than his substance,[29] it would follow that something other would be the actuation and completion of God's substance, and we should have the altogether impossible conclusion that God's substance would stand to it as potency to act – for understanding is a perfection and actuality in those who understand.

Yet how is this so? As I have said, understanding is not an action that goes out to something external.[30] It remains in an agent as its actuality and perfection (just as existing perfects things that exist). For as form brings existence, so the intelligible species brings understanding. Now, in God there is no form distinct from his existence, as I have shown above.[31] So, since his essence is also the intelligible species, as I have said,[32] it necessarily follows that understanding is his essence and his being.

So, it is clear from all that I have said that in God intellect, and that which is known, and the knowledge-species, and understanding, are entirely one and the same. Clearly, then, to say God understands is not to posit any multiplicity in his substance.

Hence:

1. Understanding is not an activity going out from an agent. It remains in it.

2. To understand an understanding that is not subsistent (as when we understand our understanding) is not to know something of first

[27] *On the Trinity* 7.2. *PL* 42.936.   [28] 1a 3.4.   [29] *Metaphysics* 12.9, 1074b18.
[30] 1a 14.2.   [31] 1a 3.4.   [32] 1a 14.2.

importance. So, the case is not parallel with God's understanding, which is subsistent.

And from this it is clear what needs to be said in reply to the third objection. For God's understanding, which is self-subsistent, is an understanding of itself, not an understanding of something else, which is what it would have to be for an endless regress to loom.

Article 5: Does God know things other than himself?

1. It seems that God does not know things other than himself. For everything other than God is external to him. But Augustine says that 'God does not behold anything external to himself.'[33] So, he does not know things other than himself.
2. Moreover, something understood perfects the one who understands. So, if God knew things other than himself, something else would perfect him and be of greater worth than he is, which is impossible.
3. Again, understanding gets its specific content from an intelligible object, as every other act gets its specific content from its object. So, the excellence of understanding is in proportion to that of the object known. But God is his own act of knowing, as is clear from what I have said.[34] So, if God knew something other than himself, he would receive a specific characteristic from something different from himself, which is impossible. So, he does not know things other than himself.

On the contrary, the letter to the Hebrews says, 'All things are naked and open to his eyes.'[35]

Reply: God must know things other than himself. For he evidently understands himself perfectly: otherwise his existing would not be perfect, since his existing is his understanding. But if something is known perfectly, its power must be known perfectly. Now the power of a thing cannot be known perfectly unless the objects to which the power extends are known. Hence, since God's power extends to other things by being the first efficient cause which produces all beings, as is clear from what I have said,[36] God must know things other than himself. This will be still more evident if we add that the very being of God, the first efficient

---

[33] *On Eighty-Three Varied Questions* 1.46. *PL* 40.30.   [34] 1a 14.4.   [35] Hebrews 4:13.   [36] 1a 2.3.

cause, is his act of knowing. So, whatever effects pre-exist in God as in the first cause must be in his understanding; and everything there must be in the condition of intelligibility. For all that is in another is there according to the condition of that in which it is.

To grasp in what way God knows things other than himself we must note that we know something in two ways: in itself, or in another. We know something in itself when we know it through a species adequate to the thing itself, coterminous with the thing known, as when our eyes see someone through the species of that person. We see something in another when we see it through the species of what contains it, as when we see a part in a whole through the species of the whole, or as when we see someone in a mirror through the species of the mirror, and so of other ways in which we know one thing in another.

So, we must say that God sees himself in himself, because he sees himself through his essence. He sees things other than himself not in themselves but in himself, because his essence contains the likeness of things other than himself.

Hence:

1. When Augustine says that God 'does not behold anything external to himself' we should not understand him as meaning, strictly speaking, that God does not behold anything external to himself, but as meaning that he beholds what is external to himself only in himself, as I have said.

2. It is not the substance of something known that perfects a knower, but its species, by which it is in the intellect as a form and perfection. As Aristotle says, 'a stone is not in the soul; its species is'.[37] God knows things other than himself because his essence contains their species, as I have said. So, it does not follow that something other than God's essence perfects his intellect.

3. We do not specify understanding itself by what we understand in something else. We do so by the primary object understood, in which we understand other things. The proper object of understanding specifies understanding itself inasmuch as intelligible form is a source of understanding. For every activity is specified by the form which is the source of the activity, as heating is by heat. So, intellectual activity

---

[37] *On the Soul* 3.8, 431b29.

is specified by the intelligible form which makes the intellect to be actually knowing. And this form is the species of the principal object known – which, in God, is nothing other than his essence, which contains all the species of things. So, there is no need for God's understanding, or rather God himself, to be specified by anything other than his essence.

Article 6: Does God know things other than himself specifically?

1. It seems that God does not know things other than himself specifically. For, as I have said, he knows things other than himself as they exist in himself.[38] But things other than God exist in him as in their first common and universal cause. But to know in that way is to know in a universal way, not specifically. So, God knows things other than himself universally and not specifically.
2. Moreover, God's essence is as far removed from a creature's essence as a creature's essence is from God's essence. But, as I have said, God's essence cannot be known through a creature's essence.[39] So, neither can a creature's essence be known through God's essence. Therefore, since God knows nothing except through his essence, it follows that he does not know any creature in its essence so as to know *what it is* (i.e. so as to have specific knowledge of something).
3. Again, something is known for what it is only through its own proper idea. But since God knows everything through his essence, it does not seem that he knows everything through its own proper idea. For one and the same thing cannot be the idea proper to many and different things. So, God does not know things specifically.

On the contrary, to know things specifically is to know them, not merely in what they have in common, but in their differences from each other, and that is how God knows things. So Hebrews says that God 'reaches to the division of the soul and the spirit, of the joints also and the marrow: and he discerns the thoughts and intentions of the heart. Nor is any creature invisible to him.'[40]

[38] 1a 14.5.   [39] 1a 12.2.   [40] Hebrews 4:12–13.

Reply: On this point some have been mistaken, holding that God knows things other than himself only through a common idea, namely, in so far as they are beings. They would say that, just as fire, if it knew itself as the cause of heat, would know the nature of heat and all other things in so far as they are hot, so God, in so far as he knows himself as the cause of being, knows the nature of being and of all other things in so far as they are beings.

This, however, cannot be so. For to know something generically and not specifically is to know it imperfectly. Hence our intellect, in passing from potentiality to actuality, attains first to a universal and confused knowledge of things, then to a knowledge of what is proper to each, thereby passing from incomplete to complete knowledge (as Aristotle makes clear in the *Physics*).[41] So, if God's knowledge of other things were merely universal and not specific, it would follow that his act of knowledge (and consequently his existence also) would not be in every way perfect, which is contrary to what I have already shown.[42] So, we have to say that God knows things other than himself in what is proper to each – not only in what they have in common as beings, but in the ways in which they differ from each other.

To make this point clear we should realize that some authors, intending to show that God knows many things through one thing, make use of certain comparisons: for example, if the centre knew itself, it would know all the lines that start from the centre; or, if light knew itself, it would know all colours. But though these comparisons bear some likeness to part of the situation (in that they illustrate God's universal causality), they fail to show how plurality and diversity are produced by the single universal principle considered as the principle of distinctiveness in things, not merely of what they share in common. For differences of colour are not only caused by light but also by differences in the state of the transparent medium that receives light. There are different lines because they have different positions. So, in these cases knowledge of their source does not give specific knowledge of the diversity and plurality of things. It only provides a general knowledge.

This is not so when it comes to God, however. I have already shown that all that makes for perfection in creatures is first of all in God, and is contained in him to an eminent degree.[43] But the perfection of creatures

---

[41] *Physics* I.1, 184a22.   [42] 1a 4.1.   [43] 1a 4.2.

is not merely a matter of what they have in common (i.e. existence) but of what they have as distinct from each other (e.g. life, understanding and other such qualities which distinguish living and non-living things, and things with intellect and those without it). In fact, every form giving a thing its own specific characteristics is a perfection. So, all things are to be found first in God, not only as regards what they have in common, but also as regards what they all have as distinct from one another. So, since God contains all perfections, his essence stands to all the essences of things not as what is common to what is special to each, in the way that a unit stands to numbers or a centre to lines, but as complete actuality stands to incomplete actualities – as, so we might say, human beings stand to animals, or as the number six (a perfect number) stands to the imperfect numbers contained within it. Now it is clear that through the complete actuality it is possible to know incomplete actualities not only in general but also specifically. Thus to know human beings is to know what is proper to animals; and to know the number six is to know what is proper to the number three.

Therefore, since the essence of God contains all that makes for perfection in the essence of every other thing, and more besides, God can know all things in himself with a knowledge of what is proper to each. For the nature proper to each thing consists in its participation in the divine perfection in some degree. But God would not perfectly know himself if he did not know all the ways in which his perfection can be shared by other things. Nor would he perfectly know the nature of existence if he did not know all its degrees. So, it is clear that God knows all things when it comes to what is proper to each, and when it comes to what makes them different from each other.

Hence:

1. To know something 'as it is in the knower' can be understood in two ways: (i) with 'as' referring to the way the thing as known is in the knower. Taken thus it is false. For a knower does not always know something known as it exists in a knower. An eye, for example, does not know a stone as it exists in it. Rather, through the species of the stone that it has in itself, the eye knows the stone as it exists outside the eye. And if people do know the known object as it exists in knowers, they still know it as it exists outside knowers. So, the intellect, in knowing that it is knowing a stone, knows the stone in the intelligible

existence it has in the intellect; but it still knows the existence which the stone has in its own nature. (ii) But if we take 'as' to refer to a knower's manner of knowing, it is true that a knower knows the thing known only as it is in a knower; because the more perfectly something known is in a knower, the more perfect the degree of knowledge. So, we must say that God does not merely know that things are in himself. We should say that, from the fact that he contains things in himself, he knows them in their own proper natures – and all the more perfectly because of the more perfect way in which they each exist in him.

2. A creature's essence stands to God's essence as imperfect to perfect actuality. So, a creature's essence is insufficient to lead us to a knowledge of God's essence. Quite the contrary.

3. Nothing is conceptually on a level with things that are different from it. But God's essence is greater than all creatures. So, we can think of it as the idea proper to each thing, in so far as different creatures can participate in it or imitate it in different ways.

Article 7: Is God's knowledge discursive?

1. It seems that God's knowledge is discursive. For God's knowing is not a matter of being able to call up knowledge but of actually knowing. But according to Aristotle the condition of being able to call up knowledge covers many objects at the same time, while actual knowledge covers only one object.[44] So, since God knows many things – both himself and other things, as I have shown[45] – it seems that he does not know everything at once, but passes from one object to another.

2. Moreover, to know an effect through a cause amounts to discursive knowledge. But God knows other things through himself, as effect through cause. So, his knowledge is discursive.

3. Again, God knows every creature more completely than we do. But we know created effects in created causes, and thus pass discursively from causes to effects. So, it would seem that God does likewise.

On the contrary, Augustine says that God 'sees all things not piecemeal or one at a time, as though turning his gaze this way and that; he sees them all at once'.[46]

---

[44] *Topics* 2.10, 114b34.   [45] 1a 14.2 and 5.   [46] *On the Trinity* 15.14. *PL* 42.1077.

Reply: There is no discursiveness in God's knowledge. This is clear from the consideration that in our knowledge there is a twofold discursiveness: (i) that of mere succession, as when after actually knowing one thing we turn to another thing; (ii) the discursiveness that involves causality, as when we come to know conclusions through principles. The first of these cannot be in God. We know a number of things successively when taken one at a time, which we know all at once if we know them in a unity. Thus we can know the parts in the whole, or see different things in a mirror. But God sees everything in one, that is, in himself, as I have concluded.[47] So, he sees everything at once, not successively. Similarly the second kind of discursiveness cannot be in God. First, because the second kind presupposes the first, for when we pass from principles to conclusions we are not considering both at the same time. Second, because this kind of discursiveness passes from known to unknown. So, it is clear that when we know the first we are still ignorant of the second. Thus we do not know the second *in* the first, but *from* the first. And the process comes to an end when the second *is* seen in the first and the effects are found in their causes, at which point the discursive process ceases. So, since God sees his effects in himself as in their cause, his knowledge is not discursive.

Hence:

1. Although understanding in itself is of something single, it is still possible to know many things in one thing, as I have said.
2. God does not know through a cause in such a way that the cause is known first and the effects are unknown. He knows the effects in the cause. So, his knowledge is not discursive, as I have said.[48]
3. God sees the effects of created causes in the causes much better than we do; but not in such a way that knowledge of created causes brings about knowledge of effects in him, as is the case with us. So, his knowledge is not discursive.

Article 8: Is God's knowledge the cause of things?

1. It seems that God's knowledge is not the cause of things. For Origen says, 'Something will not happen in the future because God knows it

---

[47] 1a 14.5.   [48] See the body of the present article.

will happen, but God knows it before it happens because it is going to happen.'[49]

2. Moreover, to posit a cause is to posit its effect. But God's knowledge is eternal. So, if God's knowledge is the cause of created things, it would seem that creatures exist from eternity.

3. Again, the knowable is prior to knowledge and is its measure, as we read in the *Metaphysics*.[50] But nothing posterior and measured can be a cause. So, God's knowledge is not the cause of things.

On the contrary, Augustine says, 'God does not know all creatures (spiritual and corporeal) because they exist; they exist because he knows them.'[51]

Reply: God's knowledge is the cause of things. For God's knowledge stands to all created things as the knowledge of artists stands to what they produce. But the knowledge of artists is the cause of their products because they work through their intellects. So, the form in their intellects must be the principle of their activity, as heat is the principle of heating. But we may note that a natural form, merely as the form remaining in the thing to which it gives existence, does not indicate a principle of activity. It does so only in so far as it has an inclination towards producing an effect. Similarly, an intelligible form does not indicate a principle of activity merely as it is in the knower unless it is accompanied by an inclination, supplied by the will, towards producing an effect. An intelligible form is indifferent to opposite courses, since one and the same knowledge covers contraries. So, a form would not produce a determined effect if it were not determined to one course by desire, as we read in the *Metaphysics*.[52] Now, it is clear that God causes things through his intellect, since his existence is his act of knowing. So, his knowledge must be the cause of things when regarded in conjunction with his will. Hence it is that God's knowledge as the cause of things has come to be called the 'knowledge of approbation'. Hence:

1. Origen in the passage quoted is taking knowledge in the sense in which, as I have said, it is not formally a cause except in conjunction with the will. We should understand his saying that God foreknows certain things because they are going to happen with reference to the

---

[49] Origen (*c.* 185–*c.* 253), *Commentary on the Letter to the Romans* 7. PG 14.1126.
[50] *Metaphysics* 10.1, 1053a33.   [51] *On the Trinity* 15.13. PL 42.1076; 6.10. PL 42.931.
[52] *Metaphysics* 9.5, 1048a11.

causality of logical consequence, not the causality which produces existence. For it follows logically that if certain events are going to happen, God foreknows them. But the events that are going to happen are not themselves the cause of God's knowledge.

2. Knowledge is the cause of things in accordance with the way things are in the knowledge. But it was no part of God's knowledge that things should exist from eternity. So, although God's knowledge is eternal, it does not follow that creatures exist from eternity.

3. Natural things mediate between God's knowledge and ours; for we get our knowledge from natural things, of which God is the cause through his knowledge. Hence, just as the knowable things of nature are prior to our knowledge, and are its measure, God's knowledge is prior to natural things, and is their measure. In the same way a house mediates between the knowledge of the architect who made it and that of those who get their knowledge of the house from the house itself once it is made.

Article 9: Does God have knowledge of non-existent things?

1. It seems that God has no knowledge of non-existent things. For God has knowledge only of what is true. But *true* and *being* are convertible terms.[53] So, God has no knowledge of non-existent things.

2. Moreover, knowledge requires a likeness between the knower and the known. But non-existent things can have no likeness to God, who is existence itself. So, God cannot know the non-existent.

3. Again, God's knowledge is the cause of what he knows. But it is not the cause of non-existent things since they have no cause. So, God has no knowledge of non-existent things.

On the contrary, St Paul says of God that he 'calls the things that are not, as the things that are'.[54]

Reply: God knows all things that are in any way whatever. But nothing bars things which, absolutely speaking, are not from being in some way. Things unqualifiedly are if they actually exist. But things that do not actually exist still exist potentially as producible either by God himself or by a creature (whether in active power or in passive potentiality; whether

---

[53] That is, whatever is a being is true, and whatever is true is a being.   [54] Romans 4:17.

in potentiality as matters of opinion, or of imagination, or as expressed in any other way). So, God knows all that can be produced, thought, or said by a creature, and also whatever God himself can produce (even if they do not actually exist). In this sense we can say that God has knowledge even of non-existent things.

Yet we have to take account of a difference among things that do not actually exist. Some of them, though they do not actually exist now, either once actually existed or will actually exist. We say that God knows all these by 'knowledge of vision'. The reason is that God's understanding, which is his existence, is measured by eternity which, itself without succession, takes in the whole of time. So, God's present gaze is directed to the whole of time, and to all that exists in any time, as to what is present before him. There are other things which God or creatures can produce – things which do not exist, things which never were, and things which will never be. With respect to these we say that God has not knowledge of vision, but 'knowledge of simple understanding'. The reason for the names is that, when it comes to us, things seen have a separate existence outside the one who sees.

Hence:

1. Things which do not actually exist have truth corresponding to their potentiality (i.e. it is true that they are potentially existent; and God knows them as such).

2. Since God is existence itself, things exist in so far as they severally participate in likeness to God – just as things are hot in so far as they participate in heat. In this way, potential things are also known by God, even though they do not actually exist.

3. God's knowledge is the cause of things taken in conjunction with his will. So, it is not necessary that all that God knows should exist at some time (past, present or future), but only such things as he wills to exist or permits to exist. And again, it is no part of God's knowledge that such things exist, but that they could exist.

Article 10: Does God know evils?

1. It seems that God does not know evils. For Aristotle says that an intellect that is not in potentiality does not know privation.[55] But evil

---

[55] *On the Soul* 3.6, 430b24.

is 'privation of good', as Augustine says.[56] So, since God's intellect is never in a state of potentiality, but always in one of actuality (as is clear from what I have said),[57] it seems that God does not know evils.

2. Moreover, knowledge either causes what is known or is caused by it. But God's knowledge is not a cause of evil. Nor is it caused by it. So, God has no knowledge of evils.

3. Moreover, all that is known is known either through its likeness or through its opposite. But God knows all that he knows through his essence, as is clear from what I have said.[58] Yet God's essence is not the likeness of evil, nor is evil its opposite. For God's essence has no contrary, as Augustine says.[59] So, God does not know evils.

4. Again, what is known not through itself but through something else is known imperfectly. But God does not know evil through itself, because then it would have to be in God, because what is known must be in the knower. However, if God knows evil through something else, he knows it imperfectly. But this cannot be so since God's knowledge is in no way imperfect. So, God's knowledge does not extend to evils.

On the contrary, the book of Proverbs says, 'Hell and destruction are before God.'[60]

Reply: Whoever knows a thing perfectly must know all that can happen to it. But there are some good things to which corruption through evils can happen. So, God would not know good things perfectly if he did not also know evils. Now, something is knowable in so far as it exists. So, since evil's nature consists in a privation of good, God, through the very fact of knowing good, also knows evils – just as we know darkness through knowing light. Hence Dionysius says that God 'through himself has sight of darkness, seeing darkness from no other source than from light'.[61]

Hence:

1. We should understand Aristotle's words as meaning that an intellect which is not in a state of potentiality does not know privation through a privation which it has in itself. And this agrees with what he had said just before, namely that we know a point, and every indivisible, by

---

[56] *Confessions* 3.7. *PL* 32.688.   [57] 1a 14.2.   [58] 1a 14.2 and 5.
[59] *The City of God* 12.2. *PL* 41.350.   [60] Proverbs 15:11.   [61] *The Divine Names* 7.2. *PG* 3.869.

way of privation of division. The reason is that simple and indivisible forms are not in our intellect actually (i.e. not as known directly) but only potentially (i.e. as known indirectly); for if they were in our intellect actually they would not be known by way of privation. Substances that are not joined to matter know what is simple in that way. So, God does not know evil through a privation which he has in himself. He knows it through the contrary good.

2. God's knowledge is not the cause of evil. It is the cause of good, through which we know evil.

3. Evil is not the contrary of God's essence, which is not liable to corruption by evil. But it is the contrary of the effects produced by God. He knows these effects through his essence. So, he knows the contrary evils in knowing them.

4. To know something only through something else is to have imperfect knowledge if the thing is knowable through itself. But evil is not knowable through itself, because evil of its very nature is the privation of good. So, it cannot be defined or known except through good.

Article 11: Does God know individuals?

1. It would seem that God does not know individuals. For his intellect is freer from matter than our intellect, and our intellect does not know individuals precisely because of its freedom from matter. As Aristotle says, 'the mind grasps universals; the senses grasp individuals'.[62] So, God does not know individuals.

2. Moreover, in ourselves the only powers of knowing which can grasp individuals are those which receive species which have not been freed from material conditions. But things in God are free from all materiality to the highest degree. So, God does not know individuals.

3. Again, all knowledge is through some likeness. Yet it would seem that the likeness of individuals as such is not in God. For the principle of individuation is matter, which, since it is merely potential, is totally unlike God, who is pure actuality. So, God cannot know individuals.

On the contrary, the book of Proverbs says, 'All the ways of people are open to his eyes.'[63]

---

[62] *On the Soul* 2.5, 417b22.   [63] Proverbs 16:2.

Reply: God does know individuals. For all perfections in creatures exist first in God in a higher way, as is clear from what I have said.[64] Now it is part of our perfection to know individuals. So, God must know them. Even Aristotle concludes that it will not do to say that God does not know something that we know.[65] Thus he argues against Empedocles that God would be anything but wise if he were ignorant of strife. But the perfections which exist separately in lower things are in God unified and without division. So, though we know universal and immaterial things by one faculty, and individuals by another, God knows both classes of object through his simple intellect.

Some writers, intending to show how this can be so, have said that God knows individuals through universal causes. They argue that there is nothing in any individual which does not have its origin in some universal cause. They offer as an example astronomers who, if they knew all the universal movements of the heavens, would be able to predict all future eclipses. But that example does not work. For individuals receive from universal causes certain forms and powers which, however closely united, are not individuated except through individual matter. Thus, to know Socrates so as to know that he is white, or the son of Sophroniscus, or as described in any other such way, is not to know him as this individual man. So, if God's knowledge were as described by these authors, he would not know individuals in their individuality.

Others have said that God knows individuals by applying universal causes to particular effects. But that line of reasoning is also of no help. For we cannot apply one thing to another unless we first know the other. So, the application just mentioned cannot be the basis on which particulars are known. Rather, it presupposes knowledge of them.

We must therefore take a different line and say that, since (as I have said)[66] God is the cause of things through his knowledge, his knowledge has the same extension as his causality. God's active power extends not only to forms which provide a universal factor, but also to matter, as I shall show later.[67] So, his knowledge must necessarily extend to individuals, which are individuated by matter. God knows things other than himself through his essence, in so far as it is the likeness of things as their productive principle. So, his essence must be the sufficient principle for knowing all things that come into existence through him, not merely in

---

[64] 1a 4.2. [65] *On the Soul* 1.5, 410b4; *Metaphysics* 3.4, 1000b3. [66] 1a 14.8. [67] 1a 44.2.

their universal natures, but also in their individuality. The same would be true of an artist's knowledge if it produced the whole of something, not merely its form.

Hence:

1. Our intellect abstracts intelligible species from individuating principles. So, an intelligible species in our intellect cannot be the likeness of the principles of individuals as such – which is why our intellect does not know individuals. But the intelligible species in God's intellect (i.e. God's essence) is not immaterial through abstraction, but of its own nature, being itself the principle of all the principles that enter into the composition of things (whether of species or individuals). Through that likeness, therefore, God knows individuals as well as universals.

2. The species in God's intellect does not have material conditions in its own nature, as the species received in imagination and sense have. But its productive power still extends to both the immaterial and the material, as I have said.[68]

3. Though prime matter, because of its potentiality, is far removed from a likeness to God, it still retains a certain likeness to God's way of being in so far as it has potential existence.

Article 12: Can God know infinites?

1. It seems that God cannot know infinites. An infinite as such is unknown. As Aristotle says, an infinite is 'that of which, if one grasps a part, there is always something more to grasp'.[69] Augustine also says that 'what is comprehended by knowing is limited by the knower's comprehension'.[70] But infinites cannot be limited. So, God's knowledge cannot comprehend them.

2. Moreover, if someone were to say that what are infinites in themselves are finite to God's knowledge, one could reply that an infinite is something that cannot be gone through, as Aristotle says.[71] An infinite cannot be gone through either by a finite or by an infinite, as Aristotle proves.[72] So, an infinite cannot be finite even to what is infinite. So, infinites are not finite to God's knowledge, which is infinite.

---

[68] See the body of the present article.   [69] *Physics* 3.6, 207a7.
[70] *The City of God* 12.18. PL 41.368.   [71] *Physics* 3.4, 204a3.   [72] *Physics* 6.7, 238b17.

3. Again, God's knowledge is a measure of its object. But it is contrary to the nature of an infinite to be measured. So, God cannot know infinites.

On the contrary, Augustine says, 'We cannot number the infinite, but it can be comprehended by one whose knowledge has no bounds.'[73]

Reply: Since (as I have shown) God knows not only things which actually exist but also those which can be produced either by himself or by creatures,[74] and since these are infinite in number, we must hold that God knows infinites. And although the 'knowledge of vision' (confined to things which are, were or will be) does not have infinites for its object, for the reason which some assign but I reject (namely, that the world existed from eternity, and generation and movement will always remain, so that individuals will be multiplied without limit), on closer consideration we must conclude that God knows infinites even by the knowledge of vision. For God also knows the thoughts and affections of hearts, which will be multiplied without limit since rational creatures will never cease to exist.

The reason for this is that the extension of a knower's knowledge depends on the scope of the form that is its principle. Now in sense-knowledge the species is the likeness of one individual only; so only one individual can be known by means of it. But an intelligible species in our intellect is the likeness of something in its specific nature, which can be shared by an unlimited number of individuals. So, our intellect, through the intelligible species of human beings, knows in a manner an unlimited number of human beings; not, however, human beings in their distinction from one another, but in their common possession of their specific nature; for the intelligible species in our intellect is not the likeness of humans in what makes them individuals, but only in what makes the species. Now, God's essence, through which God's intellect knows, is the adequate likeness of everything that is or can be, not merely with regard to the factors of what they possess in common, but also with regard to those proper to each individual, as I have shown.[75] So, it follows that God's knowledge extends to infinites, and that he knows them as distinct from each other.

Hence:

1. As Aristotle says, 'the notion of infinity coincides with that of quantity';[76] and the notion of quantity includes an ordering of parts. So, to

---

[73] *The City of God* 12.18. *PL* 41.368.   [74] 1a 14.9.   [75] 1a 14.11.   [76] *Physics* 1.2, 185a33.

know an infinite in its own nature is to know part after part; and in that way an infinite is not really known at all; for whatever number of parts is grasped, something always remains beyond. But God does not know an infinite or infinites as though by counting part after part, for, as I said above,[77] he knows everything at once, not successively. So, nothing prevents him from knowing infinites.

2. 'Going through' implies a certain succession of parts; and that is why an infinite cannot be gone through either by a finite or by an infinite. But the idea of comprehensive knowledge is satisfied if the knowledge equals the object known, for we say that something is known comprehensively when no part of it remains beyond the knower's grasp. So, it is not contrary to the notion of an infinite that it should be known comprehensively by something that is infinite. In that sense, we can say that what is infinite in itself is finite to God's knowledge (i.e. is known comprehensively by it) – though we cannot say this if we take 'that which is infinite' to mean 'that which can be gone through'.

3. God's knowledge is a measure of things, not quantitatively (which it could not be when it comes to infinites) but because it measures the essence and truth of things. For everything possesses the truth of its own nature to the extent to which it imitates God's knowledge (as the product of artists does in so far as it corresponds to the art of the artists). Even if we grant that there could be actually existing multitudes infinite in number (e.g. an infinite number of people, or an actually existing continuous quantity, like the 'infinite air' referred to by some of the ancients), it would still be clear that such infinites would have a limited, finite existence. For their existence would be limited to certain determinate natures and would therefore, be subject to the measure of God's knowledge.

Article 13: Does God know contingent future events?

1. It seems that God does not know contingent future events. For from a necessary cause there proceeds a necessary effect. As I said above, though, God's knowledge is the cause of the things he knows,[78] and since his knowledge is necessary it follows that what he knows is necessary. So, God does not know contingent events.

---

[77] 1a 14.7.   [78] 1a 14.8.

2. Moreover, if the antecedent in a conditional proposition is absolutely necessary, the consequent is absolutely necessary. For an antecedent stands to a consequent as premises to conclusions. Now, as Aristotle proves, only necessary conclusions can follow from necessary premises.[79] But 'If God knew that this is going to happen, it will happen' is a true conditional, for knowledge is only of what is true. Its antecedent is absolutely necessary (a) because it is eternal, and (b) because it is expressed as having taken place. So, the consequent is absolutely necessary as well, and whatever God knows is necessary. So, God has no knowledge of contingent events.

3. Again, all that God knows must necessarily be since even everything we know must necessarily be and since God's knowledge is more certain than ours. But no contingent future event must necessarily be. So, God knows no contingent future event.

On the contrary, the psalm speaks of God as 'He who has fashioned the hearts of every one of them [i.e. people] and knows all their deeds.'[80] But people's deeds are contingent since they are subject to free choice. So, God knows contingent future events.

Reply: From what I have shown above, namely, that God knows all things (not only those which actually exist, but those which are in the power of himself or a creature),[81] and since some of these are contingent events in our future, it follows that God knows contingent future events.

To appreciate this we should note that we can think of an event as contingent in two ways.

First, we can think of it intrinsically and in so far as it is already actual. If we think of it in this way, it is not future but present, and it is not contingent with respect to different outcomes. It is determined to one outcome. As such, it can be the object of certain and infallible knowledge, as something seen is to vision (as when I see Socrates sitting down).

But we can also think of a contingent event as it exists in its cause. If we do that, we think of it as going to happen, as a contingent event not yet determined to one outcome (for a contingent cause can end up having varying effects). Considered as such, a contingent event is not something of which we have any certain knowledge. So, someone who knows a contingent effect only in its cause has no more than a conjectural

---

[79] *Posterior Analytics* 1.6, 75a4.   [80] Psalms 32:15.   [81] 1a 14.9.

knowledge of it. But God knows all contingent events not only as they are in their causes but also as each of them actually exists in itself.

Now, although contingent events become actually existent successively, God does not know them in their actual existence successively (as we do) but all at once. For his knowledge is measured by eternity, as is his existence, and eternity, which exists as a simultaneous whole, embraces the whole of time, as I said earlier.[82] So, all that takes place in time is eternally present to God, not merely, as some hold,[83] in the sense that he has the intelligible natures of things present in himself, but because he eternally surveys all things as they are in their presence to him.

So God clearly knows contingent events infallibly since they are objects of his gaze as present to him. But they are future contingent events in relation to their proximate causes.

Hence:

1. A first cause can be necessary while its effects are contingent because of a contingent proximate cause. Thus, the sprouting of a plant is contingent because of a contingent proximate cause, although the first cause, the motion of the sun, is necessary. In the same way things that God knows are contingent because of their contingent causes, though the first cause, God's knowledge, is necessary.

2. Some hold that the antecedent, 'God knew this contingent future event', is not necessary but contingent (because, though it is past, it refers to the future).[84] That, however, does not take away its necessity, for what had in fact a reference to a future event must have had it, even though the future is sometimes not realized.

   Others take the line that the antecedent in question is contingent because it is made up of what is necessary and contingent, as the proposition 'Socrates is a white man' is contingent.[85] But that does not help either. For in 'God knew something to be a contingent future event' the word 'contingent' is merely part of the matter of the proposition, and not a principal one. So its contingency or necessity makes no difference to the necessity or contingency, or to the truth or

---

[82] 1a 10.2, *ad* 4.   [83] Ibn Sīnā, also known as Avicenna (980–1037), and his followers.

[84] St Bonaventure (*c.* 1217–74), *Commentary on Book 1 of the 'Sentences'* 38.2, 2; St Albert the Great (*c.* 1200–84), *Orations on Book 1 of the 'Sentences'* 38.4.

[85] Robert Grosseteste (*c.* 1170–1253), *On Free Choice* 6.

falsity, of the proposition taken as a whole. Thus, for example, it can be just as true that I said 'a man is an ass' as that I said 'Socrates is running' or 'God exists'. The same applies to the words 'necessary' and 'contingent'.

So we must hold that the antecedent in question is absolutely necessary. Some however go on to say that it does not follow that the consequent is absolutely necessary, because the antecedent is only the remote cause of the consequent, which is contingent because of its proximate cause.[86] But that will not do, for a conditional whose antecedent is a remote necessary cause, and whose consequent is a contingent effect, is false (e.g. 'If the sun is moving, the grass will grow').

We must therefore take a different line and say that, when the antecedent contains something that pertains to a mental act, we should understand the consequent not as it exists in itself but as it exists in a soul: for the existing of a thing in itself is not the same as its existing in a soul. For example, if we say, 'Whatever a soul knows is immaterial', we should understand the word 'immaterial' as applying to the existence of things in the mind, not to the way they exist in themselves. Similarly, if someone says, 'If God knew something, it will happen', we should understand the consequent as an object of God's knowledge (i.e. as it is in its presence to him). So it has the same necessity as the antecedent. As Aristotle says, 'that which is, when it is, necessarily is'.[87]

3. We know successively things which become actual in time while God knows them in eternity, which is above time. So we cannot be certain when it comes to future contingents, for we know them precisely as future contingents. They can be certain only to God, whose understanding is in eternity, above time. For a comparison, consider people going along a road. They do not see those who come behind them. But someone who sees the whole road from a height immediately sees all those passing along the road. So what we know must be necessary in itself, for we cannot know things that are contingent and future in themselves. But the objects of God's knowledge must be necessary considered as such, as I have said – though they are not absolutely necessary considered as existing in their particular causes.

[86] Alexander of Hales (*c.* 1185–1245), *Summa theologiae* 1.171, 184.
[87] *On Interpretation* 1.9, 19a23.

So we usually distinguish when it comes to 'All that God knows must necessarily be.' This proposition can be about a thing or a statement. If we take it in the first sense, we forget about God's knowing, and the proposition turns out to be false. For it means 'Every thing that God knows is a necessary thing.' But we can also understand the proposition as being about a statement. Thus, if taken in conjunction with the fact of God's knowing, we now end up with a true proposition which we can render as 'The statement, *a thing known by God exists*, is necessary.'

Some people argue that this distinction is appropriate only in the case of forms that can be separated from their subjects, as in 'Something white can be black', which is false in one sense, though true in another. Something white can also be black, but 'White is black' is necessarily false. They also argue that in the case of forms that cannot be separated from a subject, the distinction can have no place, as, for example, in 'It is possible for a black crow to be white', which is false in both senses. But (so runs the thinking of the argument I am now noting) 'to be known by God' is inseparable from the thing, because what is known by God cannot be not known (i.e. God cannot not know what he does know). This objection would be relevant if the expression 'thing known' (i.e. by God) referred merely to a disposition belonging to a subject. But since it refers to a knower's act of knowing, the thing itself that is known, even if it is always known, can be characterized in its own independent existence in a way it cannot be characterized in its condition as part of the act of knowing. Hence, for example, we attribute materiality to a stone because of its physical condition, but not in so far as it is something understood.

Article 14: Does God know propositions?

1. It seems that God does not know propositions. For to know propositions is proper to our intellect in its function of putting together and separating. But there is no putting together in God's intellect. So God does not know propositions.

2. Moreover, all knowledge comes about through a likeness. But in God there is no likeness of propositions since he is entirely simple. So God does not know propositions.

On the contrary, the psalm says, 'The Lord knows people's thoughts.' But people's thoughts include propositions.[88] So God knows propositions.

Reply: Since our intellect has the power to form propositions, and since (as I have said) God knows whatever is in his own power or that of creatures (as I have said),[89] God must know all possible propositions. But, just as he knows material things in an immaterial way, and composite things in a simple way of knowledge, he does not know propositions in the way they are formed (by putting together or separating their terms in his mind). He knows each thing by simple understanding, by knowing the essence of each. We would do the same if we understood all that can be predicated of people simply by understanding what they are by nature. That is not in fact how our mind works. We pass from one object to another because the intelligible species in our minds represents one thing without representing other things. So in understanding the nature of people we do not thereby immediately understand what else is true of them. We understand them one by one according to a certain succession. For this reason we have to reduce to unity what we understand separately, by putting together or separating concepts to form a statement. But the species in God's intellect (i.e. God's essence) is sufficient to present everything clearly. So by knowing his essence God knows the essences of all things, and whatever can affect them.

Hence:

1. This reasoning would hold if God knew propositions by the process by which they are formed.
2. The putting together of concepts in a proposition signifies some reality which a thing has. So, through his own being, which is his essence, God is the likeness of all that can be signified by propositions.

Article 15: Is God's knowledge changeable?

1. It seems that God's knowledge is changeable. For knowledge implies a relation to something knowable. But whatever implies a relation to creatures is something we predicate of God in time, and it changes with the changing of creatures. So God's knowledge can change with the changing of creatures.

---

[88] Psalms 93:11.   [89] 1a 14.9.

2. Moreover, God can know whatever he can produce. But God can produce more than he produces, and he can therefore know more than he knows. So his knowledge changes by growth or decrease.

3. Again, God knew that Christ was about to be born. But he does not *now* know that Christ is about to be born – for Christ is not *now* about to be born. So God does not know all that he knew, and his knowledge seems to be changeable.

On the contrary, we read that in God 'there is no change nor shadow of alteration'.[90]

Reply: Since God's knowledge is his substance, as is clear from what I have said,[91] his knowledge must be altogether invariable just as his substance is altogether unchangeable (as I showed above).[92]

Hence:

1. 'Lord', and 'Creator', and similar names imply relations to creatures as they are in themselves. But God's knowledge implies a relation to creatures as they are in God, for something is actually known in so far as it is in a knower. Now, created things exist in God unchangeably, but changeably in themselves.

   Alternatively, we may reply that 'Lord', and 'Creator', and similar names imply relations arising out of actions that we understand to target creatures as they are in themselves. So we predicate such relations of God variably with the variation of creatures. But knowledge, and love, and their like imply relations arising out of acts conceived as existing in God. So they are predicated of God invariably (as being unchangeably applicable to him).

2. God also knows what he can produce but does not produce. So from the fact that he can produce more than he does, it does not follow that he can know more things than he knows – unless we are speaking of the 'knowledge of vision' by which we speak of him knowing things which have actual existence at some time. Nevertheless, from the fact that he knows that some things which do not exist can exist, or vice versa, it does not follow that his knowledge is changeable, but that he knows the changeableness of things. If there were something whose existence God first did not know and then did know, his knowledge would be changeable. But this is not a possible scenario. For God in

---

[90] James 1:17.   [91] 1a 14.4.   [92] 1a 9.1.

his eternity knows all that is or can be in any period of time. So if we say that something exists, we must thereby concede that God knows it eternally. We should therefore not grant that God can know more than he knows. To do so implies that he was first ignorant and then gained knowledge.

3. Ancient nominalists said that the propositions, 'Christ is being born', 'Christ is about to be born' and 'Christ is born' are the same proposition because all three point to the same fact, namely, the birth of Christ: so that it follows that God knows whatever he knew, because he now knows Christ is born, which means the same as 'Christ will be born.'[93]

But that opinion is false. First, because differences in terms produce different propositions. Second, because it would follow that a proposition that is once true is always true, which contradicts Aristotle when he says that 'Socrates is seated' is true when he is seated and false when he rises.[94]

We should agree, then, that 'Whatever God knew, he knows' is false if understood as applying to facts as reported in propositions. But it does not therefore follow that God's knowledge is changeable. There is no change in God's knowledge because he knows that one and the same thing at one time exists and at another time does not. Similarly, there is no change in God's knowledge because he knows that a certain proposition is at one time true and at another time false. His knowledge would indeed be changeable if he knew propositions in the way they are formed – by putting together and separating different notions, as our minds do. That is a source of change in our knowledge; from true it can become false, or vice versa, for example, if when something changes we do not change what we think about it; or again, we can pass from one opinion to another, for example, first being of the opinion that people are sitting down and later that they are not. But neither of these kinds of change can be in God.

Article 16: Does God have theoretical knowledge of things?

1. It seems that God does not have theoretical knowledge of things. For God's knowledge is the cause of things, as I have shown above.[95] But

---

[93] Peter Abelard (1079–1142), *Introduction to Theology* 3.5. *PL* 178.1102; Peter Lombard (*c.* 1095–1160), *The First Book of Sentences* 41.3.

[94] *Categories* 5, 4a23.   [95] 1a 14.8.

theoretical knowledge is not the cause of the things it knows. So God's knowledge is not theoretical.

2. Moreover, we gain theoretical knowledge through abstraction from actual things. But that is not the mode of God's knowledge. So his knowledge is not theoretical.

On the contrary, we must attribute to God all that is more excellent. But theoretical knowledge is more excellent than practical knowledge, as Aristotle shows.[96] So God has theoretical knowledge of things.

Reply: Knowledge may be speculative only or practical only. Or it may be partly speculative and partly practical. We can see this by noting that we can call knowledge speculative on three accounts.

First, from the nature of the things known, when they are not producible by the knower, for example, someone's knowledge of natural things or of divine things.

Second, with respect to the mode of knowing – as, for example, when an architect defines, analyses and examines the qualities proper to houses in general. To do all this is to consider producible things, but in a speculative way, not as producible. Something is producible by way of the application of form to matter, not by way of a resolution of a composite into its formal principles considered universally.

Third, knowledge can be speculative with regard to its end or purpose. As Aristotle says, 'the practical intellect differs from the speculative in the end to which it looks'.[97] The aim of the practical intellect is production. That of the speculative intellect the consideration of truth. Thus, if builders consider how some house could be built, not with a view to building it but merely for the sake of knowing, their consideration, so far as concerns the end they look to, is speculative, though still about what could be produced.

So knowledge which is speculative from the nature of the thing known is speculative only. Knowledge which is speculative either in its mode or in the end it looks to is speculative in one respect and practical in another, and knowledge directed to production is unqualifiedly practical.

Bearing all this in mind, we should say that God's knowledge of himself is speculative only, for he cannot be produced. But he has both speculative and practical knowledge of all other things. He has speculative knowledge since he knows (yet much more perfectly than we do) all

---

[96] *Metaphysics* 1.1, 982a1.   [97] *On the Soul* 3.10, 433a14.

that we speculatively know about things by defining and analysing. But of things which he can produce but never does produce he does not have knowledge which is practical from the end in view. He has that kind of practical knowledge of things which he produces at some time. As for evils, though they are not producible by him, they still fall under his practical knowledge, just as good things do (in so far as he permits, or prevents, or directs them – just as illnesses fall under the practical knowledge of physicians who apply their skill to curing them).

Hence:

1. God's knowledge is the cause not of himself but of other things: of some of them, namely, those which come into existence at some time, it is the actual cause; of others (i.e. those which he can produce but which never come into existence) it is the potential cause.

2. It is not of the very nature of speculative knowledge that it should be obtained from the things that are known, but incidental to it (i.e. in so far as it is human knowledge).

As for the point raised to the contrary, for knowledge of producible things to be perfect they must be known precisely as producible. So, since God's knowledge is in every way perfect, he must know the things he can produce as such, and not merely as objects of speculation. Even so, however, his knowledge loses nothing of the excellence of speculative knowledge, for he sees all things other than himself in himself, and he knows himself with speculative knowledge. So in his speculative knowledge of himself he has both speculative and practical knowledge of all other things.

Question 15
On God's ideas

I have considered God's knowledge. Now I have to deal with God's ideas. On this topic I raise three points of inquiry:

1. Are there divine ideas?[1]
2. Are there many or only one?
3. Are there ideas for everything God knows?

Article 1: Are there divine ideas?

1. It seems that there are no divine ideas. For Dionysius says that God does not know things by way of an idea.[2] However, ideas are posited only as a means of knowing things. So, there are no divine ideas.
2. Moreover, God knows all things in himself, as I said earlier.[3] But he does not know himself through an idea. So, neither does he know anything else by ideas.
3. Again, we take an idea to be a source of knowing and acting. But God's essence is the sufficient source of knowing and producing all things. So, we need not suppose that there are any divine ideas.

On the contrary, Augustine says, 'Ideas are so powerful that one cannot be wise without understanding them.'[4]

Reply: We must hold that there are ideas in God's mind. For *idea* in Greek corresponds to the Latin *forma* (form). By 'ideas', therefore, we

---

[1] For some background, see the introduction.   [2] *The Divine Names* 7.2. PG 3.869.   [3] 1a 14.5.
[4] *On Eighty-Three Varied Questions* 1.46. PL 40.29.

understand forms of different things existing apart from the things themselves. But the form of something existing apart from the thing itself can have two functions: (a) to be the exemplar or pattern of the thing whose form we say that it is, or (b) to be the source of knowing that thing (in the sense in which we say that the forms of knowable things are in knowers). We need to hold that there are divine ideas with respect to both of these functions.

With the exception of what is generated by chance, a form must be the end in the generation of everything. But for agents to act for the sake of a form, the likeness of the form must be in them. This can happen in two ways. In some agents (e.g. those which act by nature) the likeness of the thing to be produced already exists as a natural being: thus people beget people, and fire produces fire. In other agents (i.e. those which act through understanding) the form of the thing to be produced already exists as something intelligible – as the form of a yet to be built house exists in the minds of builders. We can call this 'the idea of the house' because builders intend to make houses conforming to forms which they have conceived in their minds. Now since the world is not made by chance, but by God causing through his under-standing (as I shall show below),[5] God's mind must contain a form to the likeness of which he makes the world. That is what an idea in God's mind amounts to.

Hence:

1. God does not understand things through an idea extrinsic to himself. On this point we may recall Aristotle's objection to Plato's under-standing of 'Ideas' – things which he believed to exist in their own right, not in any intellect.[6]
2. Though God knows himself and other things through his essence, his essence is still the source of the production of other things, not of himself. So, it satisfies the definition of 'idea' with reference to other things, though not with reference to God himself.
3. God in his essence is necessarily the likeness of all things. So, an idea in God is simply God's essence.

---

[5] 1a 19.4.   [6] *Metaphysics* 3.2, 997b6; 7.6, 1031a28.

Article 2: Are there many ideas?

1. It seems that there are not many divine ideas. For an idea in God is his essence. But God's essence is something unique. So, there is only one divine idea.

2. Moreover, an idea is a source of knowledge and operation – like art and wisdom. But in God there is not more than one art and wisdom. So, there are not many ideas in God.

3. Moreover, if someone were to say that divine ideas increase in number with respect to their relations to different creatures, we can reply that a plurality of ideas exists from eternity. So, if God's ideas are many, and if creatures are temporal, it follows that the temporal will be the cause of the eternal.

4. Again, the relations referred to above are (a) real only on the side of creatures, or (b) real in God as well. If they are real only in creatures, then (since creatures do not exist from eternity), there will be no plurality of ideas from eternity – if ideas get multiplied only because of relations of the kind now in question. But if the relations are real in God, it follows that there is another real plurality in God besides that of the divine Persons (of the Trinity). But this goes against what Damascene says when he notes that everything is one in God except Ungeneration, Generation and Procession.[7] So, God's mind does not contain a number of different ideas.

On the contrary, Augustine says, 'The ideas are first or original forms, or permanent and unchangeable natures of things, contained in God's understanding – for they are not themselves formed and are therefore eternal and ever the same. While they themselves neither come to be nor perish, we say that it is in accordance with them that all that can come to be or perish, and all that does come to be and perish, is formed.'[8]

Reply: We have to suppose that there is plurality when it comes to God's ideas. To see why, we should note that in every effect the ultimate end is specifically the object of the principal agent's intention – as, for example, the order of an army is what its commander intends.

---

[7] *On the Orthodox Faith* 1.10. PG 94.837.   [8] *On Eighty-Three Varied Questions* 1.46. PL 40.30.

Now, that which is best of all in the created order is the good which consists in the order of the universe as a whole, as Aristotle shows.[9] So, the order of the universe as a whole is what God especially aims at. This is not just an incidental result produced by a succession of agents, as some claim.[10] They say that God created the first creature only, and that this in turn created a second, and so on – the result being the vast multitude of things in the world. Now according to that opinion God would only have an idea of the first creature. But if the whole universe's order is the direct object of God's creating, and if it is intended by him, he must have an idea of it. But a plan governing a whole has to involve knowledge of what is special to the parts which make it up (as, for example, builders can only plan a house when knowing what its parts amount to exactly). So, the natures of all things, including what belongs exactly to each of them, must be in God's mind. That is why Augustine says that God creates everything with its own nature.[11] So, there is a plurality of ideas in God's mind.

That this is not inconsistent with his simplicity is easy to see if we bear in mind that the idea of a work is in the mind of the agent as *that which* is known, not as the species *by which* there is knowledge (the latter being the form which makes the intellect actually knowing). Thus the form of a house in the mind of builders is something they understand, and they fashion the house to its likeness. But God's simple intellect can know many things. What would be contrary to its simplicity would be if God's intellect were informed by a plurality of species. So, many ideas are in God's mind as objects of his knowledge.

We can explain this as follows. God knows his essence perfectly. So, he knows it in all the ways in which it is knowable. But God's essence is knowable not only as it is in itself, but as creatures can share in it by some degree of likeness. Yet creatures have their own natures in so far as they share in some way in the likeness of God's essence. In this way then, God, in knowing his essence as imitable in such and such a way by such and such a particular creature, knows his essence as the nature and idea proper to that creature; and similarly in other cases. So, God clearly knows many natures proper to many things; and these natures are many ideas.

---

[9] *Metaphysics* 12.10, 1075a13.   [10] Ibn Sīnā and his followers.
[11] *On Eighty-Three Varied Questions* 1.46. *PL* 40.30.

Hence:

1. 'Idea' is not the name for God's essence as such, but only in so far as it is the likeness or intelligible nature of this or that thing. So, we speak of God's ideas as being many in so far as one essence understands many natures.
2. We attribute 'wisdom' and 'art' to God to refer to that *by which* he knows. To attribute an idea to God, however, is to refer to that *which* God knows. But God by one act knows many things, not only as they are in themselves, but also as they are as known. So, he knows many intelligible natures of things. Hence we say that builders know a house when they know its form as embodied in matter. But, when they know the form of a house as an object of their own speculative thought, they know its idea or intelligible nature in knowing that they know it. Now, God does not just know many things through his essence. He also knows that he knows many things through his essence – which means that he knows many intelligible natures of things, or that he has many ideas in his intellect as objects of knowledge.
3. Relations by which ideas are multiplied are not caused by the things themselves but by God's intellect comparing its essence to them.
4. Relations which multiply ideas are not in created things but in God. But they are not real relations, like those which distinguish the divine Persons of the Trinity. They are relations that God understands.

Article 3: Does God have ideas of everything he knows?

1. It seems that God does not have ideas of everything he knows. For God has no idea of evil – otherwise there would be evil in God. But God knows evils. So, he does not have ideas of everything he knows.
2. Moreover, God knows things which neither are, nor were, nor will be, as I said previously.[12] But there are no ideas of such things. For, as Dionysius says, 'the exemplary ideas are divine choices which determine and produce things'.[13] So, God does not have ideas of everything he knows.
3. Moreover, God knows prime matter, for which there is no idea since it has no form. So, God does not have ideas of everything he knows.

[12] 1a 14.9. [13] *The Divine Names* 5.8. PG 3.848.

4. Again, God clearly knows not only species but also genera, individuals and accidents. But according to Plato (the source of talk about ideas, according to Augustine)[14] there are no ideas of these things. So, God does not have ideas of everything he knows.

On the contrary, ideas are intelligible natures existing in God's mind, as Augustine makes clear.[15] But God possesses the intelligible natures proper to everything he knows. So, he has an idea of everything that he knows.

Reply: Plato took ideas to be sources of the knowledge of things and of their coming into existence. So, an idea as taken to be in God's mind has both these functions. As a source of things coming to be, we can call it an *exemplar*, and it belongs to practical knowledge. As a source of knowledge, we would do best to call it an *intelligible nature*, and it can also belong to speculative knowledge. As exemplar it is related to all the things produced by God at some time. As a source of knowledge it is related to all the things God knows (even if some of them never come into existence) and to all the things he knows in the intelligible natures proper to each, and as he knows them speculatively.

Hence:

1. God knows evil not through its own nature but through the nature of good. So, there is no idea of evil in God – whether we are thinking of ideas as exemplars or as intelligible natures.
2. God does not have practical knowledge of things which neither are, nor will be, nor were. He knows such things only as what he can make. So, he has no idea of them if 'idea' means 'exemplar'. He has an idea of them only in so far as 'idea' means 'intelligible nature'.
3. Some say that Plato took matter to be uncreated – meaning that he did not believe in an idea of matter but took ideas and matter to be joint causes. But my view is that matter is created by God, though not without form. So, I hold that there is an idea of matter in God, but not one distinct from the idea of the composite of matter and form. For matter in itself neither exists nor is knowable.
4. Genera cannot have an idea distinct from that of species (taking 'idea' to mean 'exemplar'), for a genus never comes into existence except in

[14] *On Eighty-Three Varied Questions* 1.46. *PL* 40.29.
[15] *On Eighty-Three Varied Questions* 1.46. *PL* 40.30.

some species. The same is true of accidents which are inseparable from a subject because they come into existence along with the subject. But accidents which supervene in a subject have a special idea. For example: working from the notion of what a house is, builders produce all the accidental qualities implied by this notion; but they add things to the house as built (e.g. pictures and so on) while working from a different notion. According to Plato,[16] individuals have no other idea than that of the species (a) because particulars are individuated by matter (which, according to some interpreters, Plato took to be eternal and jointly causal with the idea), and (b) because nature aims at producing species, and churns out individuals only for the preservation of species. But divine providence extends not only to species but also to individuals, as I shall later be saying.[17]

[16] Cf. Aristotle, *Metaphysics* 1.9, 990b29; Plato (*c.* 428–347 BC), *Philebus* 16d–e.   [17] 1a 22.2.

Question 18

On God's life

Since understanding belongs to living things, having considered God's knowledge and intellect, I need to consider his life. On this subject I raise four points of inquiry:

1. What things have life?
2. What is life?
3. Can we attribute life to God?
4. Is everything in God life?

Article 1: Are all natural things alive?

1. It seems that all natural things are alive. For Aristotle says that movement is a kind of life possessed by everything that exists in nature.[1] But all natural objects share in movement. So, all natural objects share in life.
2. Moreover, we say that plants live because they have in themselves a principle of movement to increase and decrease. But local movement is more perfect than that of increase and decrease, and prior to it by nature, as Aristotle proves.[2] So, since all natural bodies have in themselves a principle of local movement, it seems that all natural bodies have life.
3. Again, among natural bodies the elements are the least perfect; but we attribute life to them (e.g. we speak of 'living water'). All the more, therefore, do other natural bodies have life.

---

[1] *Physics* 8.1, 250b14.   [2] *Physics* 8.7, 260a28.

On the contrary, Dionysius says that 'plants live with life's last echo',[3] from which we may gather that plants have the lowest degree of life. But inanimate bodies are lower than plants. So, they do not possess life.

Reply: We may distinguish between living and non-living things by considering those which are obviously alive. Now, animals are obviously alive (Aristotle says that 'life in animals is plain to see').[4] So, we need to distinguish between living and non-living things by considering why we say that animals are alive, this being the beginning and end of what it is for them to live.

Now, we first say that an animal is living when it begins to have movement of itself, and we judge it to be alive so long as this kind of movement appears in it. When it no longer has any movement of itself, but is moved only by another, we say that life has failed and that the animal is dead. So, it is clear that only things which move themselves with one or other kind of movement are, properly speaking, alive – whether we take movement in the strict sense as 'the actuality of that which is incomplete' (i.e. in potentiality for [further] existence, or in the wider sense as including 'the actuality of that which is already completed', in the way that an act of understanding or sensation is also called movement, as we read in Aristotle.[5] Thus we call 'living' those things which produce in themselves some kind of movement or operation. It is only metaphorically that we can say that things whose nature does not contain that power are living things. Hence:

1. We can understand Aristotle's words as relating either to the first movement (i.e. that of the heavenly bodies) or to movement in general. Either way, movement is called a sort of life of natural bodies by a metaphor and not in the proper sense. Thus the movement of the heavens with respect to the universe of bodily natures has a likeness to the heart's movement, which makes an animal go on living. Similarly, every kind of natural movement is analogous to vital operations. If, for example, the whole material universe were a single living animal, its movement produced by an intrinsic cause of movement, as some have postulated, it would follow that movement would be the life of all natural bodies.

---

[3] *The Divine Names* 6.1, *PG* 3.856.   [4] *On Plants* 1.1, 815a10.
[5] *On the Soul* 3.7, 431a6; 1.4, 408b6.

2. Heavy and light bodies have movement only in so far as they are not in their natural state (not in their own place). When they are in their own natural place they cease to move. But plants and other living things have vital movement as their natural condition, not as a movement to their natural condition or away from it. In fact, if they 'move away from' vital movement they are moving away from their natural condition. Moreover, heavy and light things are moved by an extrinsic mover, namely, either that which in producing them gave them their form, or that which removes an obstacle to their natural movement, as Aristotle says.[6] So, they do not move themselves as living bodies do.

3. It is by analogy that we apply the term 'living' to water that flows continually – just as we use the word 'dead' when talking of stagnant water that is not connected to a continuously flowing source (e.g. water in cisterns and ponds). The appearance of self-movement in 'living water' gives the appearance of life. But it is not life in the true sense. For the movement is not from the water itself but from a cause which produces the water, as the movement of other heavy and light things comes from their causes.

Article 2: Is life an activity?

1. It seems that life is an activity. For all division is into parts belonging to the same kind. But life is divided into activities, as Aristotle makes clear by giving four divisions of life: taking nourishment, sensation, local movement, and understanding.[7] So, life is an activity.

2. Moreover, we say that the active life differs from the contemplative life. But it is only certain activities that distinguish contemplatives from those who engage in the active life. So, life is an activity.

3. Again, to know God is an activity. But it is life, as is clear from St John's words, 'This is eternal life, that they may know you, the one true God.'[8] So, life is an activity.

On the contrary, Aristotle says, 'For living things, to live is to be.'[9]
Reply: As is clear from what I have said, our intellect, which, as such, has for its proper object the essences of things, receives information from

---

[6] *Physics* 8.4, 255b35. [7] *On the Soul* 2.2, 413a22. [8] John 17:3. [9] *On the Soul* 2.4, 415b13.

the senses, whose proper objects are external, accidental qualities.[10] Thus we come to know the essence of something through its external appearance; and since we name a thing as we know it, as I have explained above,[11] we often impose names indicating the essences of things on the basis of the things' external properties. So, we sometimes understand names of this kind, strictly speaking, as denoting the very essences of things, and we employ them accordingly. Sometimes, however, we understand them to signify the properties which give rise to the names (this being a less proper use). Hence, for example, we understand 'body' to indicate substances of a certain kind since these have three dimensions, which is why we sometimes take 'body' to signify three dimensions (thereby taking 'body' to mean a species of quantity).

Now we should say the same when it comes to 'life'. We apply the word to things because of something in their external appearance, namely self-movement. But the word is not applied in order to signify precisely that. It is applied to signify the substance which of its nature has the power of moving itself or giving itself any kind of impulse to activity. In the latter sense 'to live' simply means 'to exist in such a nature'; and 'life' means the same, but in the abstract – just as 'running' (the noun) means the action of running in the abstract. So, 'living' is not an accidental predicate but a substantial one. Yet we sometimes understand 'life' in the less proper sense, to mean the vital activities from which we speak of things having life. Aristotle therefore says that 'to live' is chiefly 'to have sensation and understanding'.[12]

Hence:

1. Aristotle there understands life in the sense of vital activity.

   Or there is a better reply as follows.

   We sometimes understand sensation, understanding, and the like to mean certain activities; and sometimes we understand them to mean the very existing of things which have those activities. Hence, for example, Aristotle says that for living things 'to be is to have sensation or understanding'[13] (i.e. to possess a nature ready to sense or understand). And this is why Aristotle divides life into the four activities mentioned in the objection above. In our lower world

[10] 1a 17.1 and 3.   [11] 1a 13.1.
[12] *Nicomachean Ethics* 9.9, 1170a18.   [13] *Nicomachean Ethics* 9.9, 1170a33.

there are four classes of living things. Some of them have a nature ready only for the taking of sustenance and what follows from that, namely, growth and generation. Others are capable of sensation, as we see when we consider non-moving animals such as oysters. Others have a capacity for local motion – for example, perfect animals such as four-footed ones, birds, and the like. And finally there are those which are capable of understanding – namely, people.

2. We say that activities are vital when their sources are within active things – things which are therefore able to move themselves as they act. But human beings do not just have natural sources when it comes to their actions. They also have added sources, like the characteristic dispositions which incline them to certain kinds of activities in a natural way and which make those activities pleasurable. Metaphorically, as it were, we therefore call activity pleasing to human beings (and to which they are inclined, and in which they are engaged, and to which they arrange their lives) 'their life'. So, we say that some people live a dissolute life, and that others live a worthy life. This is how we distinguish between the contemplative and the active life, and this is what we mean when we say that knowing God is eternal life.

The reply to the third objection will be clear from what I have already said.

Article 3: Can we attribute life to God?

1. It would seem that we cannot attribute life to God. For, as I have said, we attribute life to certain things because they move themselves.[14] But movement does not apply to God. So, neither does life.
2. Moreover, we can assign a source of life when it comes to all living things. Hence Aristotle says that 'the soul is the cause and source of a living body'.[15] But God has no source. So, we cannot speak of him as having life.
3. Again, the source of life in living things in our world is soul producing growth; and this is found only in corporeal things. So, we cannot speak of incorporeal things as being alive.

---

[14] 1a 18.1 and 2.   [15] *On the Soul* 2.4, 415b8.

On the contrary, the psalm says, 'My heart and my flesh have rejoiced in the living God.'[16]

Reply: God has life in the truest sense. To see this we must note that we attribute life to certain things because they act of themselves and not as moved by other things; hence the more perfectly this belongs to a thing the more perfectly does it possess life. Now, in the matter of movers and things moved, there are three factors in order: first, the end in view moves the agent; and the principal agent is that which acts through its own form; and this principal agent sometimes acts through some instrument, which does not act by virtue of its own form but by virtue of the principal agent; to the instrument belongs only the carrying into effect of the action.

We find, then, that some things move themselves without consideration of the form or the end in view provided for them by nature, but only so far as concerns the carrying into effect of the movement. The form by which they act, and the end for which they act, are determined for them by nature. Plants are things like this. They move themselves by growth and they decrease according to the form with which nature endows them.

Other things move themselves in a further sense: not merely with respect to the carrying into effect of a movement, but also with respect to the form which is movement's source (a form which they acquire for themselves). Animals are like this. The source of their movement is not a form implanted in them by nature but one received through the senses. So, the more perfect their senses are, the more perfectly they move themselves. Thus in creatures which have only the sense of touch (e.g. oysters), self-movement consists merely in expansion and contraction and scarcely exceeds the movement of plants. But those with perfect sensory faculties, enabling them to know not only what is joined to them, or touches them, but also things at a distance, advance to what is at some distance from them.

Yet although such animals receive through the senses the forms which are the sources of their movements, they do not independently prescribe for themselves the end of their activity or movement. Nature implants that in them, and natural instinct moves them to a particular activity by means of a form that they apprehend by their senses. Superior to such animals, therefore, are those which move themselves with reference also

---

[16] Psalms 83:2.

to an end in view which they provide for themselves. This occurs only by means of reason and intellect, to which it belongs to know the relation between an end and the means to it, and to order the one to the other. Thus beings which have intellect have a more perfect kind of life, for they move themselves more perfectly. An indication of this is that in one and the same human being the intellective power moves the powers of sensation, and the sense powers, at the intellect's command, move bodily organs, and the bodily organs execute the movements. There is a parallel here with crafts. The craft concerned with the management of a ship (the craft of the one steering it) lays down rules for the craft of ship designing, which subsequently lays down rules for the craft concerned only with carrying out the work of ship construction.

But though our intellect controls itself in certain ways, nonetheless some things are provided to it by nature, for example first principles, about which it has no choice, and the ultimate end, which it is not free not to will. So, though our intellect moves itself to some extent, in some cases it must still be moved by another. That thing, then, whose own nature is its act of knowledge, and which does not have what belongs to it by nature determined for it by another, is something which has life in the highest degree. God is such a thing. So, God possesses life in the highest degree. Hence Aristotle, having shown that God has intellect, concludes that he has the most perfect and everlasting life because his intellect is most perfect and always actual.[17]

Hence:

1. As Aristotle says, there are two kinds of action: (i) action which passes into matter outside the agent, for example heating or cutting; (ii) action which remains in the agent,[18] for example understanding, sensation, willing. The difference between the two is that the first kind of action perfects the thing moved (not the agent that produces the movement), whereas the second type perfects the agent. Hence, since movement is an actualization of the thing moved, we call the second type of action (as being a state of actuality of an agent) 'the agent's movement', because of the similarity of the two cases: movement is an actualization of the thing moved; action of the second type is an actualization of the agent – but with this difference, that

---

[17] *Metaphysics* 12.7, 1072b27.   [18] *Metaphysics* 9.8, 1050a22.

movement is an actualization of what is imperfect (i.e. in potency for further actualization), whereas action of the second type is an actuality of what is already complete (i.e. already actualized), as Aristotle says.[19] If we take the act of understanding as 'movement' in the latter sense, we can say that something that understands itself moves itself. That is the way in which Plato, too, speaks of God as self-moving, not taking movement to be the actuality of something imperfect.[20]

2. Just as God is his very existing and understanding, he is also his life. So, his life does not proceed from any source.

3. The lower creatures of our experience receive life in a corruptible nature, which requires generation for the conservation of the species and nourishment for that of the individual. For this reason, in such lower creatures life always includes soul as producing growth. But this has no place in beings not subject to corruption.

Article 4: Is everything in God life?

1. It seems that not everything in God is life; for in the Acts of the Apostles we read, 'In him we live and move and have our being.'[21] But not everything in God is movement. So, not everything in him is life.

2. Moreover, all things are in God as in their first exemplar. But copies should be in conformity with their exemplar. So, since not everything is living in its own nature, it would seem that not everything in God is life.

3. Moreover, as Augustine says, a living substance is better than any non-living substance.[22] So, if things which in their own natures are not living are life as they exist in God, it would seem that things exist in God in a truer way than they do in their own natures. But this would seem to be false, since in their own natures they exist actually, while in God they exist only potentially.

4. Again, God knows not only good things, and those which come into existence at some time, but also bad things, and those which God can produce but which never come into existence. So, if all things in God are life in so far as he knows them, it would seem that even bad things,

[19] *On the Soul* 3.7, 431a6.   [20] *Timaeus* 30a, 34b; *Phaedrus* 245c.
[21] Acts 17:28.   [22] *On True Religion* 29. *PL* 34.145.

and those which never come into existence, are life as they exist in God, in so far as he knows them. But that seems wrong.

On the contrary, St John says, 'That which was made, in him was life.'[23] But everything except God was made. So, in God all things are life.

Reply: As I have said, God's life is his understanding.[24] But in God intellect, what he understands and his very understanding are the same. So, whatever is in God as something understood is his very living or life. So, since everything God produces is in him as something understood, it follows that in him all things are his divine life itself.

Hence:

1. We speak of creatures being in God in two senses: (i) as held and conserved by God's power (just as we say that we have something 'in us' when it is in our power). We say that, in this sense, creatures (even as existing in their own natures) are in God. We should understand the Apostle's words 'in him we live and move and have our being', in that way; for our being and living and moving are caused by God. (ii) We also say that things are in God as in one who knows them. In this sense they are in God through their own intelligible natures, which in God are the same as the divine essence. So, things, as they exist in God in that way, are God's essence. Since God's essence is life but not movement, it follows that things understood in this way are not movement but life.

2. Copies must conform with the exemplar in respect of their intelligible form, not in respect of their mode of existence. For sometimes the form has one kind of existence in the exemplar and a different kind in the copy. For example, the form of a house in the mind of an architect has an immaterial and intelligible existence, but in an actual house outside the mind it has material and sensibly perceptible existence. So, even the natures of things that are not themselves alive are life in God's mind since they have divine existence in his mind.

3. Were matter no part of the nature of material things but only form, then in every way material things would have a truer existence in God's mind through his ideas than they have in themselves. For this reason Plato held that the separate Form of Human Being is the true

---

[23] John 1:1–3.   [24] 1a 18.3.

human being and that a material human being is human by participation. However, since matter belongs to the essence of natural things, we must say that, absolutely speaking, natural things have a truer existence in God's mind than they have in themselves; because in God's mind they have an uncreated existence, while, in themselves, they have a created existence. But considered as individuals (e.g. an individual human being or an individual horse) they have their individual existence more truly in themselves than in God's mind. For a true human being includes matter, which individual material things do not have in the divine mind. Similarly, a house has a higher kind of existence in the mind of an architect than it has in matter. But a 'true house' is still a material one rather than one in an architect's mind. For the former is an actual house while the latter is only potentially a house.

4. Though evils are in God's knowledge as comprehended by it, they are not in God as created or conserved by him, nor as having intelligible natures of their own in him. For God knows them through the intelligible natures of good things. So, we cannot say that evils are life in God. But we can say that things that never exist are life in God if we understand 'life' to mean understanding only, in as much as God understands them – though not if we take 'life' as implying a source of action.

Question 19
God's will and providence

Having discussed God's way of knowing, I now need to talk about matters to do with his willing. First, I shall consider God's will in itself. Second, I shall reflect on what belongs to God's will absolutely speaking. Third, I shall treat of what belongs to God's intellect in relation to his will.

God's Will

Here there are twelve points of inquiry:

1. Is there a will in God?
2. Does God will things other than himself?
3. Does God will of necessity whatever he wills?
4. Is God's will a cause of things?
5. Can we ascribe any cause to God's willing?
6. Is God's will always fulfilled?
7. Is God's will changeable?
8. Does God's will impose necessity on the things he wills?
9. Does God have a will for evils?
10. Does God have freedom of choice?[1]
11. Can we signpost God's will?[2]
12. Can we fittingly set forth five such signs?

---

[1] That is, are there acts it is in God's power both to do and to refrain from doing?
[2] That is, are there external signs that indicate to us what God wills?

Article 1: Is there a will in God?

1. It seems that there is no will in God. For the objective of will is a good that is aimed at. But we cannot assign an aim to God. So, there is no will in God.
2. Moreover, willing is a kind of desiring. Now, desire or appetite, since it is for something not yet possessed, implies non-fulfilment, which does not belong to God. So, there is no will in God.
3. Furthermore, according to Aristotle, will both changes and is changed.[3] But God is the changeless first source of change, as the *Physics* proves.[4] So, there is no will in God.

On the contrary, St Paul urges us to 'give proof of what God's will is'.[5]

Reply: As there is intellect in God, so there is will; for will is bound up with intellect. A physical thing has its actual existence through its form of existence. Likewise, a mind actually understands something by possessing an intelligible form. Now, the bearing of a thing to its natural form is as follows: when not possessed it tends there, and when possessed it stays. Such is the case with any natural perfection that is a good for the nature in question. When cognition is absent we call this bearing on good 'natural appetite'.

An intelligible nature has a like attitude towards a good apprehended through an intelligible form, so that it makes for that good when it is still to be gained, and rests with it when it is gained: both are functions of willing. Accordingly, anything with intellect has a will, just as anything with sensation has animal appetites.

So, there must be a will in God because there is intellect in him; and as his understanding is his existing, so also is his willing.

Hence:

1. Nothing outside himself is God's aim. All the same, he himself is the aim for all the things he makes; and he is so essentially since, as I have shown, God is goodness itself.[6] To be an aim implies being a good.
2. In our case, will is an appetitive part of our soul. Despite the fact that it gets its name from wanting, 'appetite' or desire is active not only when seeking what is not yet possessed but also when loving and delighting in what is possessed. It is in the last sense that we attribute

---

[3] *On the Soul* 3.10, 433b16.   [4] *Physics* 8.6, 258b10.   [5] Romans 12:2.   [6] 1a 6.3.

will to God, for his will always possesses the good which is its objective since, as I have pointed out, God's will does not differ essentially from that good.[7]

3. A will is changed by another when its main objective lies outside the one who is willing. But the objective of God's will is his own goodness, and this is his essence. His will itself is also his essence. So, it is not changed by anything extrinsic to it, but by God alone (if we may employ language which refers to understanding and willing as changes, as Plato did when he spoke of the First Changer changing himself).[8]

Article 2: Does God will things other than himself?

1. It seems that God does not will things other than himself. For his willing is simply his being. So, since he is not anything other than himself, he does not will anything other than himself.

2. Moreover, as Aristotle says, will is stirred by what is willed – as any desire is by what is desirable.[9] So, if God were to will something other than himself, he would be changed by it, which is impossible.

3. Moreover, when content with an object the will seeks nothing outside. Now his own goodness is enough for God, and there his will is well-content. So, he does not will anything other than himself.

4. Again, there are as many acts of will as there are objects willed. So, if God willed other things as well as himself, his acts of will would be many and so would his being, for his being is his willing. But this is impossible. So, God does not will things other than himself.

On the contrary, St Paul says, 'This is God's will, your sanctification.'[10]

Reply: That God wills things other than himself, and not himself alone, appears from the comparison I introduced in the previous article.[11] For things in nature not only have a natural tendency towards their own good (to obtain it when they have not got it, and to rest with it when they have). They also spread their own good to others so far as they can. Thus we observe that all active things, in so far as they are perfect and actual, reproduce their like. In the same way it belongs to the will to share

---

[7] See the body of the present article.　[8] *Phaedrus* 245c; *Laws* 894e; *Timaeus* 34b.
[9] *On the Soul* 3.10, 433b17.　[10] 1 Thessalonians 4:3.　[11] 1a 19.1.

with others the good that it possesses. This is especially so when it comes to God's will, from which every perfection derives by a kind of likeness. If the things of nature when at their best share their good with others, much more is it the characteristic of God's will to share his goodness with others (so far as this is possible). So God wills his own being and the being of others. But he wills himself as the end, and others as means to that end – in that it befits God's goodness that others should also share in it.

Hence:

1. Although God's willing is really his being, we form distinct notions of them according to our human manner of thought and expression – as is clear from what I have previously said.[12] By saying 'God exists', we do not imply a relationship to anything else, as we do when saying 'God wills'. So, though God is nothing other than himself, he wills something other than himself.

2. When we will things because of an end, that end is our whole reason for willing as we do, and it is this that moves our will. This is most conspicuously the case when our activity is just on account of an end, as our only purpose is health when taking an unpleasant dose of medicine, and this alone prompts the will. The case is different with some pleasant medicine, which we might sample for its own sake as well as for the health it brings. So though God, as I have said, wills things other than himself only for the sake of the end that is his goodness, it does not follow that anything other than his goodness changes his will.[13] Accordingly, just as God understands things other than himself in understanding his own essence, he wills such things in willing his own goodness.

3. Because God's will is content with his own goodness it follows that he wills nothing else except on that account, not that he wills nothing else. Similarly, though God's understanding is complete because he knows his own essence, God still knows other things through his essence.

4. As God's understanding is single, because he does not see many things save in unity, so his willing is single and simple, because he does not will many things save in the unity which is his own goodness.

[12] 1a 13.4.   [13] See the body of the present article.

Article 3: Does God will of necessity whatever he wills?

1. It seems that God wills of necessity whatever he wills. For everything eternal is necessary. But whatever God wills he wills from eternity, otherwise his willing would be changeable. So he wills whatever he wills of necessity.

2. Moreover, God wills things other than himself inasmuch as he wills his own goodness. But he has to will his own goodness. Of necessity, therefore, he wills things other than himself.

3. Moreover, whatever is natural to God is bound to be, since God exists necessarily in himself and is the source of everything else that is necessary (as I have shown).[14] Now it is natural for him to will whatever he wills, for, as we read in the *Metaphysics*, in God there can be nothing over and above his nature.[15] So he necessarily wills what he wills.

4. Again, 'not-to-be-necessary' and 'able-not-to-be' are equivalent. So if it were not necessary for God to will one among the things he wills, he could possibly not will it. He could also possibly will something that he does not in fact will. But this would mean that his will would be contingent and open to alternatives, and therefore imperfect – since everything contingent is imperfect and changeable.

5. Then also, as Averroes says, no action results from what is open to opposite courses unless it is impelled to one of them by an outside force.[16] So if God's will were ever posed before alternatives, its effecting one of them would be determined by something else and it would therefore have an antecedent cause.

6. Finally, whatever God knows he knows necessarily. Now, as his knowing is his being, so also is his willing. So whatever he wills he wills necessarily.

On the contrary, there is St Paul saying, 'God works everything according to the counsel of his will.'[17] Now, when we act deliberately we do not will of necessity. So, God does not necessarily will all that he wills.

Reply: We judge something to be absolutely necessary on the basis of some relation holding between terms: either because the predicate is

[14] 1a 2.3. [15] *Metaphysics* 4.5, 1015b15.
[16] *Commentary on Aristotle's Physics* 48. [17] Ephesians 1:11.

contained in the definition of the subject (thus, 'A human being is an animal' is necessary) or because the subject is part of the meaning of the predicate (thus, 'A number is odd or even' is necessary). 'Socrates is sitting' is not necessary in this way, and is, therefore, not absolutely necessary. But we can say that 'Socrates is sitting' is hypothetically necessary in the sense that it is true that if Socrates is sitting, he is sitting.

So, when it comes to what God wills, we should note that there is something he wills of absolute necessity, but that he does not necessarily will all that he wills. His will is necessarily related to his own goodness, which is its proper objective. So, he necessarily wills his own goodness (just as we cannot but will our own happiness). For that matter, every ability is similarly related to its proper and principal objective (like sight to colour) because it tends to this of its very nature.

But God wills things other than himself in so far as they are set towards his goodness as to their end. Now, by willing an end we are not bound to will the things that lead to it unless they are such that it cannot be attained without them (as when we have to will to eat in order to stay alive, or as when we have to will to take a boat in order to cross a sea). Other things, however, without which the end can be attained, are not things we will of necessity (e.g. a horse is not necessary for a journey we can take on foot). So, since God's goodness is perfect and can exist independently of other things, and since they add no perfection to him, there is no absolute need for him to will them. We can, however, acknowledge a hypothetical necessity here. For if God does will something, he cannot not will it (since his will is immutable).

Hence:

1. Granted that God wills whatever he does from eternity, it does not follow that he wills it necessarily – unless we suppose (hypothetically) that God actually does will whatever he wills from eternity.
2. That God necessarily wills his own goodness does not imply that he must will other things as well on that account, for his goodness can well be without them.
3. God's willing of any of the things he is not bound to will is not natural, nor is it unnatural or against nature. It is voluntary.
4. Necessary causes are not always related to their effects necessarily, and this is due to something lacking in the effects, not to something lacking in their causes. For instance, the sun's power is non-necessarily related

to contingent events on earth, not because of a defect in the sun's power, but because of a defect in effects which contingently result from it. This may serve to illustrate how God does not will of necessity any of the things he does will. It is not because of some defect in God's will, but because of a defect in the effects of his will in so far as they are effects, because they are such that, even without them, God's goodness could be complete. This lack belongs indeed to every created good.

5. The determining factor in producing an effect has to be exterior to any cause that is intrinsically contingent. But God's will, which is intrinsically necessary, is self-determining about an object of the will to which it is not necessarily disposed.

6. God's existing is essentially necessary, so the same applies to his knowing and willing. But God's knowing has a necessary relation to what he knows, while his willing is not so related to what he wills. This is because knowledge arises as things come to exist in knowers, while willing has to do with things as they exist in their own right. While having no absolute necessity as existing in themselves, therefore, all things other than God do have a necessity as existing in him, from which it follows that whatever God knows he knows of necessity. But it does not follow that he necessarily wills whatever he wills.

Article 4: Is God's will a cause of things?

1. It seems that God's will is not a cause of things. For Dionysius says, 'As our sun of its nature without thinking or choosing enlightens all on whom its light can shine, so the divine goodness by its very essence sheds the rays of its goodness upon everything that exists.'[18] But every voluntary agent acts as a thinking and choosing agent. So, God does not act through will, and his will, therefore, is not a cause of things.

2. Moreover, what is essentially so comes first in any class of things that are so as well; for instance, among things that burn there is a first, namely fire itself. But God is the first agent. So he is an agent by his essence, which is his nature. Accordingly, he acts by nature and not by will, and his will is therefore not a cause of things.

---

[18] *The Divine Names* 4. *PG* 3.693.

3. Moreover, a cause by nature, not by will, is that which has its effect just from being the kind of thing it is. Thus fire is the cause of heat because it is hot, whereas builders are the cause of a house because they will to construct it. Augustine says that it is because God is good that we exist.[19] So God is a cause of things by his nature, not by his will.

4. Again, there is one cause for one thing. But the cause of created things is God's knowledge, as I have said.[20] So we should not posit his will as a cause of things.

On the contrary, the book of Wisdom says, 'How could a thing remain unless you (God) willed it?'[21]

Reply: We cannot but hold that God's will is the cause of things, and that he works through will, and not, as some have thought, through necessity of his nature. We can show this in three ways.

The first is from the very order of agent causes. Since both nature and intelligence act for the sake of an end, as the *Physics* proves,[22] in the case of anything that acts by nature both the end and the means necessary to it have to be predetermined by some superior intelligence. An arrow's target and flight is set by an archer. So an intelligent and voluntary agent has to precede a physical agent. Now, since God is first in the order of agent causes, he must act through intelligence and will.

The second fixes on the meaning implied in being a natural agent to which it belongs that it produce one determinate effect – for a nature (unless impeded) works in one and the same way. This is because, having a determinate kind of being, and from being that kind of thing, it acts as it does, and while keeping this identity it does not act otherwise. But God's being is not of a determinate kind. It contains in itself the whole perfection of being. So it does not act by the determinism of a nature – unless perhaps it were to cause indeterminate and indefinite reality, and I have shown this to be impossible.[23] So God does not act from natural necessity. Rather, determinate effects proceed from his infinite perfection by the resolution of his intellect and will.

The third is from the relation of effects to causes. Effects proceed from agent causes because they pre-exist in them. For every agent cause

---

[19] *On Christian Doctrine* 1.32, *PL* 34.32.   [20] 1a 14.8.   [21] Wisdom 11:26.
[22] *Physics* 2.5, 196b21.   [23] 1a 7.2.

produces an effect like itself. Now effects pre-exist in a cause according to its mode of being. So, since God's being is his actual understanding, creatures pre-exist there as held in his mind. They therefore proceed from him as being comprehended. As a result, they also proceed from him as being willed, for the bent of will is to what is conceived

So God's will is the cause of things.

Hence:

1. By these words Dionysius does not mean absolutely to exclude choice as such from God. He means to exclude one sort of choice, namely, of failing to communicate his goodness to some creatures. He is bringing out that God communicates his goodness to all, not only to some.
2. Because God's very being is his activity of mind and will, it follows from the fact that he causes by his essence that he causes by way of his intellect and will.
3. Good is the object of the will. So Augustine's phrase, 'because God is good we exist', signifies that his goodness is the reason for his willing all other things, as I have said.[24]
4. Even with us one and the same effect has both mind and will as shaping causes, the first as conceiving the meaning of what we do, the second as executively commanding it. Whether an idea conceived in the mind is or is not realized in fact depends on the will. Hence, mere theoretical understanding is not committed to action. Effective ability is the cause that executes an action, for 'power' signifies the immediate source of action. But all these (i.e. intelligence, will and power) are one and the same thing in God.

Article 5: Can we ascribe any cause to God's willing?

1. It seems that we can ascribe a cause to God's willing. For Augustine asks, 'Who would venture to hold that God has established all things irrationally?'[25] But the reason for the acting of voluntary agents is the cause of their willing. So God's willing has a cause.
2. Moreover, when people make something due to no cause there is no need to look for any other cause than their will. Now, I have shown that God's will is the cause of all things.[26] So if his will has no cause,

---

[24] 1a 19.2. [25] *On Eighty-Three Varied Questions* 1.46. PL 40.30. [26] 1a 19.4.

there is no need to look to anything other than God's will for the cause of things in this world. But that would mean that all the sciences, which look for causes, would be idle efforts, which is absurd. So we should ascribe a cause to God's willing.

3. Again, what people willingly make without cause depends on them just choosing to make it. So if God's willing is without cause, everything that happens comes from his simply willing it without any other cause, which is absurd.

On the contrary, Augustine says, 'Every efficient cause is greater than the thing effected. But nothing is greater than God's will. So, we should not seek any cause for it.'[27]

Reply: God's willing is not in any way caused.

To make this clear, consider that, since willing corresponds to understanding, in the case of a being capable of both we can look for a cause for the one as we can for the other.

Now, what goes on in the mind is as follows. If we know a premise and a conclusion in separate acts, the understanding of the first is a cause of the demonstrated knowledge of the second. Whereas if the mind's insight into the principle reveals the conclusion, and both are seen in one glance, the demonstrated knowledge of the conclusion is not caused by the understanding of the principle, since what is one and the same is not caused by itself. Nevertheless the mind understands that the principle is the cause of the conclusion.

The will follows the same course, and ends are related to means in the case of the will in the same way as principles are related to conclusions in the case of the mind. So if we were to will an end by one action, and if we were to will the means to the end by another action, the act of will about the first will be the cause of acts of will about the second. The case, however, will be different if at one stroke we will both, since one and the same thing does not cause itself. Still it would be true to say that the means were willed because they are directed to the end.

By one act God understands everything in his essence. Similarly, he wills everything in his goodness by one act. So, just as in God the understanding of the cause is not the cause of his understanding an effect (though he understands effects in their cause), his willing an end does not cause his willing things subordinate to it (though he does will them to be ordered to that end). In other words, he wills this to be because of that, but he does not will this because he wills that.

Hence:

1. God's will is reasonable, because he wills one thing to be for the sake of another, not because there is a cause for his willing.
2. Since God wills effects to be such that they come from various causes in order to maintain an order among things, it is not superfluous to look for other causes even apart from God's will. But it would be superfluous to seek them as though they were first causes, independent of his will. Hence Augustine remarks, 'It flattered the vanity of philosophers to attribute contingent effects to equally contingent causes, since they were not able to see the cause above them all, namely God's will.'[28]
3. Since God wills that effects come from their causes, whenever they presuppose some other effect they do not stem solely from God's will, but from something else as well. But the original effects depend on his will alone. For instance, let us say that God willed people to have hands to minister to understanding by performing various human works, willed them to have understanding in order to be people and willed them to be people in order to enjoy heaven and crown the universe. This is still not tantamount to resolving the series into further created ends. Eventually all goes back to the simple will of God, though non-ultimates also enter into a system of other causes.

Article 6: Is God's will always fulfilled

1. It seems that God's will is not always fulfilled. For St Paul says, 'God wills everyone to be saved and to come to know the truth.'[29] But things do not turn out that way. So, God's will is not always fulfilled.
2. Moreover, knowing is to things that are true as willing is to things that are good. But God knows everything true, and therefore wills everything good. Yet not everything good takes place, for many things can come to be good that fail to do so. So, God's will is not always achieved.

---

[28] *On the Trinity* 3.2. *PL* 42.871.   [29] 1 Timothy 2:4.

3. Again, although it is a first cause, God's will does not rule out intermediate causes, as I have said.[30] But an effect of first causes can be hindered by defects in secondary causes – as, for example, the power of walking is hindered by paralysis in a leg. So defects in secondary causes can prevent the effect of God's will. So, God's will is not always fulfilled.

On the contrary, there is the Psalmist saying, 'Whatever he wills, he does.'[31]

Reply: God's will is inevitably always fulfilled.

Here is the evidence. Since an effect is conformed to an agent by means of the effect's own form, the same sort of reasoning applies to efficient causes as to formal causes. With formal causes this is the rule: that although a thing can fail to have some particular form, it cannot be altogether formless; a thing may be neither human nor alive, but it cannot not be a being. Likewise with efficient causes. Something can result which is outside the order of one particular efficient cause, but not outside the order of the universal cause, which covers all particular causes. The fact that one particular cause fails to produce its effect comes from the interference of another particular cause, yet this last itself is enveloped by the universal cause. So no effect can in any way escape from the sway of the universal cause. This is clear even in the case of corporeal things. A particular star may be stopped from exerting its influence, but every effect that results in corporeal things because of hindrance by a bodily cause has to be traced back through intermediate causes to the universal power of the first heaven.

So, because it is the universal cause of all things, God's will cannot but achieve its effect, and whatever seems to depart from his will from one point of view returns to it from another. Thus people who, in so far as they can, abandon God's will by sinning fall under its order when they are punished by divine justice.

Hence:

1. We can understand the quotation from St Paul, that God wills everyone to be saved, in three senses.

   First, by restricted application so as to mean 'God wills those to be saved who are saved.' As Augustine explains, that is not so because

---

[30] 1a 19.3. [31] Psalms 113:11.

there is nobody whom God does not will to be saved, but because nobody is saved whom he does not will to be saved.[32]

Second, by application to each class of every individual, not to each individual of every class. This gives us the sense 'God wills some to be saved of every condition (men and women, Jews and Gentiles, humble and great), but not all of every condition.'

Third, and according to Damascene, St Paul's words refer to an antecedent will, not a consequent one.[33] This distinction concerns things willed, not God's willing itself, where there is no before or after.

To appreciate what this means, note that God wills everything in so far as it is good. Now, a thing may be good or bad at first sight, and looked at in isolation, only to turn out the reverse when conjoined in its context with another element. For example, it is good, absolutely speaking, for people to live, and bad for them to die. But if we are dealing with people who are murderers or public dangers, then it is good that they should be killed and bad that they should remain at large. Accordingly, we can speak of a justice that *antecedently* wishes every human being to live, but *consequently* pronounces the capital sentence. By analogy, therefore, God antecedently wills all people to be saved, yet consequently wills some to be damned as his justice requires.

Now, to will antecedently is not to will downrightly, but only in a certain respect. For willing goes out to things just as they really are and standing in all their particularity, so that we downrightly will a thing surrounded by all its circumstances; this is what is meant by 'consequent will'. Accordingly we may speak of a just judge then and there quite simply willing a murderer to be hanged, though in a certain respect, when the criminal is considered as a human being, the judge wills the criminal to live. We can call such a qualified willing more a wishing than a sheer willing.

Clearly, then, whatever God wills, simply speaking, comes about, though what he wills antecedently does not.

2. A cognitive power is active in so far as the known is in the knower, whereas activity of an appetitive power is set on things as they are in

---

[32] *A Handbook on Faith, Hope and Love (Enchiridion)* 103. *PL* 40.280.
[33] *On the Orthodox Faith* 2.29. *PG* 94.968.

themselves. The whole of what is genuinely real and true exists virtually in God, though not in Creation. So, God knows all truth. But he does not will every good, except in so far as he wills himself, in whom every good exists virtually.

3. A first cause can be prevented from achieving its effect through failure in a secondary cause when it is not the universally first cause which embraces within itself all causality. But, as I have said, God's will is the universally first cause which embraces within itself all causality. So, no effect can stray from its plan in any way at all.[34]

Article 7: Is God's will changeable?

1. It seems that God's will is changeable. For the Lord says, 'I regret that I made human beings.'[35] But those who regret what they have done have a will that changes. So, God's will is changeable.

2. Moreover, Jeremiah speaks in the person of the Lord: 'Sometimes I threaten to pluck out and pull down and destroy a nation or a kingdom. But if that nation on which I have pronounced turns from its evil, I shall also repent of the evil which I threatened to do.'[36] So, God has a changeable will.

3. Moreover, God's works are wrought through his will. Yet he is not always consistent. Sometimes he commands legal observances, while at other times he forbids them. So, he has a changeable will.

4. Again, as I have already said, God does not will what he wills of necessity.[37] So, he can both will and not will the same thing. But to be poised before alternatives is to be open to change – thus something which may or may not exist is mutable in substance, and something which may be here or there is movable in place. So, God's will is mutable.

On the contrary, there is the text in Numbers: 'God is not a human being, that he should lie, nor is he like human offspring, that he should be changed.'[38]

Reply: God's will is altogether unchangeable. Here, though, we should note that it is one thing to change one's will and another to will that some

---

[34] See the body of the present article. [35] Genesis 6:7. [36] Jeremiah 18:7–8.
[37] 1a 19.3. [38] Numbers 23:19.

things change. While remaining constant, people can will this to happen now and the contrary to happen afterwards. Their will, however, would change were they to begin to will what they had not willed before, or cease to will what they had willed before.

Such readjustment presupposes a change in either the substantial disposition or the knowledge of the people who will. Since the will is set on good, they can begin to will something new in two ways. First, because it starts to be good for them, which means that they must accommodate themselves to a fresh situation (e.g. when winter comes they like to warm themselves at the fire, which was not the case during the summer). Or secondly, they find out for the first time that something is good for them. Indeed, we deliberate in order to discover what we did not appreciate earlier.

I have already shown that God's nature as well as his knowledge is altogether immutable.[39] So, his will is immutable also.

Hence:

1. We should understand the Lord's words metaphorically and according to a human analogy. When we regret what we have made, we throw it away. Yet this does not always mean that we have second thoughts or a change of will, for we may originally intend both to make something and scrap it afterwards. By similitude with such a procedure we refer to God having regrets, for instance in the account of the Flood, in which we read that God washed off the face of the earth the people whom he had made.

2. Though God's will is the first and universal cause, it does not exclude intermediate causes that are able to produce some effects. Yet, because no intermediate cause matches the first cause in power, there are many things in God's knowledge, will and power that do not come within the scope of inferior causes: the raising of Lazarus from the dead, for instance. Looking merely at them you could have forecast that Lazarus would not rise, but allowing for the first and divine cause you could have declared that he would.

And God wills both of these – namely that something is going to result from inferior causes that will not result from a higher cause, or conversely. So we need to say that God sometimes pronounces on

---

[39] 1a 9.1; 14.5.

a future event happening according to a system of inferior causes (e.g. according to the course of nature or a person's merits), though the event, in fact, will not come about according to the ordination of the higher divine cause. For example, God told Hezekiah, 'Set your house in order, for you shall die and not live'[40] – something which did not happen, because God's knowledge and will had disposed otherwise, and because these are unchangeable. Hence Gregory says that 'God changes his sentence, but not his plan'[41] (i.e. the plan of his will).

So to speak of God as repenting is to talk metaphorically. We say that people repent when they do not carry out what they threatened to do.

3. The conclusion to this argument is not that God's will changes, but that he wills change.

4. Though God's willing something is not absolutely necessary, nevertheless, as I have shown, it is necessary on a supposition, because of the immutability of God's will.[42]

Article 8: Does God's will impose necessity on the things he wills?

1. It would seem that God's will does impose necessity on the things he wills. For Augustine says, 'No one is saved except those whom God has willed to be saved. We must therefore beseech him to will, for if he does our salvation is bound to come about.'[43]

2. Again, every cause that cannot be hindered produces its effect of necessity. As Aristotle remarks, even nature works always to the same effect unless something stops it.[44] But God's will cannot be hindered. St Paul asks, 'Who has resisted his will?'[45] So, God's will imposes necessity on the things he wills.

3. Moreover, that which is invested with necessity from something prior is absolutely necessary. Thus an animal has to die since it is compounded of contrary elements. To the things created by God his will is like something prior to them by which they have necessity. Now, since the following conditional sentence is true, 'If God wills a thing it

---

[40] Isaiah 38:1.   [41] *Morals* 16.10. PL 70.1127.   [42] 1a 19.3.
[43] *A Handbook on Faith, Hope and Love (Enchiridion)* 103. PL 40.280.
[44] *Physics* 2.8, 199b18.   [45] Romans 9:19.

is so', and since every true conditional sentence is necessary, it follows that everything God wills is absolutely necessary.

On the contrary, God wills into being every good that is made. Were his will to impose necessity on the things he wills it would follow that everything good came about inevitably, and this would do away with deliberation, and free choice, and the like.

Reply: God's will imposes necessity on some things he wills, but not on all.

Some have wanted to find the reason for this in the intermediate causes at work, explaining that what God produces through necessary causes is necessary, and that what he produces through contingent causes is contingent.

But this explanation seems inadequate, and on two grounds. First, an effect of a primary cause is hindered and rendered contingent by a defect in a secondary cause, as when the sun's power is ineffective because of some flaw in a plant. But no defect in a secondary cause can stop God's will from taking effect. Second, if the distinction between necessary and contingent effects stems only from secondary causes, it would follow that the distinction falls outside God's intending and willing, which cannot be the case.

So, it is better to say that something happens contingently because of the effectiveness of God's will. When a fully effective cause operates, an effect issues from the cause, not only in the sense that it comes to be, but also in the mode of its coming to be or existing. It is because the powers of reproduction are not fully causal that offspring are born who are unlike their parents with respect to accidental properties that pertain to their mode of existing. So, since God's will is the most effective of all causes, those things come about which God wills, and they also come about in the manner that he wills them to.

Moreover, God wills some things to become real necessarily, and others contingently, so that there may be an order among things to render the universe complete. Accordingly, for some effects he has designed necessary causes which cannot fail and from which effects result necessarily; and for other effects he has designed contingent and defectible causes, from which effects result contingently. So, the reason why effects willed by God come about contingently is not because their proximate causes are contingent, but because God has prepared contingent causes for them because he willed that they come about contingently.

Hence:

1. We should understand Augustine as saying that in things willed by God there is a necessity that is hypothetical rather than absolute. For the conditional proposition 'If God wills something, it is bound to be' is necessarily true.

2. Indeed, nothing resists God's will, and from this it follows not only that everything God wills comes about, but also that it comes about necessarily or contingently just as he wills.

3. Consequents have necessity from antecedents according to the mode of the antecedents. So things which come into being from God's will also have that necessity which God wills them to have, whether absolute or only conditional. Accordingly, not all of them are absolutely necessary.

Article 9: Does God will evils?

1. It seems that God does will evils. For he wills every good that is realized. But it is good that evils come about, for Augustine says: 'Although bad things are not good in so far as they are bad, it is good that not only good things but also evil things should exist.'[46] So, God wills evils.

2. Moreover, Dionysius says, 'There will be evil contributing to the perfection of the whole universe.'[47] And Augustine says, 'The wonderful beauty of the universe is built up of every part, and what we call evil in it, in proportion and its proper place, highlights good things, which are more pleasing and praiseworthy when they are contrasted with evils.'[48] But God wills everything that pertains to the perfection and beauty of the universe, for this, above all, is what he wills in creatures. So, God wills evils.

3. Again, 'Evils exist' and 'Evils do not exist' are logically inconsistent. But God does not will evils not to be, otherwise, since some do arise in fact, his will would then not always be fulfilled. So, God wills evils to exist.

---

[46] *A Handbook on Faith, Hope and Love* (*Enchiridion*) 96. *PL* 40.276.
[47] *The Divine Names* 4. *PG* 3.717.
[48] *A Handbook on Faith, Hope and Love* (*Enchiridion*) 10. *PL* 40.236.

On the contrary, there is Augustine saying, 'Nobody wise makes another person worse. But God surpasses all in wisdom. Much less, therefore, is he the author of making anybody worse. And when we say that God is the author of something we mean that he wills it.'[49] So, that anybody becomes worse is not by God's willing it. But every evil clearly makes something worse. So, God does not will it.

Reply: Since to be good and to be desirable signify the same (as I have already said),[50] and since evil is the opposite of good, it is out of the question that any evil as such can be directly wanted, either by natural appetite, or by animal appetite, or by intelligent appetite, which is will.

But something evil may be desired indirectly, as resulting from a good, and this appears in every kind of desiring. For no natural agent intends privation or destruction. Rather, it strives for a form which involves a privation of another form, and it desires the coming to be of something that spells the destruction of something else. Thus a lion kills a deer for the sake of food, and this involves death, and a fornicator seeks pleasure, which involves the ugliness of sin. Evil has a good attached to it, but this goes with the deprivation of another good. No one would desire evil, not even indirectly, unless the concomitant good were more desired than the good of which the evil is a deprivation.

Now, God wills no good more than his own goodness, though with regard to particular goods he wills one more than another. So, God in no way wills moral evil, which upsets the ordering of things to divine good. But he does will physical evil or suffering by willing the good to which it is attached. For instance, in willing justice he wills a penalty, and in willing to maintain the balance of nature, he wills that some things should naturally die away.

Hence:

1. Some have held that although God does not will evils, he wills them to come to be and exist, for though they are not good it is well if they enter or are present. The reason they allege, is that intrinsically evil things are ordered to some good. They suppose that they point to this arrangement by speaking of the good that arises from the arrival and presence of evils. But their manner of expression is not correct. For evil is not intrinsically ordered to good. It is ordered to good only

---

[49] *On Eighty-Three Varied Questions* 1.46. *PL* 40.11.   [50] 1a 5.1.

indirectly. That good should follow is beside the intention of anyone doing wrong: thus it was no part of the purpose of tyrants that the patience of martyrs should be displayed by their persecutions. You do not imply a real orientation towards good by talking about the goodness of evil entering or being present on the scene. For we judge things by what belongs to them intrinsically, not by what belongs to them incidentally.

2. As I have said, evil does not conspire to the achievement and beauty of the universe except incidentally.[51] When Dionysius refers to evil as contributing to the perfection of the whole he concludes by showing that he is arguing from an untenable premise.

3. 'Evils exist' and 'Evils do not exist' are contradictory statements. But 'God wills evils to exist' and 'God wills evils not to exist' are not so opposed since each is affirmative. God neither wills evils to be nor wills them not to be. He wills to allow them to happen, and this is good.

Article 10: Does God have free choice?

1. It would seem that God does not have free choice. For Jerome writes, 'God is the only one who neither sins nor can sin. All others that have free choice can be turned to one side or the other.'[52]

2. Moreover, free choice is the power of reason and will to choose good or evil. But I have just said that God does not will evil.[53] So, God has no free choice.

On the contrary, there is Ambrose teaching, 'The Holy Spirit shares with each one as he wills, that is by the free choice of will, not as bound by necessity.'[54]

Reply: We have free choice with respect to anything that we do not will by necessity or natural instinct. Now we wish to be happy by an instinctive drive which is not of our own free choice. We do not speak of other animals, which respond to their environment by natural instinct as being moved by choice. Since God wills his own goodness of necessity, but not other things, as I have noted,[55] he has free choice about the latter.

[51] See the reply to objection 1 in the present article.　[52] Letter 21. *PL* 22.393.
[53] 1a 19.9.　[54] *On Faith* 2.6. *PL* 16.592.　[55] 1a 19.3.

Hence:

1. Jerome would seem to be ruling out from God, not free choice as such, but free choice that can be turned to sin.
2. Since moral evil, by definition, is a turning away from God's goodness (whereby, as I have shown, God wills all things),[56] God clearly cannot choose to do what is morally evil. Yet there are other alternatives between which he can will such and such to happen or not. In somewhat the same manner, without being confronted with any moral issue, we can choose to sit down or not.

Article 11: Can we signpost God's will?

1. It seems that we cannot signpost God's will. For God's will is the cause of things just as his knowledge is. But we do not mark signs when it comes to God's knowledge. Why then should we expect to mark them on the part of his will?
2. Again, any sign not corresponding to what it signifies is false. So if the signposts of God's willing do not correspond to God's will, they are false; and if they do correspond, they are redundant. So, we should not mark out signs of God's will.

On the contrary, though God's will is single, being identical with his essence, it is still sometimes signified in the plural. As the psalm says, 'Great are the works of the Lord, sought out according to all his wills.'[57] On occasion, then, we should take a sign of God's will for what he wills.

Reply: As I have shown, we attribute some properties to God in their proper sense, and we attribute others to him metaphorically.[58] When we metaphorically attribute certain human emotions to God we fix on some likeness in their effect – so that we apply to him what in us is a sign of an emotion, and we do so by a figure of speech which names that emotion. We are prone to punish when we are angry, and the punishment is a sign of our anger. Thus we signify punishment when we speak of anger and employ the term with respect to God. Similarly, we sometimes metaphorically take what common usage treats as a sign of our will to signify God's will. Commands people issue are signs that they will such and such

---

[56] 1a 19.2.   [57] Psalms 110:2.   [58] 1a 13.3.

to be done. So, we sometimes refer to a divine command as God's will – as in 'May your will be done on earth as it is in heaven.'[59]

Yet notice this difference between being angry and willing. We do not attribute anger to God literally since its chief meaning implies an emotional condition. On the other hand, however, we do predicate will of God literally. That is why we distinguish between God's will in its literal and its metaphorical sense – calling the first his 'will of good pleasure', and the second a 'will of sign' (in that the sign is a pointer to his will).

Hence:

1. Knowledge is only the cause of something being done when will is at work. We do not do the things we know unless we will them. That is why we do not associate signs with knowing in the way that we do with willing.

2. We speak of these signs as divine willings, not because they are signs that God wills, but because we extend to him what we are accustomed to treat as signs of our willing. Punishment, for instance, is not a sign that indicates real anger in God. But it is a sign of anger in us, and with this implication we stretch the word when it comes to God.

Article 12: Can we fittingly set down five signs of God's will?

1. It seems incorrect to posit these five signs of God's will, namely *prohibition*, *precept*, *counsel*, *doing* and *permission*. For what God commands or advises us to do he sometimes also works in us, and what he forbids he sometimes permits. Since they overlap we cannot divide them as logical opposites.

2. Moreover, as Wisdom says, God does not bring anything about without willing it.[60] But we contrast the signs of his will that I am now discussing (his 'signed will', as we say) with his own 'will of good pleasure' (as we call it). So, *doing* should not be included among them.

3. Moreover, what God *does* and what he *permits* concerns all creatures, for he acts in all things, and in all he allows things to happen. But what he *commands*, *counsels* and *forbids* concerns intelligent creatures. So, it

---

[59] Matthew 6:10.   [60] Wisdom 11:25–6.

is wrong to enumerate these five types in the same division, for they do not fall under the same heading.

4. Again, evil occurs more variously than good, for, as Aristotle[61] and Dionysius[62] point out, 'there is one way of being good, but many of being bad'. So, it seems odd to mark one sign only with respect to evil (i.e. *prohibition*) and two with respect to good (i.e. *precept* and *counsel*).

Reply: The signs of will I am now speaking about are those by which we are accustomed to show that we will something. You make your intentions clear about what you want done either by yourself or by another. If by yourself, you carry it out on your own, whether directly or indirectly and incidentally – directly, when you perform it yourself (the sign of this will is called *doing*), indirectly, when you do not stop what is going on, for, Aristotle says, we call one who removes an obstacle an incidental cause, and we call the sign of such a will *permission*.[63] You may also declare your intention through others in that you direct them to see to it. If the lead you give is imperative then the sign is a *precept* for what you will, and a *prohibition* for the contrary; if advisory, the appropriate sign is *counsel*.

Because we manifest our will in these five fashions, we sometimes take them to refer to divine willings as being signs of them. That we may call *command*, *counsel* and *prohibition* God's will is clear from the text, 'May your will be done on earth as it is in heaven.'[64] That *permission* and *doing* fall into the same class is clear from Augustine, who says, 'Nothing is done except what the Almighty wills to be done, either by permitting it or by doing it.'[65]

Or you might say that *permitting* and *doing* refer to the present (the one with regard to evil, the other with regard to good) and that the other terms refer to the future, *prohibiting* with regard to evil, *commanding* with regard to obligatory good, and *counselling* with regard to overflowing good.

Hence:

1. There is nothing to stop people declaring their will about the same thing in different ways, just as several words can be found to signify

---

[61] *Nicomachean Ethics* 2.6, 1106b35.   [62] *The Divine Names* 4. PG 3.729.
[63] *Physics* 8.4, 255b24.   [64] Matthew 6:10.
[65] *A Handbook on Faith, Hope and Love* (*Enchiridion*) 95. PL 40.276.

the same thing. So, there is no reason why the same situation cannot fall under precept, counsel and doing, or under prohibition and permission.

2. We may metaphorically signify that God wills what he does not literally will, and also that he wills what he does literally will. There is nothing to forbid his will of good pleasure and a sign of his will coinciding in the same object. Indeed his doing is always identical with his will of good pleasure, though his commanding or counselling are not, both because his doing is in the present, whereas the others are about the future, and because his doing of itself is an effect of his will, whereas the others, as I have noted, refer to what is to be effected by another.

3. Rational creatures are in control of their actions. So special signs of God's will are assigned concerning them in that God ordains them to act voluntarily and of themselves. But other creatures do not act except as acted on by God's operation. In their case there is place only for doing and permitting.

4. Though they crop up in many ways, moral evils agree in this: that they clash with God's will. So, with respect to them we set down only one sign: prohibition. Good things, however, have all sorts of relations to God's goodness. Without some we cannot attain its enjoyment; these are the subjects of command. Others help us to reach it the better; these are the subjects of counsel. I might add that counsel is not only about striving after better goods, but also about avoiding lesser evils.

Question 20

Love in God

Here there are four points of inquiry:

1. Does God love?
2. Does God love everything?
3. Does God love some things more than others?
4. Does God love better things more?

Article 1: Does God love?

1. It seems that God does not love. For there is no passion (no capacity to be moved[1]) in God. But love is a passion. So, God does not love.
2. Moreover, love, grief, anger, and so forth are divisions of the same class. But we only attribute grief or anger to God metaphorically. The same, therefore, goes for love.
3. Again, Dionysius says, 'Love is a joining and binding force.'[2] But there can be no such thing in God since he is simple. So, God does not love.

On the contrary, there is St John writing, 'God is love'.[3]

Reply: We have to hold that God loves. For love is the first motion of will and of any appetitive power since the activities of these powers tend towards good or evil as their proper objectives. Because good is the more principal and intrinsic objective of will and appetite, and because evil is secondary and because of something else which then and there is the

---

[1] The Latin here was translated 'changed' above.   [2] *The Divine Names* 4. PG 3.713.
[3] 1 John 4:16.

opposite of good, acts of will and appetite bent on a good are prior in the nature of things to those bent on evil. Hence, for example, joy is more fundamental than sadness, and love is more fundamental than hate. For what intrinsically exists is always prior to what exists because of another.

Again, what is more universal is prior by nature. Our intellect, for instance, engages with truth as such before it bears on particular truths. Now, some activities of will and appetite engage with good qualified by certain conditions. For example, joy and delight engage with a good that is present and possessed, while desire and hope engage with a good that is not yet possessed. Love, however, is for what is good in general – whether possessed or not. Of its nature, therefore, it is the first act of appetite and will.

Consequently, all other movements of appetite and will presuppose love; it is their very root, so to speak. For no one desires or rejoices in anything except as a good that is loved. Nor is there any hatred except for what is contrary to something loved. And the same applies to grief and the rest. They all clearly must be traced back to love as their first principle. For that reason, wherever there is will or appetite, there must be love, since if you take away the first principle, the rest disappear as well. But I have shown that there is will in God,[4] and we must therefore affirm that there is love in him as well.

Hence:

1. A cognitive power does not set things in motion except through an appetitive power. Just as our abstract reason works through our sense of fact (as Aristotle says),[5] so our intelligent appetite (which we call will) works through our sense appetites. Hence, sensitive appetite is the proximate moving principle for animal bodies. So, its activity is always accompanied by bodily change, especially round the heart, the prime vital organ of animal life (according to Aristotle).[6]

   Because they are bound up with bodily changes, we call activities of the sense appetite 'passions' – a word we do not use when referring to activities of the will. Loving, enjoying and delighting are passions when they signify activities of the sensitive appetite; not so, however, when they signify activities of intelligent appetite. It is in this last sense that we attribute them to God. Hence Aristotle says

---

[4] 1a 19.1.   [5] *On the Soul* 3.11, 434a20.   [6] *On the Parts of Animals* 2.1, 647a30; 3.4, 666a35.

that God rejoices in one simple activity.[7] For this reason, God loves without passion.

2. In a passion of the sensitive appetite we can distinguish between a quasi-material element, or bodily change, and a quasi-formal element of a voluntary appetite as such. Thus, as noted by Aristotle, when it comes to anger the quasi-material element is a surging of the blood to the heart (or something of the sort), and the quasi-formal element is a desire for revenge.[8] Now, in some passions this formal element implies an imperfection; thus desire is for a good that is not yet possessed, and grief is about an evil that one has (likewise with anger which supposes grief). But other passions – such as love and joy – imply no such imperfection.

   Since, as I have shown, we rightly attribute no passions to God in so far as they contain a bodily element,[9] we can only metaphorically attribute to him passions implying even a formal imperfection – because of a likeness in their effects (as I have also explained).[10] But we can rightly and properly attribute to God passions whose formal meaning implies no incompleteness – love and joy have this character (though, as I have said, for God to have these is not for him to be acted on).[11]

3. An act of love always tends to two things: the good that one wills to someone, and the someone to whom one wills it. For, properly speaking, loving people is willing good for them. So, in loving yourself you are willing yourself good, for you seek to join yourself with a good as much as you can. We can therefore say that love is a joining force, even in God (though without implying composition). For the good he wills himself is nothing other than himself, who is good of his essence, as I have shown.[12]

   By loving other people you will good to them and treat them as yourself: good for them is good for you. So, we call love a binding force because it joins us to others whom we hold as we hold ourselves. God's love is a binding force in this sense: because he wills good to others (without there being any composition in him).

---

[7] *Nicomachean Ethics* 7.14, 1154b26.   [8] *On the Soul* 1.1, 403a30.
[9] See the reply to objection 1 in the present article.   [10] 1a 3.2, *ad* 2; 19.11.
[11] See the reply to objection 1 in the present article.   [12] 1a 6.3.

Article 2: Does God love everything?

1. It seems that God does not love everything. For according to Dionysius, 'Love carries lovers outside themselves, and it transports them somehow into their beloved.'[13] But it is improper to speak of God being carried or transported outside himself. So, it is wrong to speak of him as loving something other than himself.

2. Moreover, God's love is eternal. But things other than God are not eternal except in God. So, God does not love them except as they are in himself. Yet considered as such they are not other than himself. So, God does not love anything other than himself.

3. Moreover, there are two kinds of love: the love of desire and the love of friendship. But God does not love non-rational creatures with love of desire, for he needs nothing outside himself. Nor does he love them with the love of friendship, for, as Aristotle points out, one cannot have this for non-rational things.[14] So, God does not love everything.

4. Again, the psalm says 'You, God, hate all workers of iniquity.'[15] But one cannot hate and love something simultaneously. So, God does not love everything.

On the contrary, the book of Wisdom says, 'You, God, love everything that exists, and you hate nothing you have made.'[16]

Reply: God loves all existing things. For everything that exists is, as such, good, because the very existing of each thing is a certain good, as are each of its perfections. Now I have already shown that God's will is the cause of all things and that everything therefore has to be willed by God in so far as it has reality or any goodness at all.[17] So, God wills some good to every existing thing. Since loving is the same as willing good to something, God clearly loves everything.

Yet he does not love things as we do. For since our will is not the cause of things being good, but responds to that goodness as to its objective, our love in willing good for something is not the cause of that goodness. Instead, its goodness (real or imagined) evokes the love by which we will for the thing both that it retains the goodness it has and that it gains

---

[13] *The Divine Names* 4. PG 3.712. [14] *Nicomachean Ethics* 8.11, 1155b27. [15] Psalms 5:5.
[16] Wisdom 11:25. [17] 1a 19.4.

goodness which it lacks, and we act so as to bring this about. But God's love pours out and creates the goodness of things.

Hence:

1. Lovers are transported outside themselves into their beloved in that they will the good of their beloved and provide for it as though acting for themselves. That is why Dionysius says, 'We dare to affirm, the truth compelling us, that even he who is the cause of all by his abounding loving kindness is in ecstasy by his providence for every-thing that exists.'[18]

2. Though creatures are only eternal in God, yet because they are present to him he knows them from eternity in their own proper nature, and from eternity loves them accordingly. Similarly, by the forms of things which are in us we know things which exist in themselves.

3. There can be friendship only between rational beings who are able to return love and share in life's activities, and for whom things can turn out well or badly through the vicissitudes of good fortune and happi-ness. There can also be benevolence, in the proper sense of the term, between beings such as these. But non-rational creatures cannot attain to loving God, or sharing in the intelligence and blessedness of his life. Strictly speaking, therefore, God does not love them with the love of friendship but, as it were, with the love of desire, in that he ordains them for the sake of intelligent creatures and even for himself (not that he needs them, but on account of his own goodness and for our benefit). After all, one can desire things for others, as well as for oneself.

4. There is nothing to prevent something being loved in one respect and hated in another. God loves sinners in so far as they are natural things of some kind. Such they are, and God made them what they are. In so far as they are sinners, however, they are unreal and deficient in being. Considered as such, they are not from God. So in this respect he hates them.

Article 3: Does God love all things equally?

1. It seems that God does love all things equally. For Wisdom says, 'He has equal care for everything.'[19] But God's providence for

---

[18] *The Divine Names* 4. PG 3.712.   [19] Wisdom 6:8.

things comes from the love that he bears them. So, he loves everything equally.

2. Moreover, God's love is his essence. But God's essence does not
   admit of more or less. Nor then does his love. So, he does not love
   some things more than others.

3. Again, as God's love extends to created things so does his knowledge
   and will. But we do not say that God knows or wills some things more
   than others. So, we should not say that he loves some things more than
   others.

On the contrary, we have Augustine saying, 'God loves all things that
he has made, and among them he more deeply loves intelligent things,
and among these he more fully loves those who are members of his only-
begotten Son, and, much more than these, he loves his only-begotten Son
himself.'[20]

Reply: Since to love is to will good for something, there are two senses
in which something can be more or less loved.

The first is relative to the act of willing itself, which can admit of
degrees of intensity. In this sense God does not love some things more
than others, because he loves everything by one simple act of will that is
always steadily the same.

The second is relative to the good which is willed. In this sense we
speak of loving one person more than another because we will them a
greater good, though not by a more intense will. In this sense we have to
say that God loves some things more than others. For since, as I have
noted, his love is the cause of things,[21] one thing would not be better than
another but for God willing it more good.

Hence:

1. We speak of God having equal care for all things not because he
   dispenses the same blessings on all he looks after but because he
   directs all things with equal wisdom and goodness.

2. This argument holds with respect to the intensity of love in the
   activity of will, which is God's essence. But the good that God wills
   to creatures is not his essence, and the argument does not show why
   that may not be of greater or lesser degree.

[20] *On John* 90. PL 35.1924.   [21] 1a 20.2.

3. Understanding and willing only signify acts. They do not include in their meaning reference to objects, which are sufficiently different that we are led to say that God knows or wills them more or less – as we can say (and as I have said in this article) that he loves some things more than others.

Article 4: Does God always love better things more?

1. It seems that God does not always love better things more. For Christ is manifestly better than the whole human race since he is both divine and human. But according to Romans God loves the human race more than Christ: 'He did not spare his own Son but delivered him up for us all.'[22] So, God does not always love better things more.

2. Moreover, an angel is better than a human being. As the psalm says of people, 'You have made them a little lower than angels.'[23] But God loved people more than angels, for Hebrews says, 'He is never concerned with angels, but he is concerned with the offspring of Abraham.'[24] So, he does not always love better things more.

3. Moreover, Peter was better than John since he loved Christ more. Knowing this to be true, Our Lord asked him, 'Simon son of John, do you love me more than these others?'[25] But he loved John more. As Augustine, commenting on the text about 'the disciple whom Jesus loved'[26] says, 'This marks John out from the band of disciples – not that Jesus loved him alone, but that he loved him more than the rest.'[27] So, God does not always love better things more.

4. Moreover, it is better to be sinless than repentant. As Jerome says, 'Repentance is a second plank after a shipwreck.'[28] But God prefers those who are contrite to those who are innocent, for he rejoices over them more. As the Gospel of Luke says, 'I tell you that there will be more joy in heaven over one sinner who repents than over ninety-nine just people who do not need to repent.'[29] So, God does not always love better things more.

5. Again, good people who are foreknown to be damned are better than sinners who are predestined to be saved, though God loves the latter

---

[22] Romans 8:32.   [23] Psalms 8:6.   [24] Hebrews 2:16.   [25] John 21:15.   [26] John 21:20.
[27] *On John* 124. *PL* 35.1974.   [28] *On Isaiah* 2, on 3:8. *PL* 24.66.   [29] Luke 15:7.

more since he wills them more good (i.e. eternal life). So, God does not always love better things more.

On the contrary, everything loves what is like itself. For as Ecclesiasticus says, 'Every animal loves its like.'[30] But the better something is, the more like God it is, and he therefore loves it more.

Reply: Given what I have already said,[31] we have to conclude that God loves better things more. For I have shown that God's loving something more is nothing else than his willing it more good. For his will is the cause of the goodness of things, and the reason why some things are better than others is that God wills them more good. So, it follows that he loves better things more.

Hence:

1. God loves Christ not only more than he does the whole human race, but even more than he loves the entire created universe. For he willed him the greatest good in giving him 'the name which is above every name',[32] Christ being truly God. Nor is his excellence diminished because God gave him over to death in order to rescue the human race. On the contrary, because of this Christ became a glorious conqueror. As Isaiah says, 'The government is upon his shoulders.'[33]

2. As I have just implied, God loves the human nature that was assumed by the Word of God in Christ more than he loves all angels.[34] That nature is higher than that of angels, chiefly because of its union with God. But if we think of human nature in general, and if we compare it with that of angels, we can say that the two are equal in the order of grace and glory. For as the Apocalypse says, 'the measure of people is that of the angels'.[35] So, in this sense some people are greater than some angels, and some angels are greater than some people. But considered simply as angels, angels are better than human beings so far as nature is concerned. So, God did not assume human nature because he loved human beings more for what they are in themselves. He did so because their need was greater. In the same way, the head of a household might spend more on a delicacy for a sick servant than on a gift for a healthy son.

---

[30] Ecclesiasticus 13:14.   [31] 1a 20, a. 3.   [32] Philippians 2:9.   [33] Isaiah 9:6.
[34] See reply to the first objection.   [35] Apocalypse 21:17.

3. People have solved this doubt about Peter and John in various ways.

Augustine invokes the notion of divine mystery. He takes Peter to stand for the active life (which shows more love for God than the contemplative life), and he takes John to stand for the contemplative life. He says that the active life (Peter) is more sensitive to the miseries of life in general, and is more concerned to be free of them and to go to God. But, he adds, God loves the contemplative life (John) more than the active life since he preserves it longer – for the contemplative life does not end with bodily death, which is not the case with the active life.[36]

Others say that Peter had a greater love for Christ in his members, and Christ loved him more in this same way, which is why he entrusted his Church to Peter. But John, they say, had a greater love for Christ in his own person, and Christ loved *him* more in *that* way, which is why he entrusted his mother to John.

Others hold that we cannot be sure which of them loved Christ more with the love of charity, and that we cannot be sure which of them God loved more when it comes to the glory of eternal life. These thinkers say that Peter loved more with respect to a certain promptness and ardour. Then they add that John was loved more because of certain signs of intimacy that Christ showed him because of his youth and purity.

Others again hold that Christ loved Peter the more for his more excellent gift of charity, and that he loved John more because of his gift of understanding. Hence Peter was the better and more loved strictly speaking, but John was the better and more loved in some respect.

But I really think it presumptuous to pronounce on all this. For 'the Lord is the weigher of spirits'.[37] No one else is that.

4. The penitent and the innocent respectively are like people who are exceedingly and excessively loved. But, whether penitent or sinless, those are better loved who have more grace. All other things being equal, however, innocence is more worthy and more loved.

There is more joy in heaven over one who repents than over someone who is innocent because penitents often rise from their sins as more careful, humble and eager. So Gregory, commenting

[36] *On John* 124. *PL* 35.1974. [37] Proverbs 16:2.

on the text now in question, says: 'When it comes to a battle, a general will have more love for those soldiers who have fled and then return bravely to pursue the enemy, than for those who never fled but who also never acted bravely.'[38]

Or one might say that an equal gift of grace means more to a penitent who deserves punishment than it does to someone innocent who does not deserve it – just as a substantial sum of money means more to someone poor than it does to a king.

5. Since God's will is the cause of goodness in things, the goodness of those loved by God should be weighed at the time that they are endowed with it. Accordingly, predestined sinners are the better when granted the greater gift from God, though they were previously worse (indeed, neither good nor bad).

---

[38] *On the Gospel* 2.34. *PL* 76.1248.

Question 21

God's justice and mercy

Now that I have considered God's love, I must turn to his justice and mercy.

Here there are four points of inquiry:

1. Is God just?
2. Can we refer to God's justice as truth?
3. Is God merciful?
4. Is there justice and mercy in all of God's works?

Article 1: Is God just?

1. It seems that God is not just. Justice belongs to the classification under which temperance also falls. But God is not temperate. So, neither is he just.
2. Moreover, people who act as they will and please do not act according to justice. But St Paul says that 'God works all things according to the counsel of his will.'[1] So, we should not ascribe justice to God.
3. Moreover, justice acts by rendering what is due. But God is debtor to no one. So, justice does not belong to him.
4. Again, everything in God is his essence. But God's essence is not justice, for, as Boethius says, 'Goodness has to do with essence, but justice has to do with action.'[2] So, justice does not belong to God.

---

[1] Ephesians 1:11.
[2] *How Substances Are Good in Virtue of Their Existence without Being Substantial Goods* (*De Hebdomadibus*). PL 64.1314.

On the contrary, the psalm says, 'The Lord is just, and he has loved justice.'[3]

Reply: There are two kinds of justice.

One consists in mutual giving and receiving (e.g. as in buying and selling, and in other similar shared exchanges). Aristotle calls this 'commutative justice' (justice that directs exchanges or agreements).[4] This kind of justice does not belong to God since, as the Apostle says, 'Who has given him anything first, and shall there be a recompense for such a person?'[5]

The second kind of justice consists in sharing out, and we call it 'distributive justice'. This is the justice by which a ruler or administrator distributes to each on the basis of merit. So, as the proper order displayed in ruling a family, or any governed group, displays justice of this kind in the ruler, the order of the universe (seen both in natural and voluntary effects) shows forth God's justice. Hence Dionysius says, 'We must see that God is truly just in that he bestows on everything what is proper to each, according to the merit of everything that exists, and in that he preserves the nature of each with its own proper order and power.'[6] Hence:

1. Some moral virtues concern passions – for example temperance (which has to do with desire), fortitude (which has to do with fear and daring) and gentleness (which has to do with anger). We can attribute such virtues to God only metaphorically, since he has no capacity to be acted on (as I have said)[7] and no sense appetites (in which those virtues are located, as Aristotle says).[8] But some moral virtues concern actions like giving and spending (this is so with, for example, justice, liberality and magnanimity), and these are located in will, not the power of sense perception. So, there is nothing to stop us ascribing such virtues to God with respect to actions appropriate for God. These, however, do not include civic actions. For as Aristotle says, it would be ludicrous to praise God for his political virtues.[9]

2. Since the object of will is an understood good, God can will only what falls under his wisdom. For his wisdom is, as it were, the law of justice by which his will is right and just. So, he does justly what he does

---

[3] Psalms 10:8.   [4] *Nicomachean Ethics* 5.4, 1131b25.   [5] Romans 11:35.
[6] *The Divine Names* 8. PG 3.896.   [7] 1a 20.1, *ad* 1.
[8] *Nicomachean Ethics* 3.10, 1117b24.   [9] *Nicomachean Ethics* 10.8, 1178b10.

according to his will (as we do justly what we do according to law). But we, of course, do things according to the law of someone superior to us, while God is a law unto himself.

3. We owe to each what belongs to each, and we say that what belongs to people is ordered to them (e.g. servants belong to their masters, not the other way around, for the free are their own masters). So, the term 'due' implies a thing's needs or claims because of what it is for in a given order.

Now we can mark a double order in things: the ordering of all creatures to God, and their being ordered among themselves (e.g. parts to wholes, accidents to substances, and everything to its end).

So, throughout God's work we can consider a double due: what is owing to God, and what is owing to creatures, and under both respects God gives what is due. It is his due that things should fulfil what his wisdom and will require for them, and that they should manifest his goodness. In this way, his justice regards what befits him, as he renders to himself what he owes himself. There is also a creature's due to have what is ordered to it – that, for example, people should have hands and that animals should serve them. In this way God works according to justice in giving to each what its constitution and condition require.

Yet this due is based on the first. For to each is owing what is settled for it in the plan of God's wisdom. Though God renders what is owing on this count, he is not anyone's debtor. For everything is ordained to him, not he to anything else. So, we sometimes call his justice 'the honouring of his own goodness' or 'the requital of merits'. Anselm touches on both notions involved here when he writes, 'When you punish evil-doers it is just because the punishment matches their deserts; and it is just when you spare them because this befits your goodness.'[10]

4. The fact that justice has to do with action does not prevent it being God's essence. For what belongs to something's essence can be a source of action. But goodness does not always have to do with action. For we call something good both because of what it does and because of what is perfect in its essence. That is why Boethius says in the same place that goodness is related to justice as what is general is related to the particular.

---

[10] *Proslogion* 10. PL 158.233.

Article 2: Is God's justice truth?

1. It seems that God's justice is not truth. For justice is in the will. As Anselm says, 'Justice is rightness of will.'[11] But, according to Aristotle, truth is in the intellect.[12] So, justice does not pertain to truth.

2. Moreover, according to Aristotle truth and justice are different virtues.[13] So, truth does not pertain to the nature of justice.

On the contrary, the psalm says, 'Mercy and truth have met each other',[14] and 'truth' here means 'justice'.

Reply: Truth consists in the matching of mind and reality, as I have said.[15] Now, a mind which causes things is related to reality as a rule and measure, while the reverse is true of a mind which draws its knowledge from things. So, when things measure and rule a mind, truth consists in a matching of mind to thing – as is the case with us, for the views and positions we adopt are true or false depending on whether or not things are as we take them to be. But, when a mind is the rule and measure of things, truth consists in them matching it. Thus we say that the work of artists is true when it agrees with their art. But works of art stand to the art which makes them as just deeds stand to the law to which they conform. So, we are right to say that God's justice, which sets things up in an order conforming to his wisdom (his law), is truth (compare the way we speak about 'the truth of justice' when it comes to human affairs).

Hence:

1. While justice, considered as a law that governs, lies in reason or mind, the command governing the execution of what to do according to law lies in will.

2. Aristotle is speaking here of truth as a special moral virtue whereby people show themselves as they really are by what they say and do. So, it consists in the conformity of a sign to something signified, not in an effect conforming to its cause and rule (as I have shown to be the case with the truth of justice).[16]

---

[11] *On Truth* 12. *PL* 158.482. [12] *Metaphysics* 5.4, 1027b27.
[13] *Nicomachean Ethics* 4.7, 1127a34. [14] Psalms 84:11. [15] 1a 16.1.
[16] See the body of the present article.

Article 3: Is God merciful?

1. It seems that God is not merciful. For mercy is a kind of sadness, as Damascene says.[17] But there is no sadness in God. So, there is no mercy either.

2. Again, mercy is a relaxing of justice. But God cannot overlook what his justice demands. St Paul says, 'Though we lack faith, he (God) continues faithful; he cannot deny himself.'[18] A gloss on this text comments, 'He would deny himself were he to deny what he has said.'[19] So, we cannot attribute mercy to God.

On the contrary, the psalm says, 'The Lord is gracious and merciful.'[20]

Reply: We should especially attribute mercy to God, but in its effect, not as a sentiment or feeling.

To understand why, note that we call people merciful when they have a sad heart, so to speak (because they are sad at the unhappiness of others as if that were their own). They identify themselves with others and spring to their rescue. This is the effect of mercy.

Now, God does not feel sad about another's misery. But it especially belongs to him to drive away the misery of another (taking 'misery' to mean any defect). Yet defects are not done away with save by a perfection of some goodness, and, as I have said, God is the first source of goodness.[21]

Note, however, that lavishing perfections generously on things is a work of God's goodness, and justice, and generosity, and mercy, though in different respects. Purely and simply, other considerations apart, it is of his goodness that God communicates perfections (as I have shown).[22] That he gives them to things in proportion to the worth of their recipients comes from his justice (as I have also shown).[23] That they are not granted for his own advantage springs from his generosity. That they cast out every defect belongs to his mercy.

Hence:

1. This objection proceeds from the assumption that mercy has to be an emotion in something acted upon.

---

[17] *On the Orthodox Faith* 14. *PG* 94.932.   [18] 2 Timothy 2:13.
[19] Interlinear gloss 6.125. *PL* 192.370.   [20] Psalms 110:3.   [21] 1a 6.4.
[22] 1a 6.1, *ad* 4.   [23] 1a 21.1.

2. God acts mercifully not by acting contrary to his justice but by doing something that goes beyond that. Suppose that someone is owed a hundred units of money. You then give them two hundred units from your own pocket. There is no injustice in this deal, and you are being tender-hearted and open-handed. This is how it is when you forgive an offence against yourself, for a pardon is a sort of present. St Paul calls forgiving a giving, 'Give forgiveness to each other as Christ has given you forgiveness.'[24] So, it is clear that mercy does not do away with justice. It is, in a sense, its fullness. The letter of James therefore says, 'Mercy triumphs over judgement.'[25]

Article 4: Is there justice and mercy in all of God's works?

1. It seems that justice and mercy are not in all of God's works. For we attribute some works of God to his mercy (such as justifying the wicked) while we attribute others (such as damning the wicked) to his justice. So the letter of James says, 'Judgement without mercy will be rendered to one who has shown no mercy.'[26] So, justice and mercy are not evident in all of God's works.

2. Moreover, St Paul attributes the conversion of the Jews to God's justice and truth while attributing the conversion of the Gentiles to God's mercy.[27] So, both justice and mercy are not displayed in every one of God's works.

3. Moreover, many just people suffer in this world. But this is unjust. So, not all God's works show justice and mercy.

4. Again, justice consists in rendering what is due. Mercy consists in relieving misery. So, the just and the merciful depend on there being something there with respect to which they can act. But there is nothing there prior to God's act of creating. So, there is no justice or mercy involved in that act.

On the contrary, the psalm says, 'All the Lord's ways are mercy and truth.'[28]

Reply: It is necessary that mercy and truth be found in all of God's works, although only if we take 'mercy' to refer to the removal of just any

---

[24] Ephesians 4:33. [25] James 2:13. [26] James 2:13. [27] Romans 15:8–9. [28] Psalms 24:10.

defect. Strictly speaking, though, we cannot equate every defect with misery. The word 'misery' is only applicable when we are thinking of a defect in something with a rational nature. A thing like this can be happy (misery being the opposite of happiness).

The necessity involved here comes from the fact that, since God's justice renders either what is due to him or what is due to a creature, neither can be overlooked when it comes to any of his works. God can do nothing that conflicts with his wisdom and goodness (as I have said when speaking of what is due to God).[29] Likewise, he also does with befitting order and proportion everything that he does in created things, and the nature of justice consists in this. So, there has to be justice in all of God's works.

A work of God's justice always presupposes a work of his mercy and is based on it. For creatures are owed nothing except because of something that exists in them or is known in advance. However, if creatures are owed something, that will be so only because of something prior. Since we cannot regress endlessly, we have to arrive at something that depends only on the goodness of God's will (the ultimate end). We might say, for example, that people have the right to have hands because of their rational soul, and we might say that they have the right to have a rational soul in order to be human. But that they exist at all is due to God's goodness.

So, mercy is evident in all of God's works considered as coming from him as their first source, and the power of God's mercy is sustained as they continue to exist. It works more strongly in everything that results (as primary causes influence effects more strongly than secondary causes do). So, from the abundance of his goodness, God gives to creatures more generously than they deserve. For what would suffice to preserve the order of justice is less than what God's goodness brings, and God's goodness surpasses every proportion to creatures.

Hence:

1. We ascribe certain works to God's justice, and others to his mercy, because justice is more strongly evident in some of his actions, and mercy is more evident in others. Yet mercy appears even in the damnation of the reprobate. For, though not cancelled entirely,

---

[29] 1a 21.1, *ad* 3.

their punishment is sometimes softened, and is lighter than they deserve. God's justice appears even in the justification of sinners, when fault is forgiven because of love which God himself in mercy bestows. Thus we read of Mary Magdalen, 'Her sins, which are many, have been forgiven, because she loved much.'[30]

2. God's justice and mercy are evident in the conversion of the Jews and the Gentiles. But an aspect of justice is evident in the conversion of the Jews that is not evident in the conversion of the Gentiles. For the Jews are saved because of promises made to their fathers.

3. Even the fact that the just are punished in this world exhibits both justice and mercy when, through the sufferings they accept, they are cleansed from minor faults and are the more lifted up to God from earthly affections. As Gregory says, 'Evils that oppress us in this world drive us to find refuge in God.'[31]

4. Though creation presupposes nothing in the world of nature, it does presuppose something in God's knowledge. Accordingly, the nature of justice is preserved because creation accords with God's wisdom and goodness. And the aspect of mercy is somewhat preserved inasmuch as things are brought from not existing to existing.

---

[30] Luke 7:47. [31] *Morals* 26.13. *PL* 76.360.

Question 22
God's providence

I have so far discussed God's willing considered in isolation. Now I turn to matters relating to will in conjunction with mind. This is where the question of providence enters. It cares for all things, but especially for the ordering of people to eternal salvation. I therefore inquire

first into providence,
then into predestination and reprobation.

In studying moral science, I examine prudence (of which I view providence as a part) after the moral virtues.

Here there are four points of inquiry:

1. Should we think of providence in connection with God?
2. Is everything subject to divine providence?
3. Does divine providence directly engage in providing for everything?
4. Does divine providence impose necessity on things for which it provides?

Article 1: Should we think of providence in connection with God?

1. It seems that we should not think of providence in connection with God. For providence, according to Cicero, is a function of prudence,[1] which to Aristotle is the ability to deliberate well.[2] We cannot

---

[1] *On Invention* 2.53.   [2] *Nicomachean Ethics* 5.5, 1140a26.

entertain the notion that God does this because he has no doubts that would require him to take counsel. So, providence does not belong to God.

2. Moreover, everything in God is eternal. Yet providence is not that. According to Damascene, it concerns existent things, which are not eternal.[3] So, providence is not present in God.

3. Again, God is not a complex of parts. But providence seems to be a blend of thinking and willing. So, providence is not present in God.

On the contrary, Wisdom says, 'Your providence, Father, guides all things.'[4]

Reply: We have to declare that God has providence. For, as I have already shown, God created all the goodness in things.[5] But we do not just find good in things only so far as their substance goes. We also find it in their being ordained to an end, above all to their final end, which, as I have noted, is God's goodness.[6] So, God created the good which exists in created things when it comes to their order. Since God causes things by his intellect, and since the idea of each of his effects must pre-exist in him (as is clear from what I have already said),[7] a plan for the ordering of things to their end must pre-exist in God's mind, and, strictly speaking, providence is a plan ordering things to ends.

For providence is the principal office of prudence, served by its two other functions, namely memory of the past and insight into the present. For we bend ourselves to providing for the future by recalling what has happened before, and by sizing up what we are currently faced with.

According to Aristotle, it is prudence's proper function to arrange things to an end, whether with regard to ourselves (we say that people are prudent when they successfully adapt their actions to the purpose of their lives) or whether with regard to those subject to us within a domestic or political group, or a kingdom.[8] Thus Matthew speaks of the 'faithful and prudent servant whom the Lord has set over his household',[9] and we can attribute prudence or providence to God in the second sense here. For in him there is nothing ordered to an end, since he himself is the ultimate end. So, we take 'God's providence' to mean this plan for ordering things to ends. That is why Boethius says that 'Providence is the divine reason

[3] *On the Orthodox Faith* 2.9. PG 94.964. [4] Wisdom 14:3. [5] 1a 6.4. [6] 1a 21.4.
[7] 1a 15.2; 19.4. [8] *Nicomachean Ethics* 6.12, 1144a8. [9] Matthew 24:45.

itself grounded in the supreme principle of all things and disposing them all.'[10] (Note that 'to dispose' means 'to ordain things to their end' as well as 'to arrange parts within their system'.)

Hence:

1. According to Aristotle, 'prudence, strictly speaking, commands what good deliberation well advises and what understanding correctly decides on'.[11] So, although we should not think of God as deliberating (since one only deliberates concerning what is open to doubt), his is the executive command ordering things purposefully according to right reason. Hence the text 'He has made a decree which shall not pass away.'[12] It is in this sense that we should attribute prudence and providence to God. Though I might add that the plan of ordering things to an end is well-advised in God – not because it is the result of investigation on God's part, but because of its assurance (something we hope to reach when seeking advice). That is why St Paul says that 'God works all things by the advisedness of his will'.[13]

2. Two things belong to the care of providence: (a) planning an order (which we call 'providence' and 'disposition'), and (b) executing the order (which we call 'government'). The first of these is eternal. The second is temporal.

3. Providence exists in intellect. However, it presupposes the willing of an end. For one does not command what should be done if one has not willed an end to start with. Similarly, prudence presupposes moral virtues, which direct human appetites towards what is good (as Aristotle says).[14] Even if providence was equally the business of God's will and mind, this would still not detract from his simplicity. For, as I have said, God's will and mind are one and the same thing.[15]

Article 2: Is everything subject to God's providence?

1. It would seem that not everything is subject to God's providence. For nothing provided is fortuitous. But if everything were provided for by God then nothing would be fortuitous and there would be no chance or luck, which is contrary to general opinion.

---

[10] *The Consolation of Philosophy* 4.6. PL 63.814.   [11] *Nicomachean Ethics* 6.10, 1143a10.
[12] Psalms 148:6.   [13] Ephesians 1:12.   [14] *Nicomachean Ethics* 6.13, 1144b32.
[15] 1a 19.1; 19.4, *ad* 2.

2. Moreover, wise guardians ward off harm and evil from their charges as much as they can. But we see many evils in things. So, either God cannot prevent them, and is therefore not almighty, or he does not really care for all.

3. Moreover, whatever comes about inevitably does not call for providence or prudence. Thus Aristotle says that 'prudence is right-mindedness about things which can happen or not, and which call for counsel and choice'.[16] Since many things result from necessity it follows that all are not subject to providence.

4. Moreover, people left on their own are not under the providence of a governing authority. But Ecclesiasticus tells us that God leaves people to fend for themselves: 'When God made people in the beginning, he left them in the hands of their own counsel.'[17] This is particularly the case when it comes to evil people. As the psalm says, 'I gave them up according to the hardness of their hearts' desire.'[18] So, not everything is subject to God's providence.

5. Again, St Paul says, 'God is not concerned with oxen.'[19] And we may say the same of other non-rational creatures. So, not everything is subject to God's providence.

On the contrary, Wisdom says of God's wisdom that, 'It reaches from end to end mightily, and orders all things agreeably.'[20]

Reply: Some have denied providence altogether, like Democritus and the Epicureans, who maintained that the world was fashioned by chance. Others held that only immortal things fall under providence and that mortal things do so only with respect to their species (not as individuals), for as such they are imperishable. This view is represented in Job: 'The clouds are his hiding place; he walks upon the vaults of the sky and does not consider us.'[21] Maimonides exempted people from the generality of things that die away because of the excellence of the intellect that they share.[22] But he followed the opinion of the others with regard to other perishable things.

However, we have to say that all things are subject to God's providence, not only in general but also as individuals – as the following line of reasoning makes clear.

---

[16] *Nicomachean Ethics* 6.5, 1140a35.   [17] Ecclesiasticus 15:14.   [18] Psalms 80:13.
[19] 1 Corinthians 9:9.   [20] Wisdom 8:1.   [21] Job 22:14.   [22] *Guide for the Perplexed* 3.7.

Since every agent acts for an end, the ordering of effects towards an end extends as far as the causality of the first cause engaged does. For something unrelated to an end may come to be in what an agent brings about because some other cause produces an effect that differs from what the first cause aims at. But God (the first efficient cause) has a causality reaching to everything, both immortal and mortal, and it reaches not only to the sources of their species but also to their sources as individuals. So, everything that is real in any way whatever must be directed by God to an end. As the Apostle remarks, 'The things that are of God are well-ordered.'[23] Since, as I have said, God's providence is nothing else than the idea whereby all things are planned to an end,[24] it has to be that all things fall under divine providence in so far as they are real.

I have similarly shown that God knows everything, both general and particular.[25] Since his knowledge (as I have also explained)[26] is related to things like that of artists to their works of art, all things must be set under his ordering, like works of art under the art that makes them.

Hence:

1. A universal cause is one thing and a particular cause is another. For something can escape the ordering of a particular cause only because another particular cause interferes with the ordering in question (as when wood doused with water will not catch fire). But interference like this does not happen when it comes to the ordering of universal causes. So, since all particular causes come under a universal cause, no effect can escape the ordering of a universal cause. When an effect does stray from the ordering of some particular cause, we speak of it as fortuitous, or as a chance happening. But we do so with reference to the particular cause in question. For the effect cannot stray outside the sway of the universal cause, and with reference to this we speak of it as foreseen. Thus, for example, the meeting of two servants (a chance event from their perspective), might be foreseen by their master who (unknown to them) intentionally sent them where their paths would cross.

2. To have a limited responsibility and a universal providence are different. Someone with the first of these wards off harm to an individual in their care so far as possible. But one with universal

---

[23] Romans 13:1.   [24] 1a 22.1.   [25] 1a 14.11.   [26] 1a 14.8.

providence might allow some defect in one individual in order to preserve the good of a whole. We therefore say that defects and death are contrary to the individual's nature. But they still fall within the aim of nature as a whole – in so far as deficiency in something can lead to the good of something else, or to the good of the universe as a whole. For the passing away of one thing is the coming to be of something else, and this is a way in which species are preserved. So, since God is the universal guardian of all that is real, a quality of his providence is to allow defects in some particular things so as to safeguard the complete good of the universe. For if he prevented all evil, many good things would be lacking in the world. Lions, for instance, would never survive if they had no prey on which to feed, and there would be no patience of martyrs were there no persecution by tyrants. Thus Augustine says, 'Almighty God would in no way permit any evil in his works unless he were so good and powerful that he could bring good even out of evil.'[27]

The two difficulties I have just dealt with seem to be what influenced those who took perishable things (in which we find chance and evil) not to be subject to God's providence.

3. Human beings do not institute nature. Rather, they turn natural things to their service by applying their art and virtue. So, human providence does not extend to necessary things which follow the inevitable course of things as they are, though they are covered by the providence of God, who is the author of Nature.

The objection to which I am now replying seems to have been the argument of those, like Democritus and other early natural philosophers, who exempted from divine providence the natural course of things and attributed it to the determinism of material forces.[28]

4. The text which speaks of God leaving people to themselves is not intended to exclude them from divine providence. It means that people do not have a prefixed power of action limited to only one effect – as is the case with natural things, which are only acted on in the sense that they are directed to an end by another. Natural things do not act like self-determining agents who shape themselves to a purpose – as rational creatures do by their power of free choice

---

[27] *A Handbook on Faith, Hope and Love (Enchiridion)* 11. *PL* 40.236.
[28] *Metaphysics* 1.3 and 4, 983b7 and 985b5.

through which they deliberate and choose. Hence the pointed expression 'in the hands of their own counsel'. Yet because the very act of free choice goes back to God as its cause, whatever people freely do on their own must fall under God's providence. Indeed their providing for themselves is contained under God's providing as a particular under a universal cause.

God makes higher provision for the just than for the unjust, inasmuch as he does not let anything happen that would finally prevent their salvation. For, as St Paul says, 'All things work together for good to those who love God.'[29] We speak of him as abandoning sinners, because he does not hold them back from moral evil. But it is not that he casts them out from his care altogether. They would fall into nothingness unless his providence kept them in being.

The difficulty I am dealing with here seems to have been that which impressed Cicero and led him to except human affairs, about which we take counsel, from the sway of providence.[30]

5. As I have said, intelligent creatures are subject to providence in a special manner since they have control over their actions through free choice.[31] Blame or merit is imputed to them, and is requited with punishment or reward. It is in this sense that St Paul says that oxen are outside God's care, not in the sense of Maimonides, who thought that God's providence has no concern for individual non-rational creatures.[32]

Article 3: Does God directly provide for everything?

1. It would seem that God does not directly provide for everything. For we need to ascribe to God everything associated with dignity. But a king's dignity involves having subordinates acting as intermediaries when it comes to providing for his subjects. All the more, then, is this the case with God.

2. Moreover, you provide for something by setting it in order to an end, which in every case is its own good and completion. But the work of every cause is to conduct its effect to a good. So every agent cause is a cause of an effect of providence. So if God provided for all things by himself and without intermediaries, all secondary causes would be eradicated.

---

[29] Romans 8:28.   [30] *Divination* 2.5.   [31] 1a 19.10.   [32] *Guide for the Perplexed* 3.8.

3. Again, Augustine writes that 'not knowing some things is better than knowing them' (he is speaking of base things).[33] Aristotle writes to the same effect.[34] But we should ascribe to God what is better. So, God does not directly provide for contemptible and evil things.

On the contrary, in Job we read, 'Who has given him charge over the whole world? Or who has disposed the whole earth?'[35] On this Gregory comments, 'the world God established by himself is one that he rules by himself'.[36]

Reply: There are two sides to providence, namely the idea or planned purpose for things provided for, and its execution, which we call governance.

As for the first, God provides for all things directly. For his mind conceives of each of them, even the very least. He has given the power to produce effects to the causes he has set up to produce those effects. So he has to have had the order of those effects in his mind beforehand.

As for the second, divine providence works through some intermediaries. For God governs the lower through the higher, not from any impotence on his part, but from the abundance of his goodness imparting also to creatures the dignity of causing.

So we can dismiss Plato's opinion, recorded by Gregory of Nyssa,[37] which supposes a threefold providence. The first is that of the sovereign God himself, caring first and foremost for spiritual things, then, secondarily and in consequence, for genera, species, and universal causes in the cosmos. The second is a providence which cares for individual things which come to be and die away, which Plato attributes to divinities circling the heavens (i.e. disembodied substances moving the heavenly bodies in their cycles). The third is a providence for human affairs, which Plato attributes to dæmons, which, so Augustine tells us, Platonists thought of as occupying a stage between us and God.[38]

Hence:

1. Royal dignity requires ministers to execute its provisions. But monarchs would be inept if they had no plan when it comes to what these

---

[33] *A Handbook on Faith, Hope and Love* (*Enchiridion*) 17. *PL* 40.239.
[34] *Metaphysics* 11.9, 1074b32.   [35] Job 34:13.   [36] *Morals* 14.20. *PL* 40.239.
[37] In fact it is Nemesius of Emesa (fl. *c.* 390), *Human Nature* 44. *PG* 40.794.
[38] *The City of God* 8.14; 9.1. *PL* 41.238 and 257.

ministers should be doing. Every practical science is the better the more it attends to the details of its business.

2. As I have said, God's immediate providence over everything does not exclude secondary causes from executing its ordered policy.[39]

3. It is better for us not to know evil and contemptible things when this would hold us back from thinking of something better, partly because we cannot attend to many things at the same time, partly because dwelling on evil sometimes twists our will towards it. But this does not hold with God, who sees all things at a glance, and whose will cannot be bent to evil.

Article 4: Does providence impose necessity on the things for which it provides?

1. It seems that God's providence does impose necessity on the things for which it provides. For every effect resulting inevitably from a present or past intrinsic cause must, as Aristotle proves, itself follow of necessity.[40] But God's providence, being eternal, pre-exists, and effects result from it inevitably since it cannot be thwarted. So God's providence imposes necessity on the things for which it provides.

2. Moreover, all providers make their work as stable as they can to prevent it from mishap. But God is supremely powerful. So he gives the stability of necessity to the things for which he provides.

3. Again, Boethius writes that Fate 'coming forth from the utterances of unchangeable providence binds together people's actions and fortunes with an unbreakable chain of causes'.[41] So it does seem that providence imposes necessity on things for which it provides.

On the contrary, there is Dionysius's teaching, 'Providence does not work so as to ruin anything's nature.'[42] But some things are naturally contingent. So God's providence does not abolish their contingency and substitute necessity.

Reply: God's providence imposes necessity on some things, but not, as some have believed,[43] on all. For it belongs to providence to plan things to an end. After God's goodness, which is the end transcending all things,

---

[39] See the body of the present article.   [40] *Metaphysics* 5.3. 1027a30. /
[41] *The Consolation of Philosophy* 4.6. PL 63.817.   [42] *The Divine Names* 4. PG 3.733.
[43] St Thomas has the Stoics in mind here. See Nemesius of Emesa, *Human Nature* 37. PG 40.62.

the main good immanent to them is the completeness of the universe they compose, a completeness which would not be achieved unless every shade of reality were found among its components. So God's providence prepares (a) necessary causes for some effects, so that they come to be of necessity, and (b) contingent causes for others, so that they come to be contingently (with both types of effect corresponding to the nature of their proximate causes).

Hence:

1. The effect of God's providence is for something to come about not just anyhow but in its own proper style, necessarily or contingently as the case may be. What the plan of providence has arranged to result necessarily and without fail will so come about. What it has arranged to result contingently will likewise so come about.

2. The order of God's providence is unchangeable and sure in that everything God provides for comes about in the way he provides for it – whether as necessary or contingent.

3. The unchangingness and unbreakableness to which Boethius refers goes with the assuredness of providence, which fails neither in its effects nor in the foreseen manner of their coming; they are not qualities of the effects themselves. Notice also that to be necessary or contingent are corollaries to being as such. So the modes of necessity and contingency fall under God's providence (which provides for everything), not under the providence of what provides only for some particular things.

Question 25

God's power

After God's knowing and willing, together with their corollaries, it remains to consider God's power.

Here there are six points of inquiry:

1. Is there power in God?
2. Is his power infinite?
3. Is it omnipotent?
4. Can it make the past not to have been?
5. Can God make what he does not make, and not make what he makes?
6. Can he make the things that he makes to be better than they are?

Article 1: Is there power in God?

1. It seems that there is no power in God. For prime matter is related to power as God, the first agent cause, is related to actuality. But prime matter, considered in itself, lacks all actuality. So, the first agent cause (i.e. God) lacks power.
2. Moreover, according to Aristotle, 'better than every power is its act'.[1] For, as being its purpose, form is better than matter, and activity is better than the ability to be active. But nothing is better than what is in God since, as I have shown, everything in God is God.[2] So, God has no power to act.
3. Moreover, power is a source of activity. But God's activity is his essence (since there are no accidents in God), and God's essence has no source. So, there is no power in God.

---

[1] *Metaphysics* 8, 1051a4. [2] 1a 3.3.

4. Again, I have already shown that God's knowledge and will are the cause of things³. But a cause and a source are the same. So, there is no need for us to ascribe power to God. We need to ascribe only knowledge and will to him.

On the contrary, it says in the Psalms, 'You, Lord, are powerful, and your truth surrounds you.'⁴

Reply: There are two kinds of power: (a) passive power, and (b) active power. Now, God does not have passive power at all. But we should attribute the highest degree of active power to him.

For things are obviously active sources of other things in so far as they are actual and perfect – while things are acted upon in so far as they are lacking in some way, and in so far as they are imperfect. Now I have shown that God is sheer actuality, simply and wholly perfect, and not wanting for anything.⁵ So, he, especially, is an active source, not something acted on in any way. But to be an active source is to have active power. For, as Aristotle explains, active power is a source of acting on another, while passive power is what allows something to be acted on by something else.⁶ So, we have to conclude that God has supreme active power.

Hence:

1. We do not distinguish active power from actuality. Rather, we ground it in actuality (since things act inasmuch as they are actual). But there is a difference between passive power and actuality, for everything has passive power in so far as it is able to be in some way or other. So, God has active power but no passive power.

2. When an act is distinct from a power, the act has to be more excellent than the power. But God's activity is not distinct from his power. Each is his essence since his existing is not other than his essence. So, nothing has to be more excellent in God than his power.

3. In created things, power is a source not only of actions but also of effects. It is with reference to the notion of power as a source of effects that we justify ascribing power to God (not saying that it is a source of God's acting, which is the same as his essence, but saying that it is the source of an effect).

   Using our general ways of thinking, however, we might conceive of God's power as a source of action. For we might think of his essence

³ 1a 14.8; 19.4. ⁴ Psalms 88:9. ⁵ 1a 3.1; 4.1 and 2. ⁶ *Metaphysics* 4.12, 1019a19.

(which, in the simplicity which belongs to God, contains all created perfections) under the aspects of both action and power – just as we think of God as both an individual having a nature and as a nature in its own right.

4. We do not attribute power to God as though it were really distinct from his knowing and willing. We do so only to draw attention to something conceptually distinct from God's knowing and willing – that is, a source carrying out what mind directs and will commands (allowing for the fact that power, knowing and willing are one and the same reality in God). Or you might put it like this: God's knowledge and will as composing an effective principle entail the meaning of power. Hence we examine the first and second before the third, somewhat as we may look at a cause before turning to its operation and effect.

Article 2: Is God's power infinite?

1. It seems that God's power is not infinite. For according to Aristotle anything infinite is imperfect.[7] But God's power is not imperfect. So, it is not infinite.

2. Moreover, every power is manifested through its effect, otherwise it would be useless. So, if God's power were infinite, it could produce an infinite effect, which is impossible.

3. Again, Aristotle shows that if the power of a bodily thing were infinite it would move something instantaneously, not in stages.[8] But God does not move something instantaneously. According to Augustine he moves spiritual creatures through time, and he moves corporeal creatures through space and time.[9] So, his power is not infinite.

On the contrary, Hilary says that 'God's strength is unmeasured, living and mighty.'[10]

Reply: As I have already said, there is active power in God in so far as he is actual.[11] But his existence is infinite because it is not limited by anything receiving it. This is clear from what I have said about the infinity of God's essence.[12] So, God's active power has to be infinite.

---

[7] *Physics* 3.6, 207a7.   [8] *Physics* 8.10, 266a31.
[9] *On the Literal Interpretation of 'Genesis'* 20 and 22. *PL* 34.388 and 389.
[10] *On the Trinity* 8.24. *PL* 10.253.   [11] 1a 25.1.   [12] 1a 7.1.

For in all efficient causality we find that the more perfectly a cause possesses the form by which it acts, the more powerful is its acting. For instance, the hotter something is the more fiercely can it heat; and if heat were infinite so also would be its power of heating. So, since God's essence (through which God acts) is infinite (as I have shown),[13] it follows that his power is also infinite.

Hence:

1. Aristotle is there speaking of the infinite with regard to matter unshaped by form (infinity having to do with quantity). But, as I have shown, God's essence is not an infinity in this sense[14] and, therefore, neither is his power. So, it does not follow that God's power is imperfect.

2. An effect of a univocal agent exhaustively manifests its power. For example, the generative power of people can only produce people. But the power of a non-univocal agent is not entirely manifested in the production of an effect. Thus, for example, the sun has resources not revealed in the heat which generates an animal from decaying matter. But God is clearly not a univocal agent – for, as I have shown, he does not belong to any genus or species.[15] So, we are left with the conclusion that his effects are always less than his power. It is, therefore, not necessary that God's infinite power should be shown by his producing an infinite effect, and his power would not be useless even if it produced no effect. For something is useless when it is set towards an end that it does not reach. But God's power is not subordinate to any of its effects as to an end. Rather, it is the end of the effects that it produces.

3. Aristotle proves that if a body had infinite power it would move things non-temporally.[16] Yet he also shows that the power of the celestial mover is infinite because it is able to move things in infinite time.[17] So, his intention is to show that a body of infinite power, if such exists, would set off a motion which is not in time. He is not discussing a bodiless agent. His line of reasoning is as follows. One body which moves another is a univocal agent. So, the motion it causes manifests the agent's whole power. Since the greater the power of the body that moves it the faster it will be, it is inevitable that were this power

---

[13] 1a 25.1.   [14] 1a 7.1.   [15] 1a 3.5; 4.3.   [16] *Physics* 8.10, 266a29.   [17] *Physics* 8.10, 267b24.

infinite it would move immeasurably faster, which means that the motion would be outside time. But a bodiless agent is a non-univocal agent. So, it is not necessary that its whole power be manifested in the motion and therefore that it causes a non-temporal motion, and this is especially true when the mover causes motion in accordance with the determination of its own will.

Article 3: Is God omnipotent?

1. It would seem that God is not omnipotent. For everything can be moved and acted upon. But not God. For, as I have said, he is changeless.[18] So, he is not omnipotent.

2. Moreover, to commit sin is to do something. But according to 2 Timothy God is unable to sin or to deny himself.[19] So, God is not omnipotent.

3. Moreover, a collect says that 'God especially manifests his omnipotence by sparing and having mercy.'[20] This, then, is the best he can do. But there are much greater works (e.g. creating another world or the like). So, God is not omnipotent.

4. Again, on the text, 'Has God not made foolish the wisdom of this world?'[21] the Gloss comments, 'He made foolish the wisdom of this world by showing that what it thought impossible was possible.'[22] It seems that one should judge what is possible and impossible not as the wisdom of this world does (i.e. by lesser causes) but according to God's power. So, if God is omnipotent, all things are possible and nothing is impossible. But if one eliminates the impossible, one also eliminates the necessary. For to be is of necessity equivalent to not being able not to be. So, if God were omnipotent there would be nothing necessary in the world. But this is impossible. So, God is not omnipotent.

On the contrary, there is what is said in Luke, 'No word shall be impossible with God.'[23]

Reply: Everyone confesses that God is omnipotent. But it seems hard to explain just what his omnipotence amounts to since one might wonder

---

[18] 1a 2.3; 9.1. [19] 2 Timothy 2:13.
[20] From a collect in the text of the Mass for the tenth Sunday after the Feast of Pentecost.
[21] 1 Corinthians 1:20. [22] *Glossa ordinaria*. From St Ambrose. *PL* 17.199. [23] Luke 1:37.

about the meaning of 'all' when someone says that God can do all. Yet looked at aright, when we say that God can do everything we are best understood as meaning this: since power is relative to what is possible, divine power can do everything that is possible, and that is why we call God omnipotent.

According to Aristotle there are two senses of 'possible': one relative, and the other absolute.[24] We use the first sense with an eye on some particular power. Thus, for example, we say that what falls under human power is possible for us. But we should not say that God is omnipotent because he can do everything that created natures can do, for his power extends to many more things. Yet if we say that God is omnipotent because he can do everything possible to his power, our explanation of omnipotence goes round in a circle – stating nothing more than that God is omnipotent because he can do all that he can do.

So, employing the second sense of 'possible', we should conclude that we call God omnipotent because he can do everything that is absolutely possible. We judge something to be absolutely possible or impossible from the implication of terms: absolutely possible when a predicate is compatible with a subject (as in 'Socrates is seated'); absolutely impossible when it is not so compatible (as in 'Human beings are donkeys').

Consider this: since every agent produces an effect like itself, every active power has a possible objective corresponding to the nature of the activity which the active power is for. Thus, for example, the power of heating supposes that things can be heated. But God's being, on which the notion of his power is based, is infinite existing, not limited to any kind of being, but possessing in itself the perfection of all existing. So, whatever can have the nature of being falls within the range of things that are absolutely possible, and we call God omnipotent with respect to these.

Nothingness, and only that, contradicts the real meaning of being. So, whatever implies simultaneous existing and non-existing is contrary to what is absolutely possible and subject to God's omnipotence. For that which is contradictory is not subject to God's omnipotence – not because of a lack of power in God, but because it simply does not have the nature of being something achievable or possible. So, whatever does not imply a contradiction is included in the class of possible things with respect to

[24] *Metaphysics* 4.2, 1019b34.

which we call God omnipotent. But nothing implying a contradiction falls within God's power since all such things are impossible. The best thing to say, however, is that they cannot be brought about, not that God cannot bring them about. Nor is this against the angel's saying, 'No word shall be impossible with God.'[25] For a contradiction in terms cannot be a word since no mind can conceive it.

Hence:

1. As I have said, we call God omnipotent with regard to active power, not passive power.[26] His omnipotence is not compromised by the fact that he cannot be in motion or undergo action.
2. To sin is to fall short of perfect action. So, to be able to sin is to be able to fail in doing, which is incompatible with omnipotence. So, it is because God is omnipotent that he cannot sin. Aristotle indeed says that 'God and the cautious person can go wrong.'[27] But we can interpret his statement in different ways. We can take it as a conditional whose antecedent is impossible (the meaning then being 'God could do evil if he wanted to'). For a conditional can be true when both its antecedent and consequent are impossible (as in 'If human beings are donkeys, they have four feet'). Alternatively, we can read Aristotle as saying that God could do things that seem evil now, though they would be good if he were to do them. Or again, we can take Aristotle to be adopting the common usage of pagans who said that people became gods (like Jupiter or Mercury).
3. God especially manifests his omnipotence by sparing and having mercy. For by freely forgiving sins he shows that he has supreme power, and no one bound by the law of a superior is free to forgive sins freely. Again, by sparing and having pity on people God brings them to share in an infinite good, which is the greatest effect of his power. Then again, and as I have said, the product of God's mercy is the foundation of all his works.[28] For we are entitled to nothing except on the basis of what has come from God as a sheer gift. Here, in particular, God manifests his omnipotence – as first instituting everything good.
4. We do not call something absolutely possible by reference to causes (whether higher or lower) but by reference to itself. But we do say that

---

[25] Luke 1:37. [26] See the body of the present article. [27] *Topics* 4.5, 126a34. [28] 1a 21.4.

something is possible with respect to a proximate cause when we speak of it as possible with respect to a particular power. So, we call 'possible with respect to a higher cause' things such that only God can directly bring them about (e.g. creation, justification, and the like). Those things that are such that they can be produced by inferior causes we call 'possible with respect to inferior causes'. For, as I have said, an effect is contingent or necessary depending on the nature of its proximate cause.[29] That is why the wisdom of the world is foolish when it reckons that what is impossible for things in nature is also impossible for God.

In the light of these considerations it is clear that God's omnipotence does not rule out impossibility or necessity from things.

Article 4: Can God make the past not to have been?

1. It seems that God can make the past not to have been. For what is intrinsically impossible is much more impossible than what is accidentally impossible. But God can do what is intrinsically impossible (like giving sight to someone blind, or raising a corpse to life). Much more, therefore, can he do what is accidentally impossible. But for something in the past not to have happened is accidentally impossible (e.g. for instance, Socrates not having run is accidentally impossible because Socrates actually having run is now part of history). So, God can make what has happened not to have happened.

2. Moreover, whatever God could have done he can do now, since his power has not diminished. But before Socrates ran God could have seen to it that he would not run. So, God could bring it about that he has not run after he has run.

3. Again, charity is a greater virtue than virginity. But God can restore charity that has been lost and he can therefore restore lost virginity. So, he can make what was destroyed not to have been damaged.

On the contrary, Jerome says, 'Though God can do everything, he cannot make the undestroyed from the destroyed.'[30] For the same reason he cannot make something that has been not to have been.

---

[29] 1a 14.13, *ad* 1.   [30] Letter 22 to Eustochius. *PL* 22.397.

Reply: As I have explained, nothing implying a contradiction falls under God's omnipotence.[31] But for the past not to have been implies a contradiction. For example, to say that Socrates is and is not seated is contradictory, just as it is contradictory to say that he was and was not seated. To affirm that he was seated is to affirm a past fact. To affirm that he was not seated is to affirm what was not the case. So, for the past not to have been does not lie under divine power. This is what Augustine says: 'People who say "If God is omnipotent, he should make the things that have been done not to have been done" are not aware that they are saying that if God is omnipotent, he should make things that are true also false, precisely in so far as they are true.'[32] Aristotle, too, says, 'This alone is lacking in God, the power to make undone the things that were once done.'[33]

Hence:

1. If you think of a past event, for instance that Socrates once ran, merely as a contingent event, then it is only accidentally impossible that it did not take place. But if you think of a past event precisely as a past event, then it is both intrinsically and absolutely impossible that it did not take place. For 'It took place and it did not take place' is contradictory. As such it is more impossible than the raising of the dead to life, which implies no contradiction, and is something we call impossible only with an eye on what nature can bring about. Impossibilities of this sort are subject to divine power.

2. When it comes to the perfection of his power, God can do everything. But some things are not subject to his power because they do not belong to the realm of the possible. Similarly, when it comes to the immutability of his power, whatever God could do he still can do. But some things, which were in the realm of the merely possible when they remained yet to be brought about, have ceased to be possible now that they have been brought about. So, we say that God cannot bring them about since they are not things which can be brought about.

3. God can take away all corruption, mental and physical, from a woman who has lost her integrity. But he cannot abolish the fact that she once did lose it. Similarly, God cannot make it the case that someone who once sinned and failed in charity did not do so.

---

[31] 1a 25.3.   [32] *Against Faustus* 25.5. *PL* 42.481.   [33] *Nicomachean Ethics* 6.2, 1139b10.

Article 5: Can God bring about what he does not bring about?

1. It seems that God cannot bring about what he does not bring about. For God can bring about only what he has foreseen and preordained that he shall bring about. That is exactly what he does bring about. So, he cannot bring about what he does not bring about.
2. Moreover, God can bring about only what he ought to bring about and what it is right for him to bring about. But God is under no obligation to bring about what he does not bring about. Nor is there any question of it being right for him to bring about something that he does not bring about. So, God can only bring about what he brings about.
3. Again, God can bring about only what is good and fitting for the things he makes. But it is neither good nor fitting that they should be other than what they are. So, God can only bring about what he does bring about.

On the contrary, we have the text in Matthew, 'Do you think that I cannot ask my Father, and he will immediately give me more than twelve legions of angels?'[34] But our Lord did not ask, nor did the Father summon them to repel the Jews. So, God can bring about what he does not bring about.

Reply: Two mistakes have been made on this point.

Some hold that God acts as though from necessity of nature. They argue that, just as the actions of things in nature can produce only what comes to be (as, for example, human seed produces people, and olive seeds produce olive trees), God's actions cannot produce things, or an arrangement of things, other than those which now exist.

I have, however, shown that God does not act from any necessity of nature, that his will is the cause of all things and that his will is not determined naturally and by necessity to produce them.[35] So, the present order of things does not proceed necessarily from God in such a way that different things could not have come about.

Others hold that God's power is restricted to the present order of things because of the plan of his wisdom and justice, without which he does nothing.

---

[34] Matthew 26:53.   [35] 1a 19.3.

But since God's power, which is his essence, is nothing other than his wisdom, we may fairly say that they are commensurate, for his wisdom covers the whole range of his power.

Still, as I have said, the order which God's wisdom establishes in things (in which justice consists) is not such an adequate expression of God's wisdom that this wisdom is enclosed within its boundaries.[36]

The whole reason for an arrangement set up by the wise in the things they do is drawn from their end. So, when an end is proportionate to the things that are done in order to achieve it, the maker's wisdom is committed to a determinate pattern. But God's goodness is an end that immeasurably surpasses created things. So, God's wisdom is not limited to one fixed system so that no other course of things could flow from it. Therefore, we should quite simply declare that God can bring about things other than he actually does bring about.

Hence:

1. In us, power and essence are different from will and intellect, and intellect is different from wisdom, as is will from justice. So, some things lie within our power which cannot be in a just will or a wise intellect. With God, however, power, and essence, and will, and intellect, and wisdom, and justice are all identical. So, nothing can be in God's power which cannot be in his just will and wise intellect.

   All the same, since his will is not bound of necessity to this or that particular objective (except, perhaps, hypothetically, as I have said),[37] and since his wisdom and justice are not committed to any one particular order of things (as I have explained),[38] there is no reason why something should not be within God's power which he does not, in fact, will, and which is not part of the present order he has established. Because we conceive of power as executing, but will as commanding, and intellect and wisdom as directing, we say that what God can do by virtue of his power is something he can do by his absolute power. This, as I have said, covers everything that is consonant with the meaning of being real.[39] When it comes to what lies within God's power as carrying out the command of his just will, we speak of him being able to do whatever he does by virtue of his ordinate power.

---

[36] 1a 21.4.   [37] 1a 19.3.   [38] See the body of the present article.   [39] 1a 25.3.

Accordingly we should state that, by his absolute power, God can bring about what is other than what he foresaw and preordained that he would bring about. Nevertheless nothing can come to pass that he has not foreseen and preordained. For his acting is subject to his foreknowing and preordaining while his ability to act, being natural to him, is not so subject. For God brings something about because he wills to do so, and he is able to do so because he is so by nature, not because he wills to do so.

2. God owes nothing to anything except himself. So, when we say that God can bring about only what he ought to bring about, we simply mean that he can bring about only what is proper and right with respect to himself. But we can understand 'proper and right' here in two senses.

We can construe it with 'is' as restricted to present things, and then as referred to God's power. On this construal the claim 'He can bring about only what is proper and right with respect to himself' is false. For, so understood, it means that God can bring about only what is presently proper and right.

But if we construe 'proper and right' first with the word 'can' (which has the effect of extending reference to possible things) and then with the verb 'is', the claim ('He can bring about only what is proper and right with respect to himself') will refer to any (possible) present and is true in the sense that God can bring about what would be proper and right were he to bring it about.

3. Things that now exist determine the present course of things. But God's wisdom and power are not determined by this. So, though no other order would be good and appropriate for things as they now exist, God could make other things and instil a different order in them.

Article 6: Can God make things better than he does?

1. It seems that God cannot make things better than he does. For he makes everything with the utmost power and wisdom. But the more powerfully and wisely something is made, the better it is made. So, God cannot make anything better than he makes it.

2. Moreover, Augustine argues, 'God would be jealous if he could beget a Son equal to himself but did not do so.'[40] Likewise, God would be

---

[40] *Against Maximinus* 2.8. *PL* 42.762.

jealous if he could make things better than he has made them but refused to do so. But jealousy has no place in God. So, he has made things as best he can and cannot, therefore, make things better than he has.

3. Moreover, what is far and away the best cannot be bettered, for nothing is better than the best. But Augustine says, 'Everything God makes is good. But, considered as a whole, all things are very good indeed, for they make up the wondrous beauty of the universe.'[41] So, God cannot improve on the good of the universe.

4. Again, in his human nature Christ is full of grace and truth, and he possesses the Spirit beyond measure. So, he cannot be better. Similarly, we say that our happiness with God after we die is the supreme good, and therefore cannot be better. Likewise, the blessed virgin Mary is raised above all the choirs of angels, and so cannot be better than she is. So, God cannot improve on what he has made.

On the contrary, there is the text in Ephesians, 'God is powerful and able to make all things greater than we understand or desire.'[42]

Reply: Things have goodness in two ways. First, they have it essentially (as, for example, people are essentially rational), and God cannot make something better than it is essentially, though he can make something else that is better than it. It is analogous to how God cannot make the number four to be more than four, for then it would not be four but another number (Aristotle notes that the addition of an essential difference in the definition of a species is like the addition of a unit to a number).[43] But things can also have goodness which goes beyond their essence or nature – as a human being can come to be virtuous and wise. God can make things better than they are by giving them goodness like this.

Yet to speak without reservation, God can make something better than anything he has made.

Hence:

1. When we say 'God can make something better', we can understand 'better' substantively, in which case what we say is true. For God can make something that is better than something else that he has made.

---

[41] *A Handbook on Faith, Hope and Love* (*Enchiridion*) 10. *PL* 40.236.
[42] Ephesians 3:20.   [43] *Metaphysics* 7.3, 1044a1.

As I have said, he can make something better in one way though not in another.[44] But if we understand 'better' adverbially (to refer to the manner of the making), then God cannot do better than he does because he cannot make something from any greater wisdom and goodness than he employs in making anything. If, however, we understand 'better' as referring to the mode of the things made, then God can make better since he can give things a better manner of existing when it comes to their accidental properties, though not to their essence.

2. To be his father's equal is in the nature of a son when he grows up. But to be better than as made by God is not in any creature's nature. Hence the comparison fails.

3. Supposing the things that are, the universe cannot be better than it is. For its good consists in a most fitting order given to its components by God. If one part of it were improved, that would spoil the proportions of the whole design (overstretch one harp string and the melody is lost). All the same, God could make other things, or add them to those he has made, and there would then be another and better universe.

4. Christ's humanity (because it is united with God), our happiness with God after death (because it amounts to enjoying God), and the blessed Virgin (because she is God's mother), all have a certain infinite dignity deriving from the infinite good that is God. Considered as such, there can be nothing better than these, just as there can be nothing better than God.

---

[44] See the body of the present article.

Question 26

God's beatitude

In my discussion of what belongs to God's essence, I now end by turning to the topic of God's beatitude.

Here there are four points of inquiry:

1. Does beatitude belong to God?
2. Should we say that God is blessed with respect to his intellect?
3. Is God essentially the beatitude of each of the blessed?
4. Is all beatitude included in God's beatitude?

Article 1: Does beatitude belong to God?

1. It seems that we should not ascribe beatitude to God. For, according to Boethius, beatitude is a state made perfect by the accumulation of all good things.[1] But there is no accumulation of goods in God just as there is no compositeness. So, we should not attribute beatitude to God.
2. Again, according to Aristotle beatitude (or happiness) is virtue's reward.[2] But reward, like merit, does not apply to God. So, neither does beatitude.

On the contrary, St Paul says, 'he, the blessed and only sovereign, the King of kings and Lord of lords, shall show in his times'.[3]

Reply: Beatitude is God's above all. For by 'beatitude' we mean nothing else than the perfect good for an intelligent being who is conscious that it has a sufficiency of the good it possesses – a being which

---

[1] *The Consolation of Philosophy* 3.2. PL 63.724. [2] *Nicomachean Ethics* 1.9, 1099b16.
[3] 1 Timothy 6:15.

may face good or ill and is in control of its actions. Yet God is both perfect and intelligent. So, beatitude belongs especially to God.

Hence:

1. The accumulation of good things in God occurs, not by composition, but in a simple manner. For, as I have said, that which is manifold in creatures pre-exists in God in simplicity and unity.[4]
2. Being the reward of virtue is an accident that belongs to beatitude or happiness when someone arrives at beatitude – just as being the end product of an act of generation is an accident that something has when it moves from potentiality to actuality. So, just as God has existence (though he does not come into existence) he also possesses beatitude (though this is not something he has because he merits it).

Article 2: Should we say that God is blessed with respect to his intellect?

1. It seems that we should not say that God is blessed with respect to his intellect. For beatitude is the highest good. But we speak of God as good while thinking of his essence. For Boethius says that something is good with respect to its essence.[5] So, we should ascribe beatitude to God while thinking of his essence, not his intellect.
2. Again, beatitude is an end. But an end is the objective of will, just like goodness. So, we should say that God's beatitude lies in his will, not in his intellect.

On the contrary, on these words in Job, 'Clothe yourself with glory and splendour',[6] Gregory says, 'The glorious are those who rejoice in themselves and need no additional praise.'[7] But to be glorious is to be happy. So, since we enjoy God by virtue of our intellect (as Augustine says, our entire reward lies in the vision of God),[8] it seems that we should talk of God's beatitude in relation to his intellect.

Reply: As I have noted, beatitude is the perfect good for an intelligent being.[9] Hence it is that, as everything desires the perfection of its nature,

---

[4] 1a 4.2, *ad* 1; 13.4.
[5] *How Substances Are Good in Virtue of Their Existence without Being Substantial Goods* (*De Hebdomadibus*). *PL* 64.1314.
[6] Job 40:10.   [7] *Morals* 32.6. *PL* 76.639.   [8] *Explanations of the Psalms* 90.2, 16. *PL* 37.1170.
[9] 1a 26.1.

everything with intellect naturally desires to be blessed. But that which is most perfect in something with intellect is the operation of its intellect, by which it somehow grasps everything. So, the beatitude of every intelligent creature lies in intellectual activity. Now, when it comes to God, to be and to understand are one and the same thing. They differ only in so far as we are able to think of them. So, we should ascribe beatitude to God with reference to his intellect, just as we ascribe it to others enjoying beatitude. We call them blessed because they are drawn into God's beatitude.

Hence:

1. This argument shows that God is essentially blessed, not that his beatitude derives from his essence rather than his intellect.
2. Since beatitude is good, it is an object of desire (or will). But an object pre-exists any ability to acquire it. So, we have to think of God's beatitude as pre-existing his desire to retain it – meaning that it cannot be anything other than an act of intellect. So, beatitude, for God, lies in his intellect.

Article 3: Is God the beatitude of everyone who is blessed?

1. It would seem that God is the beatitude of everyone who is blessed. For God is the supreme good, as I have explained.[10] But, as I have also explained, there cannot be many supreme goods.[11] Yet beatitude, by definition, is supremely good. So, it would seem to be nothing other than God.
2. Again, beatitude is the ultimate end for something rational. But only God can be such an end. So, the blessedness of those who are beatified is God alone.

On the contrary, those beatified are not all equally happy. For, as St Paul says, 'Star differs from star in glory.'[12] But nothing is greater than God. So, we need to distinguish between beatitude and God.

Reply: The beatitude of an intellectual nature consists in an act of the intellect. We can think of intellect in two ways: as having an object (something to understand), or just as being itself (as being something that understands). And if we think of beatitude with a view to an object,

---

[10] 1a 6.2 and 4.   [11] 1a 11.3.   [12] 1 Corinthians 15:41.

then God alone is beatitude since people are blessed only in so far as they understand God. As Augustine says, 'Blessed are those who know you, even though they know nothing else.'[13] When it comes to understanding, however, beatitude is something created in creatures who are blessed. In God, though, even beatitude resulting from understanding is uncreated. Hence:

1. Considered with respect to its object, beatitude is unquestionably the supreme good. But, considered as what someone blessed actually is, beatitude is not unquestionably the highest good. Rather, it is highest in the class of goods in which creatures can share.
2. As Aristotle says, there are two kinds of end: objective ends, and subjective ends (i.e. ends as they are in themselves, and ends as we manage to lay hold of them).[14] So, for example, misers are interested in money considered simply as money (i.e. as an objective end), but they are also interested in having it (i.e. they are interested in it as a subjective end). Now, the end of rational creatures is God (considered as an objective end). But their end is also created beatitude (something which they can hold on to or enjoy).

Article 4: Does God's beatitude include all beatitude?

1. It seems that all beatitude is not included in God's beatitude. For there are certain false kinds of beatitude. But there is nothing false in God. So, his beatitude does not include all beatitude.
2. Moreover, some find a certain beatitude in bodily things (e.g. pleasure, riches, and so on). But, since he is incorporeal, God is not blessed because of bodily things. So, his beatitude does not include every sort of beatitude.

On the contrary, beatitude is a kind of perfection. I have already shown that God's perfection includes every other perfection.[15] So, his beatitude also includes every other beatitude.

Reply: Whatsoever is desirable in any beatitude whatever, whether it be true or false, wholly and most highly pre-exists in God's beatitude.

As for contemplative happiness, God has an ever-constant and most assured knowledge of himself and of everything else. As for active

[13] *Confessions* 5.4. PL 32.708. [14] *On the Soul* 2.4, 415b20. [15] 1a 4.2.

happiness, he has the governing of the whole universe. Then, as to earthly happiness (which Boethius takes to consist in pleasure, riches, power, dignity and fame),[16] God has joy in himself and everything else. For riches, which promise sufficiency, he has his own on every count. For power, he has omnipotence. For dignity, he has the rulership of all. And for fame, he has the admiration of all creatures.

Hence:

1. In so far as it falls short of the meaning of true beatitude, some beatitude is false. So, it is not to be found in God. But it pre-exists in God's beatitude in so far as it has even the slightest resemblance to true beatitude.
2. Goods that are in corporeal things physically are also in God, though in a non-physical way.

I think that I have now said enough concerning what belongs to the unity of God's essence.

---

[16] *The Consolation of Philosophy* 3.2. *PL* 63.724.

Index of scriptural citations

Index of names and subjects

literal sense 17, 18, 19, 44, 143–5, 238
logic xxix
love 241–50; God's 241–7
Luther, Martin xxxi

Maimonides, Moses vii, xii, 141, 262, 265
Manichees 83
Marcella 96
martyrs 236, 264
Mary Magdalen 258
Mary, the Virgin 281, 282
mathematics xxix, 56, 57, 72, 74, 110
matter xvii, xx, 32, 89, 169, 186, 194, 205; form
   and 32, 70, 133, 168; individualization by 32,
   33, 186, 187; limitlessness of 71, 74; in
   potentiality 42, 45, 74; and privation 55, 56;
   see also form and matter; prime matter
meaning xxvi, 161; *see also* allegorical sense;
   anagogical sense; historical sense; literal
   sense; moral sense; parabolic sense; spiritual
   sense; tropological sense
measurement 22, 36, 38, 59, 60, 147, 150, 189,
   190; eternity and 94, 95, 97, 98, 99
mercy 255, 256–8; God's 251–8, 273, 275
merit 252, 265
metaphors 15–17, 31, 32, 89, 94, 143, 151, 158,
   237, 238, 241, 243, 252; bodily 30, 31, 79, 144,
   145, 208
metaphysics xxvi, 14
Metaphysics (Aristotle) 4, 173, 182, 221
Miller, Barry xvi
mind 114, 118, 122, 129, 226, 254, 259
   God's 201, 203; and God's essence 113–17,
   119–21, 122–9; ideas in God's 200–6;
   see also intellect
miracles 133
mirror, seeing in a 116, 120, 127, 128, 130,
   132, 176
misery 255, 257
modality xxx
mode 58–61, 63, 64
moral science 8
moral sense 17, 18
Moses xxiv, 19, 132, 134, 135, 163
movement xi, 30, 31, 61, 73, 87, 88, 103, 213,
   271, 272; as life 207, 208, 211; *motus* as spatial
   xxiii; and time 73, 74, 98, 103; understanding
   as 170, 171, 208
mover xi, 87, 212, 214
multiplication 73, 75
mysticism x

names 68, 140, 156, 158, 196, 210; God's 54,
   158, 159, 160–4; proper 158, 159

Naples viii
natural philosophy 264
nature 183, 198, 205, 207–9, 213, 224, 235, 264;
   and animals 212; and God 33–4, 156–7; and
   grace 15, 23; unity of 47
nature of God ix, x–xi, xvii, xxiii, xxviii, 40,
   41, 223
necessary things 96, 262, 264
necessity 267, 273, 276; absolute xxix, xxx, 232;
   and contingent future events 192, 268; God's
   knowledge and 190–4; and God's will
   xxviii–xxx, 221–3, 232–4, 278; hypothetical
   xxix, 222, 234; and possibility xxv, 25; and
   providence 267–8
Nemesius of Emesa 266
Neoplatonism viii
New Law 8, 18
nominalism xxxi, 197
non-existence 28, 55, 90, 183–4, 274
nouns: abstract 34, 139, 140, 210; common
   and proper 158, 160; concrete 34, 139,
   140, 159
number 59, 60, 76, 84, 86; perfect 179; unity
   generates 38, 108, 110; unity of 102, 106;
   unlimited 75–7

object 12, 83, 164; of activity 170; of
   understanding 116, 175, 176
Ockham, William of xxxi
Old Law 8, 18
Old Testament 18
omnipotence xxv, 273–6
omnipresence xxiii, xxx
omniscience xxiii, xxiv; *see also* God's
   knowledge
On Interpretation (*De Interpretatione*) 161
one: and being 66, 105–7, 108, 111; and many
   106, 107–9
oneness, God's 29, 105–12, 145, 162–4
ontology xii, xxvi
opposites 21, 46, 107, 108
order 60, 203, 233, 261; double in things 253;
   goodness and 58–61, 63, 64; and justice 252,
   257; relations of different 117, 154, 155; and
   unity 110
Origen 103, 181, 182

pagans 160, 161, 162, 275
parabolic sense 18, 19
Paris, University of vii, viii
participation 50, 66, 68, 215
parts: and composites 40, 80, 81; and whole
   xviii, 20, 40, 81, 85, 92, 107,
   176, 203

Cambridge texts in the history of philosophy

Titles published in the series thus far

Aquinas *Disputed Questions on the Virtues* (edited by E. M. Atkins and Thomas Williams)

Aquinas *Summa Theologiae, Questions on God* (edited by Brian Davies and Brian Leftow)

Aristotle *Nicomachean Ethics* (edited by Roger Crisp)

Arnauld and Nicole *Logic or the Art of Thinking* (edited by Jill Vance Buroker)

Augustine *On the Trinity* (edited by Gareth B. Matthews)

Bacon *The New Organon* (edited by Lisa Jardine and Michael Silverthorne)

Boyle *A Free Enquiry into the Vulgarly Received Notion of Nature* (edited by Edward B. Davis and Michael Hunter)

Bruno *Cause, Principle and Unity* and *Essays on Magic* (edited by Richard Blackwell and Robert de Lucca with an introduction by Alfonso Ingegno)

Cavendish *Observations upon Experimental Philosophy* (edited by Eileen O'Neill)

Cicero *On Moral Ends* (edited by Julia Annas, translated by Raphael Woolf)

Clarke *A Demonstration of the Being and Attributes of God and Other Writings* (edited by Ezio Vailati)

Classic and Romantic German Aesthetics (edited by J. M. Bernstein)

Condillac *Essay on the Origin of Human Knowledge* (edited by Hans Aarsleff)

Conway *The Principles of the Most Ancient and Modern Philosophy* (edited by Allison P. Coudert and Taylor Corse)

Cudworth *A Treatise Concerning Eternal and Immutable Morality* with *A Treatise of Freewill* (edited by Sarah Hutton)

Descartes *Meditations on First Philosophy*, with selections from the *Objections and Replies* (edited by John Cottingham)

Descartes *The World and Other Writings* (edited by Stephen Gaukroger)

Fichte *Foundations of Natural Right* (edited by Frederick Neuhouser, translated by Michael Baur)

Fichte *The System of Ethics* (edited by Daniel Breazeale and Günter Zöller)

Herder *Philosophical Writings* (edited by Michael Forster)

Hobbes and Bramhall on Liberty and Necessity (edited by Vere Chappell)

Humboldt *On Language* (edited by Michael Losonsky, translated by Peter Heath)

Kant *Critique of Practical Reason* (edited by Mary Gregor with an introduction by Andrews Reath)

Kant *Groundwork of the Metaphysics of Morals* (edited by Mary Gregor with an introduction by Christine M. Korsgaard)

Kant *The Metaphysics of Morals* (edited by Mary Gregor with an introduction by Roger Sullivan)

Kant *Prolegomena to any Future Metaphysics* (edited by Gary Hatfield)

Kant *Religion within the Boundaries of Mere Reason and Other Writings* (edited by Allen Wood and George di Giovanni with an introduction by Robert Merrihew Adams)

La Mettrie *Machine Man and Other Writings* (edited by Ann Thomson)

Leibniz *New Essays on Human Understanding* (edited by Peter Remnant and Jonathan Bennett)

Lessing *Philosophical and Theological Writings* (edited by H. B. Nisbet)

Malebranche *Dialogues on Metaphysics and on Religion* (edited by Nicholas Jolley and David Scott)

Malebranche *The Search after Truth* (edited by Thomas M. Lennon and Paul J. Olscamp)

Medieval Islamic Philosophy (edited by Muhammad Ali Khalidi)

Melanchthon *Orations on Philosophy and Education* (edited by Sachiko Kusukawa, translated by Christine Salazar)

Mendelssohn *Philosophical Writings* (edited by Daniel O. Dahlstrom)

Newton *Philosophical Writings* (edited by Andrew Janiak)

Nietzsche *The Antichrist, Ecce Homo, Twilight of the Idols and Other Writings* (edited by Aaron Ridley and Judith Norman)

Nietzsche *Beyond Good and Evil* (edited by Rolf-Peter Horstmann and Judith Norman)

Nietzsche *The Birth of Tragedy and Other Writings* (edited by Raymond Geuss and Ronald Speirs)

Nietzsche *Daybreak* (edited by Maudemarie Clark and Brian Leiter, translated by R. J. Hollingdale)

Nietzsche *The Gay Science* (edited by Bernard Williams, translated by Josefine Nauckhoff)

Nietzsche *Human, All Too Human* (translated by R. J. Hollingdale with an introduction by Richard Schacht)

Nietzsche *Untimely Meditations* (edited by Daniel Breazeale, translated by R. J. Hollingdale)

Nietzsche *Writings from the Late Notebooks* (edited by Rüdiger Bittner, translated by Kate Sturge)

Novalis *Fichte Studies* (edited by Jane Kneller)

Schleiermacher *Hermeneutics and Criticism* (edited by Andrew Bowie)

Schleiermacher *Lectures on Philosophical Ethics* (edited by Robert Louden, translated by Louise Adey Huish)

Schleiermacher *On Religion: Speeches to its Cultured Despisers* (edited by Richard Crouter)

Schopenhauer *Prize Essay on the Freedom of the Will* (edited by Günter Zöller)

Sextus Empiricus *Against the Logicians* (edited by Richard Bett)

Sextus Empiricus *Outlines of Scepticism* (edited by Julia Annas and Jonathan Barnes)

Shaftesbury *Characteristics of Men, Manners, Opinions, Times* (edited by Lawrence Klein)

Adam Smith *The Theory of Moral Sentiments* (edited by Knud Haakonssen)

Voltaire *Treatise on Tolerance and Other Writings* (edited by Simon Harvey)